W0036157

SAGE was founded in 1965 by Sara Miller McCune to support the dissemination of usable knowledge by publishing innovative and high-quality research and teaching content. Today, we publish over 900 journals, including those of more than 400 learned societies, more than 800 new books per year, and a growing range of library products including archives, data, case studies, reports, and video. SAGE remains majority-owned by our founder, and after Sara's lifetime will become owned by a charitable trust that secures our continued independence.

Los Angeles | London | New Delhi | Singapore | Washington DC | Melbourne

'Laden with anecdotes, examples and data, *Reluctant Technophiles* paints successfully on a very wide canvas, analysing the past, dissecting the present and presenting a plausible vision for the future.'

N. R. Narayana Murthy,
Founder, Infosys

'*Reluctant Technophiles* brilliantly underscores the complicated and often contradictory relationship India has with technology, which must be acknowledged and navigated to chart a path to technology-based prosperity.'

Naresh Chandra Saxena,
Former Secretary, Planning Commission of India

'*Reluctant Technophiles* describes the evolution of various technologies over the years and their relationships that exist today with the Indian society. It is very lucidly written with examples and is useful for common people to understand the societal impact of advanced technologies and derive the benefits out of them, given the strengths, limitations and contradictions in our society. Congratulations to Professor Rakesh Kumar on his achievement.'

Sankar Pal,
Padma Shri and National Science Chair

'It is a much-needed work by a technologist to deconstruct the engagement of the Indian society with technology, taking into account underlying contradictions and complexities.'

Dinesh C. Sharma,
Author, The Outsourcer;
*winner of the Computer History
Museum Book Prize*

'*Reluctant Technophiles* cuts through vision documents and road maps, puts an ear to the ground and narrates technology–society stories from India's heartlands. That is where technology or the lack thereof matters most.'

Subhra Priyadarshini,
Chief Editor, Nature India

'Kumar's deep knowledge enables him to serve as an outstanding and entertaining guide to both India and technology, two complex subjects that are often misunderstood.'

Ross Bassett,
Author, The Technological Indian

'Technology is both demonized and epitomized in India, but seldom well understood. Rakesh's book brings in an evidence-led perspective to understand technology in the Indian context and significantly raises the level of debate. He forcefully argues why India must aspire to be a technology superpower, a gap that needs urgent attention.'

Varun Aggarwal,
*Founder, India Science Festival;
Co-founder, Aspiring Minds; Author,* The Bird Farm

Reluctant Technophiles

Reluctant Technophiles

India's Complicated Relationship with Technology

Rakesh Kumar

Los Angeles | London | New Delhi
Singapore | Washington DC | Melbourne

First published in 2022 by

SAGE Publications India Pvt Ltd
B1/I-1 Mohan Cooperative Industrial Area
Mathura Road, New Delhi 110 044, India
www.sagepub.in

SAGE Publications Inc
2455 Teller Road
Thousand Oaks, California 91320, USA

SAGE Publications Ltd
1 Oliver's Yard, 55 City Road
London EC1Y 1SP, United Kingdom

SAGE Publications Asia-Pacific Pte Ltd
18 Cross Street #10-10/11/12
China Square Central
Singapore 048423

Published by Vivek Mehra for SAGE Publications India Pvt Ltd. Typeset in 11.5/14 pt Sabon by Fidus Design Pvt Ltd, Chandigarh.

Library of Congress Control Number: 2021948653

ISBN: 978-93-5479-177-2 (PB)

SAGE Team: Namarita Kathait, Neena Ganjoo and Anupama Krishnan

To my parents
for teaching me
about life and living

Thank you for choosing a SAGE product!
If you have any comment, observation or feedback,
I would like to personally hear from you.

Please write to me at **contactceo@sagepub.in**

Vivek Mehra, Managing Director and CEO, SAGE India.

Bulk Sales

SAGE India offers special discounts
for purchase of books in bulk.
We also make available special imprints
and excerpts from our books on demand.

For orders and enquiries, write to us at

Marketing Department
SAGE Publications India Pvt Ltd
B1/I-1, Mohan Cooperative Industrial Area
Mathura Road, Post Bag 7
New Delhi 110044, India

E-mail us at **marketing@sagepub.in**

Subscribe to our mailing list

Write to **marketing@sagepub.in**

This book is also available as an e-book.

CONTENTS

They say that India is a land of contradictions. I learned that growing up in the 1980s and early 1990s in a village (Pusa) in India with no more than 2,000 people. Villages outside Pusa were dirt poor, while Pusa itself hosted a nationally renowned agricultural research university. My father was a professor at the university, so were most of his friends. However, it was common to see discrimination against the 'lower' castes, women and minorities both in and around Pusa. People both within family and friends held many superstitions and practised dogma. It was quite common, in fact. There was not much penetration of technology. As a child in the 1980s, I still remember often running to watch *Ramayana* and *He-Man* at the home of this (extremely kind!) family who had the only television in the locality. Most families did not have telephones, let alone heating and air conditioning. However, people clapped when Rakesh Sharma went to space or when Agni launched. The decade ended with horrifying communal riots in Bhagalpur, a city which I had familial connections to.

Things changed in the 1990s. As I remember it, several forms of discrimination worsened—*mandal* and *kamandal* exacerbated existing fissures. However, I noticed more women going for college and career. Also, there was much technological change. Televisions and telephones became common. Some even started owning washing machines. Software jobs became status symbols.

Fast-forwarding several decades later, even though I live in the USA, I routinely visit India, talk to friends and family in India, work with different organizations in India, and also spend (perhaps excessive amount of) time following news and events from India. I would say that I still have an ear to the ground.

It is clear that technology is a big part of Indian life today. *Paanwallahs* and *rickshawallahs* use cell phone, Aadhaar card and the Internet. At the same time, the superstitions and discriminations continue. Godmen thrive. Modern-day India reports lynchings, horrific sexual violence and riots.

All of these lead one to ask: What is the relationship between technology and the Indian society? How does the uniqueness of the Indian society impact attitudes towards technology? How does it impact access to technology? How does it affect technological innovation? Conversely, how is technology uniquely impacting the Indian society? What unique opportunities and challenges does technology present in India? What path should India tread if it must rely on technology to become a better, more prosperous nation?

Some more context is useful here. As a professor in an elite electrical and computer engineering programme, as someone who has been fortunate to be associated with technologies which now are used widely, and as an entrepreneur and advisor to several technology companies, I routinely find myself in panels, debates and thinktank meetings where I am often charged with evaluating different current and emerging technologies, their trade-offs and how they can impact the society. I am also often involved in preparing technology road maps and visioning documents. However, these exercises tend to be inherently optimistic, assume that technology can solve societal problems and often ignore the human and social factors. Most importantly, they assume a Western socio-economic context and do not reflect the reality I grew up with or that I still see in India. The resulting gnawing, uncomfortable feeling I have had for some time has led to this book.

There are several general interest books related to technology in India. However, these books either simply trace the historical evolution of technology in India or are narrowly focused on the state of technology in India today. There is no book which focuses on the relationship which exists today between technology and the Indian society. *Reluctant Technophiles* fills this gap.

This book follows an example- and anecdote-based approach to provide an account of India's complicated and often contradictory relationship with technology: how we often blame technology for our shortcomings, how we exaggerate our technological past to shift attention away from the present, how our faith and superstitions coexist with technology, how we routinely pretend that technology can solve our deep-rooted problems and how only some succeed in technological India while others struggle. It traces how we have been cavalier about enabling and promoting technology in spite of belief in its power, how the current technological ecosystem does not reward critical thinking and innovation, and how some of the reasons are fundamental. It asserts that we must succeed as a technological nation in spite of these complications and contradictions, since the promise from technological progress is too immense. It underscores that there are both reasons for optimism and causes for concern. It argues that we need to chart our own path which not only recognizes the uniquely Indian strengths, limitations and contradictions but also benefits from them.

The book has a very wide canvas. I do not pretend to be an expert in a large number of areas being touched upon in the book. However, I rely on data and historical understanding both for making arguments and recommendations. I invite you, the reader, to engage with me on both data and arguments. The goal of the book will be served if it generates a better understanding of how technology and society impact each other and if it leads to new ideas on how to move India forward technologically.

ACKNOWLEDGEMENTS

To my parents and teachers who I owe everything. To my son for giving new meaning to my life. To my wife for our son, and for her encouragement and support. To my brother for his faith in me. To my sister for keeping me grounded. To my cousin for being a brother. To my friends for joy and countless thought-provoking discussions. To my colleagues who I learn from every day. To my current and past students who give me purpose. To my collaborators at different stages of the book to make this a reality. To all who have been kind or ever said a word of encouragement.

CHAPTER 1

THE PERFECT SCAPEGOAT

In April of 2020, with India in the middle of a long Coronavirus lockdown, two sadhus (holy religious men) passing through a village in Maharashtra were killed, along with their driver, by a vigilante mob which suspected them of being child kidnappers and organ harvesters.[1] Rumours had been floating around on WhatsApp about organ-harvesting gangs being active in the area—a vigilante group had been formed in the village to teach these gangs a lesson, and the sadhus who were on way to a funeral in Gujrat, and were simply passing through the village, had to pay the price.

Unfortunately, this was simply one in a long line of lynchings and attacks fuelled by rumours spread on WhatsApp.[2] At least 15 innocent people had been killed in

---

[1] Zeeshan Shaikh, 'Palghar Lynching: A Recap of What Happened', *The Indian Express*, 24 April 2020, https://indianexpress.com/article/explained/palghar-mob-lynching-mahant-kalpavruksha-giri-6370528/

[2] Vindu Goel, Suhasini Raj, and Priyadarshini Ravichandran. 'How WhatsApp Leads Mobs to Murder in India', *The New York Times*, 8 July 2018, https://www.nytimes.com/interactive/2018/07/18/technology/whatsapp-india-killings.html

different parts of India in the previous three years by vigilante mobs, simply based on WhatsApp messages, with many more injured.

These horrific killings raised many uncomfortable questions. Are we a violent and revengeful society? How effective is rule of law in India? However, instead of confronting these questions, both the government and the general public immediately identified a culprit to direct their scorn and anger on: WhatsApp. It was alleged that WhatsApp enabled the viral spread of information which led to these horrific incidents. There were calls for WhatsApp to be banned or regulated. The Ministry of Electronics and Information Technology of India threatened legal action if WhatsApp did not provide traceability of messages. The minister-in-charge even suggested abetment charges. 'When rumors and fake news get propagated by mischief mongers, the medium used for such propagation cannot evade responsibility and accountability.... If they remain mute spectators, they are liable to be treated as abettors and thereafter face consequent legal action,' said a press note from the ministry.

Never mind the fact that subsequent investigations found that each lynching's true reason was traceable to some angst from a socio-historical divide: caste, class, religion, gender, etc. Or that caste- and religion-based mob killings have had a long history in India—since much before WhatsApp. Or that the killing of the sadhus in Maharashtra happened more than a year after the WhatsApp had to make several changes to its messaging platform to comply with the government's wishes and threats. It was also telling that communities' lack of faith in government's ability to protect them led them to organize vigilante mobs.

In November of 2008 took place one of the most horrific acts of terror on Indian soil.[3] In a series of coordinated and widely televised shooting and bombing attacks lasting 4 days, a group of 10 terrorists who came through the sea killed 165 people and wounded over 300 across Mumbai. The attacks raised many uncomfortable questions. Most prominently, how could such a flamboyant attack be launched in India's financial capital which has arguably some of the best security in India? How effective really is India's intelligence and security apparatus? However, again, instead of confronting these questions head on, a technology culprit was identified—BlackBerry (the company) in this case—and the government decided to focus its might on bringing BlackBerry to its knees.[4] BlackBerry phones made by Canadian company Research In Motion (RIM) were reputed for their end-to-end encrypted real-time messaging services. The encryption made it impossible for anyone, including intelligence services, to monitor any communication over BlackBerry which used these services. After a post-mortem of attacks, the government concluded that the end-to-end secure encryption supported by the erstwhile BlackBerry platform prevented acquisition of the intelligence required to prevent the attacks. RIM was issued an ultimatum to allow access to encrypted information by a certain date or face a blockage of its encrypted messaging services. RIM had over a million customers in India then. It eventually buckled under pressure, relocated some of its servers which were responsible for encryption and decryption to India, and started providing

---

[3] Adrian Levy and Cathy Scott-Clark, *The Siege: 64 Hours inside the Taj Hotel* (New York, NY: Penguin Books, August 2014).

[4] Josh Halliday and Graeme Wearden, 'India Sets Deadline for Blackberry Compliance', *The Guardian*, 12 August 2010, https://www.theguardian.com/technology/2010/aug/12/blackberry-email-messaging-india

Indian law-enforcement agencies access to secure BlackBerry data, including ability to track email and email attachments, monitor which websites were visited, etc.

It became clear to any information technology (IT) company wanting to do business in India that their business model could not wholly rely on providing security or privacy guarantees. In the meanwhile, terror incidents continued.

The Finger-pointing is Pervasive

Horrific rape and sexual violence incidents are reported in India with alarming regularity.[5] Several of them earn worldwide shame, horror and condemnation—India routinely finds itself in the list of world's most dangerous countries for women. In 2012, a 23-year-old student was gang-raped on a public bus in Delhi, the capital of India, with such brutality that she died of her injuries. In 2018, an 8-year-old girl was raped in Kathua in Jammu and Kashmir in a temple by several men over multiple days and then murdered—strangled and battered to death with a stone. In 2019, a 23-year-old rape victim was set on fire in Unnao, Uttar Pradesh, by a gang of men, including the rapist, as she was on her way to a court hearing. The National Crime Records Bureau (NCRB) estimates that a woman is raped in India every six hours.[6]

These incidents raise a lot of uncomfortable questions. Has the status of women improved much in certain regions of India? Has gender dynamics changed much even as the rest of the society changes? While some of these questions are being asked, perhaps a more visible reaction has been to blame the Internet and cell phones for these crimes.

---

[5] Priyanka Dubey, *No Nation for Women: Reportage on Rape from India, World's Largest Democracy* (Noida: Simon and Schuster India, December 2018).

[6] https://ncrb.gov.in/en/crime-against-women-statesuts

A minister in Rajasthan blamed the Internet for the 'perverted mentality' and demanded censoring of all online content. A political leader in Uttar Pradesh went further, 'Minor boys and girls should be barred from using mobiles phone and the Internet.' *The Guardian* blared, 'For repressed men to be fed a constant diet of porn on their phones is a recipe for disaster.'[7] Experts opined that easy access to porn, including violent and revenge porn, desensitizes men to rapes and sexual harassment.

Never mind the fact that the history of brutal rape and sexual violence in India has been long, often systematic, and much predates the Internet and cell phones.[8] Even considering only time since Independence, an estimated 75,000–100,000 women were abducted and raped during the partition of India. In 1973, Aruna Shanbaug, a 26-year-old nurse, was raped and strangled by a ward attendant and left in coma for more than 40 years until she died (in 2015). The first hanging in India for this millennium was for a 1990 rape and murder of a 14-year-old girl in Kolkata. In 1995, Bhanwari Devi, a lower-caste woman working on a women's development project in Rajasthan, was gang-raped by five men who were angered by her efforts to prevent a child marriage in their family. The Internet or cell phones could not be blamed.

Technology in the Dock

Disinformation ('fake news') is rampant in India.[9] In 2020 alone, the year began with considerable disinformation about the Citizenship (Amendment) Act, a law which

---

[7] https://www.theguardian.com/commentisfree/2018/aug/09/sexual-violence-india-rape-pornography

[8] Kalpana Sharma, *The Silence and the Storm: Narratives of Violence against Women in India* (New Delhi: Aleph Book Company, November 2019).

[9] Samir Patil, 'India Has a Public Health Crisis. It's Called Fake News', *The New York Times*, 19 April 2019, https://www.nytimes.com/2019/04/29/opinion/india-elections-disinformation.html

provided citizenship to certain classes of non-Muslim citizens of three neighbouring countries. Then there was disinformation related to communal riots in Delhi. Subsequently, Coronavirus hit and there was considerable misinformation about its cause, spread and treatment, including disinformation targeting minority communities. The discussion of this disinformation problem by Indian policymakers, public and media would suggest that it is a problem birthed by technology. An argument is made that smartphones and social media have made it easier to propagate fake news, and, therefore, they are to blame. Little discussion happens around the uncomfortable questions this raises about tribalism in the Indian society and people's inability to ascertain truth beyond social media.

Similarly, summons and threats of legal action are routinely issued to technology companies such as Facebook in India in the context of data privacy issues. In 2018, when it was found that a political consultancy firm (Cambridge Analytica) harvested Facebook data of 50 million users to benefit different political campaigns,[10] the government threatened Facebook with legal action if it found that Indian users' data was misused. The minister-in-charge also said that Facebook's CEO will be summoned if needed.

While the concern about user data privacy is admirable, technology is being put in the dock even though the deeper questions about the right trade-off between public good and an individual's privacy are still unresolved in India. Data privacy bill has been pending for almost two years, and there are no laws governing data privacy. Even the draft bill has highly contentious provisions such as

---

[10] Georgina Lee, 'Q&A on Cambridge Analytica: The Allegations So Far, Explained', Channel 4, 26 March 2018, https://www.channel4.com/news/factcheck/cambridge-analytica-the-allegations-so-far

requiring companies to hand over 'non-personal' user data to the government when requested as well as allowing government to collect data of its citizens without consent to serve sovereignty and larger public interest.

Platforms such as Twitter and Facebook are also routinely in the dock for free speech-related issues. They get blamed for allowing content that a section of society or government finds objectionable. They also get blamed for disallowing or deleting content that they find objectionable. No clear direction exists for them, since the larger questions around freedom of speech are unresolved.

A Frequent and Soft Target

It should not be a surprise that technology is a frequent target.

There are several reasons. First, India has always had socialist tendencies and has had deep distrust of industry. Coupled with the fact that there is inequality, it is politically expedient to vilify industry. Poverty is often blamed on the greed of the rich. Corruption is blamed on their morals (or lack thereof). Black money is blamed on their methods. In fact, rarely are industrialists and their successes celebrated. Industry and industrialists are often viewed by the political class as necessary evil. In that context, any potential role of technology in a crisis or a tragedy allows the political class grandstanding opportunities. The pronouncement of a minister to summon billionaires evil rich simply would be an attempt at establishing the power of the people.

Second, technology industry is a soft target. In a highly regulated environment such as India, any protestations would lead to repercussions. Also, Indian technology industry does not have the same muscle or pulpit that the Western counterparts have. This makes it difficult for the industry to defend itself against accusations. Consider social media and cloud companies, for example. They are increasingly under scrutiny in the debates about privacy and free flow of information. The likelihood of such companies pushing back on criticisms by policymakers and politicians would be small. Similarly, e-commerce companies are under constant scrutiny related to impact on informal economy and local jobs. Such companies, again, are unlikely to protest characterizations which may be unfair. The same applies to foreign companies trying to enter the Indian market or Indian companies impacted by policies and politics.

Perhaps most compelling reason why technology is targeted frequently is that such targeting allows the political class and the society to create an illusion of progress—progress at addressing deep-rooted problems without having to confront uncomfortable realities and address hard questions about political decision-making, intelligence and society.

Consider, for example, the fact that mob lynching and riots have a history at least as long as modern India—a history that much predates WhatsApp. Paul Brass's book *Forms of Collective Violence: Riots, Pogroms, and Genocide in Modern India*[11] details some of the worst such incidents since Independence. The 1967 riots in Ranchi in present-day Jharkhand started with an anti-Urdu agitation and killed almost 200 people. The 1969 Gujarat communal riots over desecration of places of worship killed over 500. The 1980 Moradabad riots over policemen's refusal to remove a pig from *Idgah* (a Muslim place of worship) killed almost 400 people. A 1983 massacre arising out of Hindu–Muslim tension in Nellie, Assam, killed 2,000–10,000 people. The 1984 Bhiwandi riot killed

---

[11] Paul R. Brass, *Forms of Collective Violence: Riots, Pogroms, and Genocide in Modern India* (New Delhi: Three Essays Collectives, December 2006).

almost 300 people in Maharashtra over placement of a saffron flag on top of a mosque. The 1984 anti-Sikh riots after assassination of Indira Gandhi by her two Sikh body-guards killed over 2,800 people. The 1985 Gujarat riots killed almost 300. The 1987 Meerut riots killed almost 350. The 1989 Bhagalpur violence killed over 1,000 people. At least 300 people were killed in Kashmir in 1989. The 1990 Hyderabad riots killed over 200. Thousands of people were killed in 1992 over Babri Masjid dispute. The 1993 Bombay riots killed over 1,500. The 2002 Gujarat riots killed over 2,000 people. The list goes on. Blaming WhatsApp for a deep, long-running societal malaise is disingenuous at best.

Also, if WhatsApp was the cause for mob lynching, it would have the same effect in other countries where WhatsApp is popular. However, to no one's surprise, there is no conversation around whether WhatsApp incentivizes violence in most countries it operates in. The most closely related incident was the violence which happened in Kenya after 2007 general election.[12] Incumbent President Mwai Kibaki was declared the winner of the election, in spite of trailing during the entire counting process. The opponent, Raila Odinga, alleged electoral manipulation and encouraged mass protests. Once the protests started, violence erupted where Odinga's supporters went on a killing rampage against Kikuyus, the ethnic group that Kibaki belonged to. This, in turn, devolved into full-fledged inter-tribe violence over 59 days which killed 1,400 people and displaced almost half a million. During this violence, mobs organized using SMS groups and many killings were triggered by rumours which flew around on mobile networks. WhatsApp had not arrived yet.

---

[12] Kimani Njogu, ed., *Healing the Wound: Personal Narratives about the 2007 Post-election Violence in Kenya* (Nairobi: Twaweza Communications, December 2009).

Blaming smartphones and the Internet for horrific sexual violence is also disingenuous. There are many fewer horrific incidents of sexual violence (even per capita) in countries with far greater Internet and mobile penetration. India ranks 120 among countries of the world in terms of Internet penetration (percentage of population which accessed the Internet in last 12 months using any device). India was ranked 74 among 87 countries ranked by Opensignal in 2019 in terms of mobile download speed and 63 among 78 in terms of average Internet speed. The percentage of people with smartphones has indeed been increasing quickly (ranked 40). However, greater access to porn still does not explain similar cases in the pre-smartphone era or many fewer horrific sexual violence cases than countries with greater consumption of porn (even per capita) or with greater fraction of users with Internet accesses. Ultimately, it is simply easier to blame smartphones than to look critically at patriarchy codified over centuries, lack of effectiveness of the criminal justice system and general lack of education about consent.

Blaming technology companies as the primary enabler of election meddling also seems to be an attempt to shift focus from deep-rooted problems. While Cambridge Analytica's harvesting of Facebook information for influencing voters is concerning, Indian voters have for long been swayed using cash, alcohol and drugs. In a fascinating study, Jennifer Bussell from the University of California, Berkeley, found that more than half of incumbent politicians in Bihar, Jharkhand and Uttar Pradesh were pressured to distribute gifts to the electorate.[13] Nearly all the politicians at the state and national levels felt the pressure. In fact, there are parts of India where votes are literally bought using cash or alcohol. The politicians in Bussell's

[13] Jennifer Bussell, 'Funding Elections in India: Whose Money Has the Most Influence', *The Hindustan Times*, 24 July 2018.

study estimated that roughly quarter of voters received a gift. Thousands of crores worth of contraband was seized just during the last general election. A study from Columbia University found that politicians in Mumbai region can easily spend over half their budget in gifts to voters.[14]

If the primary concern with Cambridge Analytica was foreign meddling into Indian politics, we have had plenty of that as well.[15] In 1967, *Ramparts*, an American magazine, exposed the details of Central Intelligence Agency (CIA) operation in India. CIA had bankrolled throughout the 1950s and early 1960s election campaigns of pro-Western politicians and subsidized anti-Communist newspapers and magazines. Several reports have described KGB funding of left-leaning parties in the 1960s and 1970s. *The New York Times* covered the outing of a Union minister as a CIA agent. These scandalous examples of meddling make Cambridge Analytica's learning of user preferences to perform micro-targeting during elections look pale in comparison. Fast-forward to now, the current campaign finance regulations allow Indian subsidiaries of foreign companies to fund elections. Similarly, foreign entities can buy electoral bonds. These are easy, direct conduits for foreign entities to influence elections.

Similarly, disinformation has also always been around in India.

Mowgli, the child protagonist of Rudyard Kipling's books, had given rise to a worldwide interest in the 1920s in 'feral children'—children who were raised by animals, specifically wolves. The story that got the most traction, and travelled worldwide, was that of Amala and Kamala, two sisters in India who had been reportedly discovered

---

14 Simon Chauchard, 'Electoral Handouts in Mumbai Elections: The Cost of Political Competition', *Asian Survey* 58, no. 2 (2018): 341–364.

15 Paul McGarr, '"Quiet Americans in India": The CIA and the Politics of Intelligence in Cold War South Asia', *Diplomatic History* 38, no. 5 (November 2014): 1046–1082.

from a wolf den by a local priest running an orphanage.[16] For years, the story was covered by media, scientific journals, and even children's books worldwide! At the same time, as the story gained interest, questions started being asked to ascertain the veracity of the news. Eventually, it was discovered that the two girls were not feral children— they had neuro-developmental disorders and the story had been crafted and promoted to raise money for the orphanage. The disinformation lasted over three-quarters of a century!

On 21 September in 1995, word spread that the statues of Ganesha, a Hindu deity, were drinking milk offerings. The news travelled wide and fast over telephone and word of mouth. Long lines formed at temples. Stores ran out of milk. Traffic was gridlocked. Television (TV) channels started broadcasting scenes at temples live. Some of the most popular temples shut down, since they couldn't handle the level of the footfall. The incident was covered by major news outlets all over the world, including BBC, CNN and *The New York Times*.[17] In particular, BBC screamed, 'The milk miracle that brought India to a standstill.' Of course, over time, it became clear that it was simply a case of confirmation bias and mass hysteria—science of surface tension and capillary action was able to explain the rest.

In the 1990s, several parts of Karnataka were gripped by the fear of a witch. News spread that a witch would roam the streets at nights and knock on doors. If you opened the door, you would die. To deceive you into opening the door, the witch would speak in the voice of your kin. The fear of this witch writ large. At some point, the residents started writing '*Nale Baa*' ('come tomorrow'

---

[16] Serge Aroles, *L'Enigme des enfants-loups* (Paris: Publibook, November 2007).

[17] The Associated Press, 'Does the God of Learning Drink Milk?' *The New York Times*, 22 September 1995, https://www.nytimes.com/1995/09/22/world/does-the-god-of-learning-drink-milk.html

in English) outside the doors and the walls of their houses, hoping that the ghost would read it, come later, would read it again, and the cycle would repeat. Even to this day, houses in parts of rural Karnataka have 'Nale Baa' written outside houses. The 2018 Bollywood movie *Stree* was based on the Nale Baa incident.[18]

The list of examples of disinformation is endless. Technology simply provides new media for communication. Disinformation has preceded many newer communication technologies.

Finally, there has been considerable vilification of technology companies in context of privacy. However, much of the criticism simply distracts from the hard questions surrounding data privacy. For example, while social media indisputably brings privacy challenges, the challenges of keeping digital data private are much more general. In January 2018, a journalist from *The Tribune* was able to access personal data—name, address, telephone number, photo, etc.—of anyone with an Aadhaar number for 500 rupees.[19] Another 300 rupees allowed printing of Aadhaar card for anyone. The government is the custodian of Aadhaar data, not social media companies; it's failure to keep Aadhaar data private was simply a reflection of the inherent difficulty in keeping any data secure and private in the interconnected digital age.

A Mirror for Self-reflection

Despite this, instead of holding mirror to itself, the society and the political class find it more expedient to blame

---

[18] India Today Web Desk, 'Nale Ba: The Scary Urban Legend Rajkummar–Shraddha's Stree Is Based On', *India Today*, 6 June 2018, https://www.indiatoday.in/movies/bollywood/story/nale-ba-the-scary-urban-legend-rajkummar-shraddha-s-stree-is-based-on-1252289-2018-06-06

[19] Rachna Khaira, 'Rs 500, 10 Minutes, and You Have access to Billion Aadhaar Details', *The Tribune*, 5 January 2018, https://www.tribuneindia.com/news/archive/nation/rs-500-10-minutes-and-you-have-access-to-billion-aadhaar-details-523361

technology, often without lack of clarity on what concrete follow-up actions will be effective.

In general, it is impossible to remove all 'objectionable' online content. Governments have often asked social media companies to hire people simply to monitor content being created and uploaded so that objectionable content can be filtered. However, the amount of content that is generated online is staggering, and no amount of manual policing from the administration or the platform providers (e.g., Facebook) will ensure that there is no such content online. As a reference, 300 hours of video are uploaded on YouTube every minute. Instagram users upload over 100 million photos and videos every day. Over 2 trillion searches are performed online every day. Over 100 million messages are sent every minute using SMS and in-application messaging systems. Monitoring this content manually is an impossible task.

Automatic filtering tools are often used. Such tools rely on sophisticated machine learning algorithms to identify content which is potentially objectionable. Marked content can be either directly blocked or flagged for manual review. The challenge with using such tools is that they have lower-than-needed accuracy in terms of both false positives and false negatives. High false positive rates mean that even harmless content is blocked or flagged frequently, adversely impacting the overall online experiences. High false negative rates mean that objectionable content frequently escapes the attention of these tools. In both the cases, such tools cannot be exclusively relied upon, and manual policing is needed.

Many platforms popular in India are headquartered elsewhere and operate across the globe. This makes it particularly difficult to enforce regulations. For example, several social media companies like WhatsApp, have their servers, including ones responsible for encryption and storage, outside India. This makes it hard for these companies to enforce India-specific regulations. Several companies operate in India also without any physical or legal local presence. This makes it hard for the government to regulate such companies.

Even if it were possible to regulate, both content generators and consumers could always migrate to newer platforms if they found regulations stifling. The recent surge in the popularity of end-to-end encrypted platforms such as Telegram and Signal, as well as increasing use of darknet for communication, suggests migration away from regulated platforms. The speed at which Indian users migrated from TikTok, a video-sharing application with Chinese origin which was banned in India after skirmishes at the border, to Triller suggests that this migration can be quick.[20] In fact, in this cat-and-mouse game, the government and the platform providers will always trail due to the ease of content creation and consumption compared to regulation and filtering.

Attempts to weaken encryption and introduce backdoors (so that monitoring can be performed) are even more misguided. India currently does not have broad restrictions on encryption. It does have sector-specific restrictions, however.[21] For example, the use of bulk encryption— where large amounts of data are encrypted at a time—is prohibited by telecom licence holders. Similarly, all Internet and voice traffic must be encrypted with key length no longer than 40 bits (in general, the longer the length of the encryption key, the stronger the encryption). There are also laws in the books which empower the government to allow general restrictions on encryption.

---

[20] Anumeha Chaturvedi, 'Triller Registers around 40 Million Downloads in India', *The Economic Times*, 15 August 2020, https://economictimes.indiatimes.com/tech/software/triller-registers-around-40m-downloads-in-india/articleshow/77552069.cms.

[21] Information Technology Act, 2000.

However, again, one could always migrate to a different tool or a different channel for communication which does provide strong encryption or limited regulation. In fact, it may be counterproductive to weaken encryption through legislation or policy changes. The reach and magnitude of access to governmental programmes and services have grown with increased digitization and connectivity. Weakened encryption or backdoors could make these programmes and services vulnerable to cyberattacks. The security keys will invariably land in the hands of criminals, mischief makers and hostile actors, as has been seen umpteen times, which will enable more criminal and terrorist activity. As one notorious example, Juniper Networks, a large producer of networking equipment for many large corporate and government customers, discovered in 2015 two sophisticated backdoors in its firewalls. One of the backdoors allowed attackers to decrypt traffic through its devices. Researchers found out, based on the documents released by Edward Snowden, that the backdoors may have been created at the urgings of National Security Agency (NSA), the American spy agency, so that NSA could spy on secrets. Interestingly, the source code of Juniper's firewall had been previously hijacked by a hacking group, who used this backdoor for their own spying purposes. This was a real-world example of government-forced weakening of backdoors directly benefiting criminals and compromising security for everyone else.[22]

In fact, encryption with 40-bit key mandated by the government for all telecom licensees can be broken by today's computers within seconds. If the telecom companies did truly follow the 40-bit regulation, all our banking and

---

[22] Nicole Perlroth, 'Government Announces Steps to Restore Confidence on Encryption Standards', The New York Times, 10 September 2013.

Aadhaar-based transactions which rely on SMS-based authentication would become vulnerable. Interestingly, the 40-bit key length limit also has NSA origins. In the early 1990s, the USA placed all export restrictions on all software which used key length greater than 40 bits. This was done to allow NSA to spy at will using any software that the USA exported (NSA had capability then to break 40-bit encryption). The 40-bit restriction made its way into India's policy documents and continues today, although the USA abandoned the restriction over 20 years back!

If Indian electronic and software products have weakened encryption compared to the rest of the world, it would also make these products uncompetitive globally. There would be lack of trust in doing business with India, especially in some sectors such as finances and banking. As it is, companies which deal with encryption are wary of doing business in India. The way BlackBerry was threatened after the Mumbai attacks despite it not being a telecom provider created a lasting scepticism about the rule of law (encryption limitations apply only to telecom operators).

Weakened encryption may lead to frauds and data thefts becoming common, which will reduce citizens' trust in their own government, industry and banking institutions. Since information may now flow over weakened channels, even security and intelligence may be compromised.

Counterintuitive as it may sound, weakened encryption may make content regulation and monitoring even more difficult. It is easy to monitor if most objectionable content is created on a small number of platforms. If encryption is weakened on these platforms, the terrorists and the mischief mongers will simply migrate to other platforms. Platform fragmentation may make monitoring and regulation further complex and arduous.

'Ears and Eyes' Are Equally Threatening

Analogously, an institutionalized mechanism for regulating online content could be susceptible to misuse by authorities. Examples abound. In 2018, the Ministry of Information and Broadcasting decided to set up a social media hub to monitor online data. The ostensible goal was to have a

> guiding tool for Ministry of Information & Broadcasting to understand the impact of various social media campaigns conducted on various schemes run by the Government of India. In addition, the tool should have the capacity to provide inputs to the Ministry on how to improve the reach of various social media campaigns, how to make a particular topic trending and for the overall general improvement of social media campaigns.[23]

In addition to the software tool, the Broadcast Engineering Consultants India Limited (BECIL), a public sector undertaking (PSU) under the ministry, had already floated a tender to supply a software for the project which the ministry had proposed to hire local journalists and stringers on a contractual basis to serve as 'ears and eyes' to receive feedback from the ground. Unsurprisingly, there was a big hue and cry. The Supreme Court of India took up the matter and slammed the government for an attempt to create a surveillance state.[24] Thankfully, the social media hub was not heard about again.

---

[23] Request for Proposals (RFP) invited for Selection of Agency for SITC of Software and Service and Support for function, operation and maintenance of Social Media Communication Hub, Ministry of Information and Broadcasting, Government of India. RFP Ref No: BECIL/Social Media/MIB/02/2018-19 Dated 25th April 2018.

[24] Express Web Desk, 'Govt Withdraws "Social Media Hub" Plan after SC's Surveillance State Remark', *The Indian Express*, 3 August 2018, https://indianexpress.com/article/india/govt-withdraws-proposal-to-create-social-media-hub-after-snooping-allegations/

In 2012, Mumbai shut down when the controversial politician Bal Thackeray died. A 21-year-old woman, Shaheen Dhada, who was unhappy with the shutdown, wrote in her Facebook post: 'People like Thackeray are born and die daily and one should not observe a "bandh" [shutdown] for that.' After the post appeared, a mob attacked and vandalized her uncle's clinic. More shockingly, Shaheen was arrested and charged with 'creating or promoting enmity, hatred or ill-will between classes'. She was also charged under the Information Technology Act (IT Act). A friend of hers, Renu Srinivasan, who had 'like'ed the comment, was also arrested under the same charges.

Unfortunately, it is not an isolated incident.[25] In the same year (2012), there were multiple incidents where authority to regulate online content was misused. A teacher was arrested in West Bengal for emailing to his friends a cartoon which was critical of Chief Minister Mamata Banerjee. A cartoonist was arrested in Mumbai on sedition charges for his anti-corruption drawings. A businessman was arrested in Puducherry for a tweet criticizing the son of India's finance minister. The Ministry of Telecommunications asked Internet service providers to block 16 Twitter accounts, including those of right-wing groups, such as Sangh Parivar, right-wing leaders such as Pravin Togadia, and journalists such as Kanchan Gupta and Shiv Aroor, who were considered sympathetic to right-wing causes. The directive did not quote any sections of the IT Act or any other law which empowered the government to make such a decision.

---

[25] *The New Indian Express*, 'Arrest over Mamata Banerjee Meme Latest in Long Line of Similar Rows', 15 May 2019.

Deep-rooted Malaise

Most crises and tragedies are rooted in fundamental problems such as caste and class divide, communalism, weakened law and order, untrustworthy criminal justice system, gender bias, corruption, radicalization, worsened external relations and questionable intelligence. Scapegoating technology in face of crises and tragedies shifts valuable attention and resources away from addressing roots of these problems.

Consider law and order. India ranks a measly 69 out of 128 in the 2019 World Justice Project Rule of Law Index. India's police personnel-to-population ratio is 144 to 100,000 as opposed to the United Nations (UN) recommendation of 222. Less than 25 per cent of Indian population trusted the police according to a 2018 Centre for the Study of Developing Societies (CSDS) study. Training is poor. A 2018 report claimed that up to 119 out of the 122 Indian Police Service trainee officers failed in at least one subject. Poor training at all levels translates into lack of patience in dealing with the public. Conviction rates for kidnapping and robbery have fallen by over 45 per cent in last 50 years. The conviction rate for rape is only around 25 per cent, and the process often takes more than 2 years. Prejudice against minorities and marginalized communities runs rampant. Anachronistic 1861 Police Act governs conduct often resulting in colonial-style feudal relationship with the public. Police reforms are stalled and can be largely attributed to the increasing number of elected officials with criminal cases and the fact that police reforms do not win votes (as opposed to handouts). In fact, the fraction of a state's gross domestic product (GDP) devoted to law and order has been decreasing for most states.

Fixing many of the above issues will be hard and will require sustained effort and resources. Political class has found it easier to blame technology for many law and order problems instead.

Similarly, consider the status of women. In 2019 UN Gender Development Index, which 'measures gender gaps in human development achievements by accounting for disparities between women and men in three basic dimensions of human development—health, knowledge and living standards', India ranked 129 among the 189 countries ranked. National Family Health Survey (NFHS) data reports that over 35 per cent of Indian married women experience violence by a spouse. Labour force participation rate for women in India is less than 30 per cent. Working women, on average, get paid 30 per cent less than their male counterparts. The Economic Survey of 2017–2018 stated that 21 million girls had 'notionally unwanted' birth because of couples' tendencies to keep trying till a boy is born. India also has one of the most skewed sex ratios in the world (107 males to every 100 females)—in fact, India is the only large country in the world where more girls die than boys (girls are also more likely to drop out of school). According to a 2017 World Economic Forum report, India is ranked 139th in terms of economic participation and opportunities for females—one of the worst countries—and 118th for education of women and girls. A large fraction (over 30%) of married women in India were married as children. One of every three child brides belongs to India.

It is certainly easier to blame smartphones and the Internet for crimes against women than to address deep-rooted prejudices against women in the society.

Partners, Not Adversaries

Both to improve trustworthiness and in face of increased pressure from the government and the public, technology industry is already employing several tools and resources to combat misinformation.[26]

YouTube now promotes 'authoritative' sources in search results during breaking news as well as Watch Next list to de-emphasize possibly mis-informing sources. It has also modified its ranking systems to decrease the visibility of trash comments. It funds trusted news organizations to improve news quality and organizes panels for fact-checking. It has invested heavily in machine learning algorithms which can classify videos as harmful, risky or fake.

WhatsApp now restricts the number of forwards to 5 at once and labels forwarded messages to remove prior ambiguity about the source of a message. It is testing a Search Messages on WhatsApp Web feature which allows users to check the authenticity of forwarded messages. It has also been funding research on online fact-checking as well as street plays, full-page newspaper ads and workshops to educate people on how to spot fake news.

Twitter has suspended hundreds of millions of fake accounts. It now uses labels such as 'Harmful Misleading' to mark tweets which it considers objectionable. It has removed tweets from public figures which it considers are harmful. Search results for some items (e.g., COVID-19) link to credible news sources. Ad credits are provided to select trustworthy organizations.

Facebook automatically links to authoritative sources for news and posts centred around certain topics It also employs third-party fact-checkers and machine learning to identify and mark misleading information. Facebook

---

[26] Peter Roudik et al., *Initiatives to Counter Fake News in Selected Countries: Argentina, Brazil, Canada, China, Egypt, France, Germany, Israel, Japan, Kenya, Malaysia, Nicaragua, Russia, Sweden, United Kingdom* (Washington, DC: Law Library of Congress, April 2009).

Journalism Project assists journalists with tools, products and services to improve quality of news and decision-making. Facebook founded a CUNY Graduate School of Journalism-administered News Integrity Initiative to improve trust in journalism.

Google News Initiative both builds tools for news industry and partners with them to increase trust and promote journalism. Google News Lab founded First Draft News, a project to fight disinformation online using other industry and philanthropic partners. Google has a round-the-clock response team to scrape misinformation from Search and YouTube.

Technology companies have similarly taken measures to counter online extremism and radicalization. The Tech Against Terrorism initiative supported by the UN works with technology companies to provide support to prevent terrorist use of the Internet. Partners include some of the biggest companies such as Facebook, Google, Microsoft and Twitter. Google, Facebook, Twitter and Microsoft formed in 2017 the Global Internet Forum to Counter Terrorism (GIFCT)[27] to counter terrorism online. GIFCT members not only use a combination of machine learning and human moderators to prevent uploading of content which has been previously classified as terrorist, but they have also created a shared industry database of 'hashes'. When terrorist image or video content is blocked on one platform, the corresponding hash (or unique digital signature) is shared with other platforms. This allows other platforms to quickly identify the same content on their platforms as well as prevent the uploading of the content on their platforms. Over 200,000 hashes have been created thus far. The quality of machine learning

---

27 https://gifct.org/

algorithms is also getting better—YouTube reported that over 98 per cent content which was marked as terrorist content by humans was marked similarly by their learning algorithms. Some companies such as Jigsaw learn the tendencies of the target audience of the extremists and create online advertisements targeting this audience. These advertisements redirect to sources which could address questions without risking radicalization.

Technology companies also routinely hand over data, especially meta data, to law-enforcement agencies when a lawful request is made. Almost 20,000 requests were made by the Indian government to Google in 2019 for about 40,000 user accounts; Google responded with some data in over 62 per cent cases. Over 48,000 requests were made by the Indian government to Facebook in 2019; for over 55 per cent of the requests, some data was provided by Facebook to the government. Similarly, Apple produced some data for the government for 45–85 per cent of the requests, depending on the type of the request.

Data privacy has certainly been a challenge, considering that the business model for some of the biggest technology companies relies on collection and analysis of data. However, companies have recently started putting privacy at the forefront. Microsoft CEO Satya Nadella declared privacy to be a human right. Mark Zuckerberg announced plans to remake Facebook into a privacy-focused platform. Google's Sundar Pichai has started advocating for ubiquitous privacy. Jack Dorsey, the CEO of Twitter, has endorsed General Data Protection Regulation (GDPR).[28] Apple has been advertising itself as a champion of privacy for some time now. While it is yet to be seen how

---

[28] Paul Voigt and Axel von dem Bussche, *The EU General Data Protection Regulation (GDPR): A Practical Guide* (Switzerland: Springer, August 2017).

well recent talk translates into actions, intent is clearly positive if the pronouncements are taken at face value. Furthermore, a slew of start-ups have emerged with focus on privacy—they provide services ranging from personal data scrubbing to ensuring compliance. Interest in these start-ups has been growing as well. As an example, privacy-focused start-up OneTrust, whose software helps businesses manage data privacy, has already been valued at over 1 billion dollars and counts more than 40 per cent of Fortune 500 companies as its customers.

A Complicated Relationship

India's scapegoating of technology is simply one example of a complicated and often contradictory relationship Indians have with technology. We blame WhatsApp for lynchings, smartphones for rapes, encryption for terrorists attacks, Facebook for disinformation, etc. But we fail to admit that lynchings, sexual violence, terrorism and disinformation were rampant in India even before the advent of these new technological tools and that other countries with even greater usage of these tools do not suffer the same way. We constantly reimagine and fabricate (Chapter 2) India's technological past and prowess for false pride, going as far as undermining modern science and technology and using governmental resources to promote potentially harmful self-aggrandizing pseudoscience. But we are willing to turn a blind eye to the widening gap between us and the rest of the world in technological innovation, especially related to transformative technologies such as robotics, artificial intelligence (AI) and quantum computing. We are famed as a land of superstitions and religious (Chapter 3). But we enthusiastically embrace new technologies. We routinely assume (Chapter 4) that technological solutions, such as direct benefit transfer, online marketplace and access to broadband, can eliminate deep-rooted problems such as corruption, lack of opportunities and inequality, while we disregard the mounting evidence which suggests the contrary. We often posture as a technological nation. But the reality is that only a small fraction of the population enjoys access to and benefits from some of the most cutting-edge technologies and technical knowledge, while others struggle to get their basic needs met and are often denied access to technology (Chapter 5). We appear to be overly sensitive to real and perceived slights on and by Twitter, WhatsApp or Facebook. But we appear to be relatively unprepared (Chapter 6) for the several challenges technology does present, such as magnifying existent biases due to increasingly algorithmic decision-making, exacerbating social and economic inequality due to progressive automation of jobs, impact of technology on environment and health, and increased hate speech and extremism due to unregulated online content.

These complications and contradictions sometimes distract from the simple truth; we must succeed as a technological nation, since the promise from widespread and equitable technological progress is too immense. Fruits of success will be many (Chapter 7)—prosperity, health, security, environment, quality of life and national pride.

Unfortunately, we have been cavalier (Chapter 8), throughout our history, in nurturing technology and have mostly treated science and technology as a largely unaffordable luxury and invested minimally and erratically into innovation. As a result, the current innovation ecosystem is largely rigid and slow to adapt to the fast-changing technological landscape, and does not reward critical thinking, risk-taking or entrepreneurship. Some of the reasons are fundamental (Chapter 9). Poverty, inequality, entrenched attitudes, License Raj, subpar access to health, education, and welfare safety-nets, and lack of political will present grave challenges to improving this ecosystem in the short term.

A pragmatic combination of homegrown technologies and technologies acquired from elsewhere (Chapter 10) may be needed to allow massification of technology and improve country's technological and innovation DNA.

Yes, India has a complicated and often contradictory relationship with technology, which reflects both in our technological past and the present. However, it can still become a center of technological innovation and technology-based prosperity (Chapter 11) in spite of these complications and contradictions. A path for technological India which not only recognizes India's various contradictions and complications but also benefits from them must be outlined and put into effect.

CHAPTER 2

THE DELUSION OF GRANDEUR

A Rich Past

Metallurgy in India has had a distinguished history. When Alexander the Great invaded India towards the end of the 4th century BC, he was presented with 100 talents of Indian steel. This steel had already been in production in South India for over 200 years and had exceptional flexibility and strength. The uniqueness of this crucible steel impressed Alexander and the word spread. It started getting traded widely. There are several ancient Tamil, Greek, Chinese and Roman literary references to this steel.[1] In the medieval world, Arabs started taking this steel to Damascus, where it was used to make weapons and armour. The fame of this steel spread further to Europe during the crusades, as the Europeans encountered Muslim warriors wielding Damascus swords made of this steel.[2] There are (possibly fictitious) accounts of these swords being able to cut even gauze handkerchiefs

---

[1] Sharada Srinivasan and Srinivasa Ranganathan, *India's Legendary Wootz Steel: An Advanced Material of the Ancient World* (Hyderabad: Orient BlackSwan, January 2013).

[2] Gunther Lobach, *Damascus Steel: Theory and Practice* (Atglen, PA: Schiffer Publishing, May 2013).

through the air. By the late 17th century, tens of thousands of ingots of this steel were being shipped from the Coromandel Coast to Persia alone. This drove a frenzy to identify the chemical composition of this steel and reproduce the manufacturing process (which was closely guarded by the Indians to retain monopoly).

The corresponding studies led to a fundamental technological breakthrough. For centuries, steel was thought of as an element belonging to the ferrous family. Chemical assaying of this Indian steel (which the British started calling Wootz steel likely as a corruption of *wook* which, in turn, was likely derived from the Tamil root word *urukku* or Kannada and Telugu word for steel *ukku*) led to the discovery that steel is in fact an alloy of iron and carbon. The large number of studies into the composition and properties of this steel are widely believed to have led to the birth of modern metallurgy and materials science. Wootz steel is arguably India's greatest contribution to technology.

Sugar is often described as the food everyone craves and no one needs. Sugarcane is native to Papua New Guinea and was first cultivated there 10,000 years back. People chewed on the reeds to enjoy the sweetness. There was no concept of sugar. Around 6000 BC, sugarcane spread to the Philippines and India via sea, carried by Austronesian and Polynesian seafarers. When Emperor Darius of Persia invaded India in 510 BC, he found 'the reed which gives honey without bees'.[3]

It was in India that sugar was first produced and chemically refined around 2,500 years back. Once Indians invented how to refine sugar at scale, it became widespread in Indian cooking. The book *Mahabhashya* by Patanjali talks about sugar-based recipes such as milk-based rice

---

[3] Ji Xianlin, *A History of Sugar* (Beijing: New Star Press, November 2013).

pudding, sweet barley meal and fermented drinks with ginger, which became popular during 350–400 BC.

In the 4th century BC, Greeks and Romans learned about sugar on their visits to India. Nearchus, a general of Alexander, wrote of 'a reed in India that brings forth honey without the help of bees, from which an intoxicating drink is made, though the plant bears no fruit'. An Indian text from 100 AD describes a sugar mill—it was the first such mill recorded in history. Sugar was called *khanda* locally, which is the source of the word 'candy'. In fact, the word 'sugar' is thought to be derived from the Sanskrit word *śarkarā*, meaning 'ground or candied sugar', originally 'grit, gravel'.

Around 600 AD, Western scholars who gathered at Jundi Shapur, a university in Iran, wrote about a potent medicine from India—sugar—and developed better methods for refining sugar. Subsequently, sugar was discovered, along with techniques for refinement, by the Arabs on their invasion of Persia in the 7th century AD, and by the Europeans as a result of the Crusades in the 11th century AD. Small amounts of sugar were brought to the Mediterranean and traded to physicians who used it for medical purposes. Simultaneously, India traded sugar to the neighbouring countries, including knowhow about sugar production. China, for example, learned about sugar refining from India and created its first sugar plantations in the 7th century. By many measures, sugar has been India's most impactful invention, and its chemical refinement it's the most exported technology.[4]

The modern society is built upon standard weights and measures which are needed for trade, business, construction and engineering. The Harappan civilization developed

---

4 Andrew Smith, *Sugar: A Global History* (London: Reaktion Books, May 2015).

between 2500 and 1700 BC world's first standardized system for weights and measures likely used for trade and/or collecting taxes.[5] Excavations in the Punjab region found cubical weights in graduated sizes which suggest that Harappans had two different series of weights. The first series was represented by the ratio 1:2:4:8:16:32:64 with the smallest weight being 0.8375 g. The smaller weights were likely used to measure luxury goods such as jewellery, while the larger weights were likely used in the trade of bulkier items such as food grains. The second series corresponding to the ratios 0.05:0.1:0.2:0.5:1:2:5: 10:20:50:100:200:500 was decimal where each decimal number was multiplied and divided by two. Archaeologist Shigeo Iwata described excavation of 558 weights from Mohenjo-daro, Harappa and Chanhu-daro. There were not statistical different weights which were excavated from five different 1.5 m deep layers, suggesting strict control over the construction of these weights. Later, Manusmiriti (8th Chapter, Shloka 803) described the following as being one of the duties of a king: 'The king should examine the weights and balances every six months to ensure true measurements and to mark them with the royal stamp.' This was further evidence of the strict standardization and authentication of weights and measures.

Length was similarly standardized. An excavated bronze rod was marked in units of precisely 0.93 cm. An excavated ivory scale was marked in units of 0.1704 cm! Another scale of measurement was based on decimal system with a unit of measurement of 3.34 cm. Excavations have shown that these unit of lengths were used accurately during construction. For example, length, breadth and height of

5 Ian Whitelaw, *A Measure of All Things: The Story of Man and Measurement* (New York, NY: MacMillan Publishers, August 2007).

the fire-baked bricks used by the Harappans to build baths and sewerage were in the ratio 4:2:1, and the dimensions of the bricks were the same in the entire region. Similarly, it is apparent that the measuring sticks such as the ones which were excavated were used to plan construction of cities, roads, drains and houses.

The Harappan weights and measures eventually reached Central Asia and Persia, where they were further modified, which, in turn, subsequently spread to the rest of the world. The world owes much of the concept of standard weights and measures to India today.

A Chequered Present

Unlike the rich ancient history, modern history of technology in India has been chequered at best. As Infosys co-founder N. R. Narayana Murthy said in 2015, 'No invention, technology or idea from India has set the world on fire in the last 60 years.'[6] It can be seen in much mundane metrics as well.[7] Government research and development (R&D) funding as a fraction of overall GDP is relatively small (0.6% for India vs 2.1% for China and 2.8% for the USA; countries such as Israel, South Korea and Japan have much larger expenditures at 4.2%, 4.3% and 3.4%, respectively). In fact, it has been stagnant 0.6–0.7 per cent for the last two decades. Publications from India generate many fewer citations than the world average. India has fewer scientists per capita than Kenya. It also has far fewer patents per capita than other science-focused nations.

---

[6] https://economictimes.indiatimes.com/news/science/no-invention-earth-shaking-idea-from-india-in-60-years-nr-narayana-murthy/articleshow/48085732.cms?from=mdr

[7] Varun Aggarwal, *Leading Science and Technology: India Next?* (New Delhi: SAGE Publications, March 2018).

Over 70 per cent patents in India are filed by multinational companies (MNCs); Indian companies and academia contribute only the remaining 30 per cent. No innovative technology which has come out of India in recent memory appears to be getting used widely.

It is also instructive to compare India against China. Many forget that India and China have similar histories. For most of the first millennium, India and China accounted for a third and a quarter of world economy. However, subsequently they lost their economic prominence first to Japan and Western Europe and then also to the USA, not because their economies shrunk, but because they let the Industrial Revolution pass them by. Countries that led and adopted industrial production technology prospered and grew rapidly, leaving India and China in the dust.

In 1949, when China became a communist country and India adopted its constitution, India was the largest economy in Asia. In fact, India had higher GDP per capita than China even in 1990. The story is much different now.[8] The Chinese per capita GDP is almost five times that of India. A similar story played out in the science and technology space. The number of research articles in India used to be much higher than China. The trend reversed in 1995. Similarly, the ratio of research output of China to India has been accelerating since 1977. The two countries are now poles apart. China has more than five times the number of researchers than India. It has five times the growth rate in terms of number of researchers as India. It has produced almost 4.5 times the number of science and engineering papers than India. It has almost nine times more highly cited papers than India. It has over 320 times

[8] Rebecca Fannin, *Tech Titans of China: How China's Tech Sector Is Challenging the World by Innovating Faster, Working Harder, and Going Global* (Boston, MA: Nichola Brealy, September 2019).

more filed patents than India. It has three times the number of 'unicorns' (start-ups valued at over 1 billion dollars). Its smartphone penetration is almost twice of India. Its investment in R&D is almost 20 times that of India.

In fact, starting far behind India, China is, by most measures, is now a technological superpower.[9] India, on the other hand, cannot boast of much technological impact. China recently entered the ranks of the top 20 nations in the Global Innovation Index. World Intellectual Property Organization which publishes the index opined that China's ranking 'represents a breakthrough for an economy witnessing rapid transformation guided by government policy prioritizing research and development-intensive ingenuity'.

Another instructive comparison is against South Korea. India established its first Indian Institute of Technology (IIT) when South Korea was still ravaged by war. In fact, Korea was an agrarian-based Japanese colony in the first half of the 20th century, just as India had been an agrarian-based British colony for most of the first half of the 20th century. Also, per capita income for both countries was similar at the beginning of the 1960s when South Korea truly started its development. Today, South Korea's per capita income is 15 times that of India, its spending on R&D is 4 times that of India as a fraction of its GDP, and it is a technology powerhouse with global leaders such as Samsung and LG.[10] India, on the other hand, uses foreign technology overwhelmingly and it's export of technology is minimal. In fact, South Korea is second only to Germany in Bloomberg's 2020 Innovation Index. It had been at the top of the list for the previous five years. In contrast, India is ranked 54 in this 60-country list.

---

[9] Kai-Fu Lee, *AI Superpowers: China, Silicon Valley, and the New World Order* (Boston, MA: Houghton Mifflin Harcourt, September 2018).

[10] Leigh Dayton, 'How South Korea Made Itself a Global Innovation Leader', Nature, 27 May 2020, https://www.nature.com/articles/d41586-020-01466-7

Romanticizing Fables

Unsurprisingly, the history of India's past technological contributions keeps getting rewritten and overstated to fantastical levels to shift focus away from the sorry state of the present.

Headquartered in Kolkata, Indian Science Congress Association is a premiere science organization in India, boasting of membership of over 30,000 scientists. Founded in 1914, it meets annually in the first week of January and attracts scientific luminaries, including Nobel Prize winners. The 106th Indian Science Congress was held in January 2019 in Jalandhar and was inaugurated by the prime minister of India. One paper presented at the conference attributed the birth of the Kauravas in the Mahabharat to stem-cell research and in-vitro fertilization (IVF). The presenter said, 'It happened a few thousand years ago. This was science in this country. Mahabharata says, 100 eggs were fertilised, and put to 100 earthen pots. Are they not test-tube babies? Stem cell research in this country was present thousands of years ago.'[11] He then claimed that Vishnu's *dashavatar* or 10 incarnations provided a better and more accurate understanding of human evolution than the Darwinian theory. He further claimed that Ravana, from the Ramayana, had airports in Sri Lanka, which were used for his collection of over 24 different kinds of aircrafts.

Another paper presented at the conference claimed,

---

[11] *Business Standard*, 'Of Kauravas, Stem Cells and Other Baloney at Indian Science Congress', 7 January 2019, https://www.business-standard.com/article/current-affairs/of-kauravas-stem-cells-and-other-baloney-at-indian-science-congress-119010700281_1.html

"There is nothing that Lord Brahma, who is creator of this universe, did not know. He was completely aware of the existence of dinosaurs and even mentioned them in Vedas. Before anyone else in the world, it was Lord Brahma who discovered dinosaurs' existence on earth. India was a hotspot for dinosaur evolution and breeding before extinction. A dinosaur named Rajasaurus had originated in India.[12]"

The 102nd Indian Science Congress was held in Mumbai. The programme included a session on aviation in ancient India. A paper presented by a former principal of a pilot training institute and a college teacher, claimed that aviation technology in ancient India was far advanced than what we see today: 'The knowledge of aeronautics is described in Sanskrit in 100 sections, eight chapters, 500 principles and 3,000 verses. In the modern day, only 100 principles are available,' the authors said, 'In those days aeroplanes were huge in size, and could move left, right, as well as backwards, unlike modern planes which only fly forward.' There were also claims of inter-planetary travel. The authors lamented, 'There is official history and unofficial history. Official history only noted that the Wright Brothers flew the first plane in 1903.'

Of course, the fantastical claims implying a glorious technological past are even more common among non-scientists. Perhaps more famously, the prime minster of India is on record claiming that the Hindu god Ganesha, whose elephant head is attached to a human body, was an example of plastic surgery in ancient India. Another lawmaker claimed in Indian Parliament that astrology

---

[12] Ashu Khosla interview with the Indian Express (https://indianexpress.com/article/india/lord-brahma-first-to-discover-dinosaurs-mentioned-them-in-vedas-pu-geologist-5526043/) about his paper "Biotic assemblages from the Deccan trap-associated sedimentary sequences of penninsular India" presented at the 106th Indian Science Congress.

was 'the biggest science' and that India conducted nuclear tests more than 100,000 years ago. He said, 'Today we are talking about nuclear tests. Lakhs of years ago, Sage Kanad had conducted a nuclear test. Our knowledge and science do not lack anything.'

Attempts to fabricate and inflate India's technological past have also led to attacks against modern science and technology.

At the 106th Indian Science Congress, Kanan Jegathala Krishnan, a senior research scientist proclaimed that Isaac Newton and Albert Einstein knew little about physics. 'Space is heavier than the sun and every other planet and hence compresses all the planets. Equal pressure is applied to them, which is why they are moving,' he said, 'The quality of space is self-compressive, which is something that Newton and Einstein could not understand. Einstein did not guide the world in the correct way.'[13] He also said, 'The present understanding of physics will be destroyed once my theories are proved,' and that after his theories on gravitational phenomena are proven and accepted, gravitational waves would be called 'Narendra Modi Waves'.

In 2018, the higher education minister of India threatened to remove Charles Darwin's evolution theory from school and college curricula: 'Nobody, including our ancestors, in written or oral [texts], has said that they ever saw an ape turning into a human being.'

Acceptance and Propagation of Pseudoscience

Pseudoscience rooted in imagined technological past is both prevalent and being propagated.

---

13 BBC News, 'India Scientists Dismiss Einstein Theories', 7 January 2019, https://www.bbc.com/news/world-asia-india-46778879

When COVID-19 hit India, Amitabh Bachchan, India's most popular Bollywood star with over 80 million followers on Twitter and Facebook combined, claimed that clapping vibrations destroy the potency of the virus. He also promoted the use of homeopathic remedies for the virus.

The 103rd Indian Science Congress featured a paper claiming that the process of ageing can be reversed if one sat on tiger skin and performed yoga. Another paper claimed that cows carry in their bodies bacteria which can convert food into gold.

A chief minister proclaimed, 'Astrology is the biggest science. It is in fact above science. We should promote it.' One Union Minister for Human Resource Development had wanted astrology to be taught in colleges as a branch of science.

The education minister of a state considered it imperative to 'understand the scientific significance' of the cow, since 'it was the only animal in the world to both inhale and exhale oxygen'.

Western validation has also been sought to propagate fantastical claims.

In March of 2020, it was announced that Charles, Prince of Wales, had successfully recovered from effects of COVID-19. An Indian minister declared that the Prince had been cured using Ayurveda, a system of traditional Indian medicine. In a press conference, he declared that the treatment's success 'validates our age-old practice'. The British government had to issue a swift retort: 'This information is incorrect. The Prince of Wales followed the medical advice of the National Health Service in the UK and nothing more.'[14]

---

[14] Gerard de Souza and Prasun Sonwalkar, '"Incorrect Info": Spokesperson of Prince Charles on Ayurveda Treatment', *Hindustan Times*, 3 April 2020, https://www.hindustantimes.

At the 105th Indian Science Congress, India's science and technology minister falsely claimed that Stephen Hawking had once endorsed a particular Vedic theory to be better than Einstein's theory of relativity. It was found later he based this assertion on a Facebook post on a page run by an Indian man whose display name was Stephen Hawking!

What is perhaps most disconcerting is the institutionalization of pseudoscience.

The AYUSH Ministry, responsible for promotion of traditional medicine, has, at times, promoted questionable treatments for COVID-19. It issued a dubious advisory titled 'Homoeopathy for Prevention of Corona Virus Infections: Unani Medicines Useful in Symptomatic Management of Corona Virus Infection' when the virus had started spreading outside China and suggested traditional remedies. In another advisory, the ministry claimed that an arsenic-based homeopathic medicine—Arsenicum Album 30—serves as an effective prophylactic; a vast number of studies have shown that homeopathy does not work. The ministry also recommended at different times an Ayurvedic malaria drug, sesame oil inside the nose, drinking warm water, and eating holy basil leaves. It is worth noting that AYUSH received a 15 per cent budget increase from 2019 to 2020; the Defence Ministry was the only ministry which saw a larger increase that year.[15]

In 2017, a national programme called Scientific Validation and Research on Panchgavya (SVAROP) was initiated by the Department of Science and Technology

com/india-news/incorrect-info-spokesperson-of-prince-charles-on-ayurveda-treatment/story-ituGiZuqhoke46HNFttWbM.html

[15] The Wire, 'Govt Invites Applications for Research on "Indigenous" Cows', 19 February 2020, https://thewire.in/government/research-indigenous-cows-sutra-pic-svarop-panchgavya

(DST), Department of Biotechnology (DBT) and the Council of Scientific & Industrial Research (CSIR), in collaboration with IIT Delhi to study the medicinal properties of *panchagavya*, a concoction that includes cow milk, curd, ghee, urine and dung, and 'to carry out research & development (R&D), and also build capacities, even at grassroots level'. The goal is to validate scientifically[16]:

- Uniqueness of indigenous cows
- *Panchgavya* for medicine and health
- *Panchgavya* and its products for agriculture applications
- *Panchgavya* for food and nutrition
- *Panchgavya*-based utility products

In 2015, the vaastu consultant of the notoriously superstitious chief minister of Telangana was hired as a governmental 'advisor on architecture'. In 2020, Telangana's 150-year-old secretariat building, Errum Manzil, was demolished to make way for a new, vaastu-compliant one. Essentially, vaastu experts had advised the chief minister that the building had *vaastu dosha* (flaws according to vaastu). The chief minister promptly decided to operate from his official residence till a new secretariat is built.[17]

Similar institutionalization is happening in education as well. Perhaps the best science and technology institute in India, the Indian Institute of Science (IISc), organized a

[16] R. Prasad, 'Panchagavya... If Cow Urine Could Cure Cancer', *The Hindu*, 21 July 2017, https://www.thehindu.com/thread/science-health-environment/panchagavya-if-dung-and-urine-could-cure-cancer/article19325496.ece

[17] Aihik Sur, 'Vastu Major Reason for CM's Decision to Raze Errum Manzil?' *The New Indian Express*, 17 July 2019, https://www.newindianexpress.com/states/telangana/2019/jul/17/vastu-major-reason-for-cms-decision-to-raze-errum-manzil-2005126.html

conference on astrology, while vaastu shastra has become a part of many architecture courses.

Increasing Complacency and Low Scientific Temper

Outlandish boasts of India's past technological prowess induce complacency and shift focus away from reality. As Kaushik Basu, one-time chief economist of the World Bank, said, 'For a nation to progress it is important for people to spend time on science, mathematics and literature instead of spending time showing that 5,000 years ago their ancestors did science, mathematics and literature.'

India's first prime minister, Jawaharlal Nehru, coined the term 'scientific temper' to define an attitude of logical and rational thinking. He had said,[18]

> India must break with much of her past and not allow it to dominate the present. Our lives are encumbered with the dead wood of this past, all that is dead and has served its purpose has to go. But it does not mean a break with, or a forgetting of, the vital and life-giving in that past. We can never forget the ideals that have moved our race, the dreams of the Indian people through the ages, the wisdom of the ancients, the buoyant energy and love of life and nature of our forefathers, their spirit of curiosity and mental adventure.... There is in fact essential incompatibility of all dogmas with science. Scientific temper cannot be nurtured by ignoring the fact that there are major differences between the scientific attitude and the theological and metaphysical attitude; especially in respect of dogma.

---

[18] Mridula Mukherjee, 'Nehru's Word: Scientific Temper and an Integral Vision of Life', *National Herald*, 16 May 2021, https://www.nationalheraldindia.com/india/nehrus-word-scientific-temper-and-an-integral-vision-of-life

The 1958 science policy resolution and the 1976 constitutional amendment (Article 51A) reaffirmed India's commitment to cultivating scientific temper.

For a country which has the need for scientific temper enshrined in its Constitution, a realistic assessment of technological past and a modernistic approach to technological future should be a requirement.

The Innovation Problem

The delusion of grandeur also prevents an honest assessment of recent past and present. In 2019, India stood 52nd out of 129 countries on the Global Innovation Index which measures the 'capacity and success in innovation'— 35 ranks behind China. This is an abysmal record for a country which is among world's largest economies and where the people are raised to be proud of the country's technological past. In fact, the global start-up economy was valued at 3 trillion dollars in 2019, a 20 per cent increase in 2 years, primarily driven by investments in AI, blockchain, robotics, advanced manufacturing, autonomous vehicles, agri-tech, medicine and genetics. These sectors still see limited investment in India, let alone impactful and newsworthy output. Even in cases where investment is seen, companies fail at a rate much higher than other countries due to lack of innovation. IBM Institute for Business Value and Oxford Economics performed a study on Indian start-ups and found that 90 per cent of Indian start-ups fail within the first five years. They also found through a survey of venture capitalists that the most common root cause was lack of innovation. Seventy-seven per cent of the surveyed venture capitalists believed that Indian start-ups lacked new technologies or unique business models.

A deeper dive into different technology sectors lays bare the lack of innovation. Consider India's IT industry. It contributes almost 10 per cent of India's GDP. By some estimates, it has generated 4 million jobs and provided indirect employment to over 10 million people. Many believe that we are one of the leaders of the IT revolution. It is true that start-ups abound. It is also true that many start-ups have reached the vaunted unicorn status (market valuation over 1 billion dollars). However, the truth is also that these start-ups largely lack innovation. In fact, Indian unicorn IT start-ups can be best described as imitations of successful ideas which originated elsewhere (with some fine-tuning to serve local needs). Predictably, most of these start-ups wilt anytime there is direct foreign competition.

Large Indian companies are also not building innovative products for the world. Even Indian labs of MNCs are largely engaged in serving local needs.

Similarly, consider the electronics industry. A good barometer for the industry is the smartphone market which, of late, has been a strong technology driver. The top five phone companies in India in terms of market share are Xiaomi (China), Samsung (South Korea), Vivo (China), Oppo (China) and Realme (China). There is no Indian company with a meaningful market share.

India's struggle with semiconductor manufacturing has also been well-documented. One hundred per cent of the chips, memory and display used in India (worth over 10 billion dollars a year) are imported. India has only two semiconductor-manufacturing units—SITAR, a unit of Defence Research and Development Organisation (DRDO), and Semiconductor Complex Limited (SCL), owned by the DST and making chips for India's space and defence programmes. The reported technology used by the two units is 180 nm, a technology which was commercialized over 20 years back!

The Deep Tech Apathy

Innovation in potentially transformative deep technologies is also minimal.

Autonomous vehicles are expected to become a multitrillion business and transform the transportation industry.[19] The World Economic Forum expects that autonomous transportation could also result in multitrillion cost savings due to improved safety, high productivity and reduced environmental impact.

It is no surprise, therefore, that there is a worldwide race towards making cars self-driving.[20] A large number of automotive companies, technology firms as well as fleet service providers have been investing high amount of R&D resources towards development of such vehicles. Even test trials have begun in countries such as the USA, China, Germany, the UK and Japan, among others, with millions of miles logged by autonomous vehicles on local roads. China expects to commercialize autonomous vehicles by 2025. ABI, a marketing firm, predicts 8 million self-driving cars on American roads by the same time.

Indian automobile industry is one of the largest in the world, accounting for over 7 per cent of India's GDP. One would expect, therefore, for Indian automobile industry to have significant R&D devoted to autonomous vehicles.

Instead, the government has repeatedly stated that autonomous driving will not be permitted in India due to

19 Samuel I. Schwartz, *No One at the Wheel: Driverless Cars and the Road of the Future* (New York, NY: PublicAffairs, November 2018).

20 Alex Davies, *Driven: The Race to Create the Autonomous Car* (New York, NY: Simon & Schuster, January 2021).

fear of job losses. The argument made was that India, with its 40 lakh drivers and 25 lakh shortage of drivers, is not ready for autonomous vehicles. The lack of government support, coupled with poor condition of Indian roads and transportation infrastructure as well as high R&D costs, has meant that India will likely miss the opportunities to innovate and lead in this space. India ranked 24th out of 25 countries in the 2019 KPMG Autonomous Vehicles Readiness Index, a list which ranks countries in terms of their readiness.

There are some fledgling efforts. Escorts has been developing technology to allow tractors auto-steer in geo-fenced areas. Mahindra & Mahindra, the largest tractor manufacturer in the world by volume, recently proto-typed a semi-autonomous tractor, which is said to be working on fully autonomous tractors. Not many more efforts exist.

The story is similar with robotics. India's fascination with robotics is old.[21] An 11th-century *Lokpannatti*—Pali translation of old, lost Sanskrit texts—narrates the story of an army of robots (also known as *bhuta vahana yanta* or 'Spirit movement machines' in Pali and Sanskrit) which was erected by the king Ajatashatru in the 5th century BC to protect Buddha's remains after his death in a secret stupa near Pataliputra, modern-day Patna. In the story, robots were designed based on a plan which was original to the Yavanas (or the 'Greek speakers') in 'Roma-visaya' (Greco-Roman culture). Yavanas used these robots for trade, farming and law enforcement. The robots would also kill anyone who threatened to reveal their design. The plan was stolen by one of Ajatashatru's subjects who had

---

[21] Adrienne Mayor, *Gods and Robots: Myths, Machines, and Ancient Dreams of Technology* (Princeton, N: Princeton University Press, November 2018).

married the daughter of one of the Greek robot makers. Ajatashatru's robot army killed anyone who tried to intrude into the stupa. Over time, people forgot about the existence of Buddha's remains and the robots. Two centuries later, king Ashoka heard about the remains and decided to look for them. His army finally found the stupa which had the remains. A fierce battle ensued between the robots and Ashoka's army. Eventually, his army managed to disable and control the robots, and Ashoka became the lord commander of the robot army.

This old fascination with robots has not translated to any significant contribution to robotics or significant use of robots. There are 2.5 million robots being used worldwide today—this is a threefold increase in last two decades. India accounts for only 5,000 of the 2.5 million robots.

A large fraction of the robots is being used to automate production.[22] Globally, there are 74 robot units for every 10,000 employees. The robot density (number of operational industrial robots per 10,000 workers) is 99, 84 and 63 in the UK, the USA and Asia, respectively. China's robot density currently stands at almost 80—it was 25 in 2013. The robot density in India, on the other hand, stands at 3. This is over 25 times lower than China. In fact, it is over four times lower than Indonesia.

Besides, while the world has moved on to autonomous and service robotics, India is still struggling with industrial robotics.

While the number of robots and robotics-related start-ups are steadily increasing in India, the extent in increase is much lower than many developing and comparable developing countries.

---

[22] Martin Ford, *Rise of the Robots: Technology and the Threat of a Jobless Future* (New York, NY: Basic Books, July 2016).

There are several reasons for India to lag severely in robotics. First, India began late. Robots already had significant penetration in many economies before they started being used significantly in India. Second, building a robot requires a large number of hardware parts. Due to the lack of hardware ecosystem in India, these parts need to be imported, increasing the development cycle, cost and inconvenience. Third, robots are capital-intensive, at least in the short term. Since access to cheap labour is easy in India, the use of robots becomes unattractive in the short term. Fourth, there is inadequate training to pursue a highly interdisciplinary area such as robotics. Finally, the government has been concerned about the impact of automation on jobs and, therefore, its policies have been less than encouraging of robotics.

In August 2015 in a first of its kind accident in India, a 23-year-old employee of an automobile factory in Manesar, Haryana, was killed by an industrial robot.[23] The Government of Haryana ordered an enquiry into the accident. As a part of the enquiry, it asked the concerned authorities to get a count of the number of robots being used in Haryana. As the officials scrambled to get the number, they realized that no official count of estimate exists! The same question when asked at the national level produced the same answer. Not only did India not have a count of robots, but it also did not have an official robotics policy either. At the time of writing, India still does not have a robotics policy.

---

[23] Isha Sahni and Dhananjay Jha, 'Manesar: Factory Worker Crushed to Death by Industrial Robot', *Hindustan Times*, 13 August 2015, https://www.hindustantimes.com/gurgaon/manesar-factory-worker-crushed-to-death-by-industrial-robot/story-0Hc7V2uu2L2jlYfo9gEdXK.html

The Great Lag of AI and Other Key Technologies

AI is increasingly being touted as a necessary technology for progress and security.[24] As a result, countries are investing heavily into AI.[25] Far from having its own equivalent of DeepMind or IBM Watson, India is woefully behind in terms of even producing AI-trained engineers.

Again, comparison against China is instructive. By most measures, China is already a leader in the field of AI today. Companies such as Baidu and Tencent routinely produce world-class AI innovations. AI-based companies such as ByteDance are world leaders in their market segment. China hosts some of world's most exciting AI hardware start-ups. It also perhaps is the country with deepest and widest rollout of AI in different spheres of the society. It has created an AI innovation ecosystem which is attractive to some of the world's brightest minds today. The government is actively working on a plan to create a $150 billion domestic AI industry with the goal of China becoming the world's 'innovation centre for AI' by 2030.

In contrast, India has yet to make any significant global or domestic impact in AI. Most of current AI research has been publicly funded and limited to a small number of institutions. Private participation is largely led by the companies which have hitherto mostly focused on supporting outsourcing.

Another key technology of future is quantum computing.[26] A quantum computer can not only lead to an

---

[24] Max Tegmark, *Life 3.0: Being Human in the Age of Artificial Intelligence* (New York, NY: Vintage, July 2018).

[25] Erik Brynjolfsson and Andrew McAfee, *The Second Machine Age: Work, Progress, and Prosperity in a Time of Brilliant Technologies* (New York, NY: W.W. Norton, January 2014).

[26] Chris Bernhardt, *Quantum Computing for Everyone* (Cambridge, MA: MIT Press, March 2019).

exponential increase in a performance-enabling solution to some of world's hardest computing problems, but it can also be used to decrypt enemy communication.[27] Expectedly, there has been a scramble among nations to build a quantum computer. European Union (EU) announced a 1 billion Euro funding in 2016. Several groups in Europe (e.g., Delft University in the Netherlands) are now world leader in quantum computing. The USA announced a 1.2-billion-dollar funding in quantum computing in 2018. The US private sector has already led quantum computing efforts with Google and IBM already building world's most powerful quantum computers. Similarly, Amazon and Microsoft are already offering cloud services for quantum computing. China has already put in 2 billion dollars towards quantum computing research and now boasts of being a major innovation centre in quantum computing.

India, again, has been a laggard with no visible contribution or company in the quantum space. There are several reasons. Fewer than 200 uncoordinated researchers in India work on quantum computing. This is a smaller number than the size of quantum computing-focused groups in many large companies! No single Indian institution seems to have more than five quantum computing researchers, eliminating potential of any experimental breakthrough in this multidisciplinary and highly collaborative field. Second, lack of hardware fabrication ecosystem in India means that infrastructure and experimental facilities for quantum computing research are hard to build. Third, the private sector is largely uninvolved. So even though the government recently promised a significant outlay for quantum computing

[27] Robert S. Sutor, *Dancing with Qubits: How Quantum Computing Works and How It Can Change the World* (Birmingham: Packt, November 2019).

research (1.2 billion dollars over five years), success is unlikely due to lack of trained manpower and commercial pull.

'Jugaad' Isn't Enough

Of course, the continued failings at technology race encourage many to focus on 'jugaad' as an example of 'India's innovative spirit'.[28] While whipping yogurt drinks using washing machines and building vehicles using irrigation pumps and parts of other vehicles may make some fawn, jugaad is a testament to how things have gone wrong. Instead of enjoying the productivity and income advantages which true technological innovations would have produced, people are forced to invent workarounds simply to make a living. For a country that is wholly reliant on others for almost all its electronics, military equipment and fast trains, it must snap out of its delusion of grandeur; a bit of technological humility will go a long way.

---

[28] Jaideep Prabhu, Navi Radjou, and Simone Ahuja, *Jugaad Innovation* (Noida: Penguin, June 2012).

CHAPTER 3

THE FAITH PARADOX

A smartphone-based ridesharing taxi driver steps out of home in the morning after eating a spoonful of curd and sugar for good luck, gets into his GPS-fitted vehicle which has a bundle of a lemon and chillies hanging at front to ward off evil, and drives all day wearing multiple rings with gemstones, bought online and each serving a different celestial purpose, while stopping and waiting for someone else to pass when a black cat crosses a busy neighbour-hood road at a distance. During the day, he uses his mul-tiple phones, with multiple SIM cards, to get ride requests through Ola, Uber and Meru apps at the same time, plays PUBG during his short lunch break, watches cricket matches when they are on, live streams *aarti* from the tem-ple he frequently visits, and fields multiple WhatsApp calls from friends, family and his vehicle owner, each announced by a Bhajan ringtone.

This taxi driver's day can be a typical day in India, which portrays reconciliation of superstitious beliefs with a tight embrace of technology. In fact, India's fascinating relationship with technology is nowhere seen better than in this intertwining of technology and seemingly antithetical beliefs and practices.

India, a Land of Superstitions[1]

Some superstitions are seemingly harmless. Putting a bundle of a lemon and a few chillies in front of homes, shops or vehicles is supposed to ward off evil. So does kohl on infants' foreheads or women's eyes. Eating a spoonful of curd and sugar before an important task is supposed to bring good luck. Being underneath a peepal tree at night is an invitation to be possessed or killed by a ghost. Not sweeping house at night and keeping lights on encourage Laxmi, the goddess of wealth, to visit. Cutting nails and hair on Saturday brings bad luck. Taking in bath in the Ganges absolves one of all sins. Sneezing thrice and looking into broken mirrors bring bad luck. Black cat crossing one's path is bad omen. Right eye twitching is good for men, while left eye twitching is good for women. Numbers 8 and 13 are unlucky. Shaking legs portends loss of prosperity.

Some are harmful to varying degrees. Widows are considered inauspicious, often shunned, and expected to wear white and not remarry. Menstruating women are considered impure and are expected to not enter temples or kitchens. Holy men and tantrics can give *prasad*, which guarantees success. Women born with *mangal dosh*—an astrological anomaly—bring quick death to the husband when they marry. So they should ritualistically marry an animal or a tree before the actual marriage.

Some have been downright evil.

---

[1] John Oman, *Cults, Customs and Superstitions of India* (Chestnut Hill, PA: Adamant Media, November 2005).

Sati was a practice where a widow was burned alive on the funeral pyre of her husband.[2] It was believed that a woman was at least partially culpable if the husband died before her. Burning alive alongside the husband would remove culpability and allow her to protect the husband from new dangers in the afterlife. The practice was widespread in certain parts of India and continued unabated till it was abolished in 1829. Incidences of sati continued, however, and were largely described as voluntary acts. An Act was passed in 1987 criminalizing the glorification of sati. There continue to be sporadic incidences.

Another heinous superstition encourages human and animal sacrifice to appease the rain gods and the fertility gods. Several hundreds of cases of child sacrifice have been reported in last two decades just in Uttar Pradesh.

Yet another evil superstition brands women as witches who are then subsequently attacked and killed.[3] More than a thousand people have been killed in India for practising witchcraft in last 12 years.[4]

Our embrace of technology continues alongside these superstitions. These superstitions are common across caste, class and regions, and span all education levels and backgrounds.

The God-man Celebration

India is a land of many faiths and beliefs. There is also a large diversity in who people follow.

---

[2] Sakuntala Narasimhan, *Sati: Widow Burning in India* (New York, NY: Anchor Books, July 1992).

[3] R. N. Saletore, *Indian Witchcraft: A Study in Indian Occultism* (New Delhi: South Asia Books, December 1990).

[4] https://www.arcgis.com/apps/Cascade/index.html?appid=44f8a8cc132b4b76b8aedb86 72580edf

A very Indian superstition-based phenomenon is the popularity of god-men.[5] God-men are apotheosized as higher beings, may or may not belong to a religious order, tend to have a large number of followers, often followed by large wealth, and many of them are claimed to perform miracles.

Some god-men (there are female equivalents as well) have enormous clout in India, including in the highest corridors of power.[6]

Chandraswami, a god-man popular in the 1980s and 1990s, earned notoriety as a spiritual adviser to P. V. Narsimha Rao, former Indian prime minister.[7] He was later arrested for fraud and foreign exchange violations. He was also investigated in the assassination of Rajiv Gandhi, another former Indian prime minister.

Sathya Sai Baba was a god-man with a large following and a reputation for miracles such as materializing sacred ash, jewellery and watches. Such was his clout that in 2001, when he was accused of manipulation and abuse, an official governmental letter was made public, defending the god-man. Among the signatories were Atal Bihari Vajpayee, erstwhile prime minister of India, and P. N. Bhagwati and Ranganath Mishra, former chief justices of the Supreme Court of India. Sathya Sai Baba's burial after his death in 2011 was attended by veritable who's who of India, including the then Indian prime minister. It is said that over 500,000 attended his burial.

Another god-man, Gurmeet Ram Rahim Singh of Dera Sacha Sauda, claimed several miraculous powers.[8]

---

[5] Peter Brent, *Godmen of India* (London: Allen Lane, January 1972).

[6] Khushwant Singh, *Gods and Godmen of India* (Noida: HarperCollins, November 2014).

[7] Bhavdeep Kang, *Gurus: Stories of India's Leading Babas* (Bengaluru: Westland, June 2016).

[8] Anurag Tripathi, *Dera Sacha Sauda and Gurmeet Ram Rahim: A Decade-long Investigation* (New Delhi: Penguin, May 2018).

He enjoyed considerable political clout and was openly courted for support by different political parties before elections in Punjab. In fact, he was on *The Indian Express*'s list of 100 most powerful Indians of 2015. He is currently serving life imprisonment for multiple counts of rape and murder.

Shoban Sarkar, a local god-man of Unnao, Uttar Pradesh, is responsible for perhaps the most bizarre god-man-related story. He claimed in 2013 that he saw in his dreams that over 1,000 tonnes of gold were buried under the ruins of on old fort of a 19th-century king, Ram Baksh Singh. He then wrote to the president of India, Ministry of Mines, as well as the Archaeological Survey of India (ASI), requesting them to excavate the site. Such was his clout that one of his disciples contacted Charan Das Mahant, Union Minister of State for Food Processing Industries, who, in turn, convinced other officials in the government to start excavation. So an entire government machinery was activated based on the dream of this god-man! ASI excavated the site for a little over a month—simply based on this god-man's dream—and, unsurprisingly, found nothing.

There are stories even of dreams *about* god-men. Pratibha Patil, then a nominee for being the president of India, openly declared in 2007 that a long-dead god-man had visited her in her dream. The god-man had let her know (in the dream!) that she would be nominated as the president. Pratibha Patil went on to serve a full five-year term as the president of India. This highlights how common—and commonly acknowledged—the seeming paradox of beliefs is in India.

India's love of technology continues alongside love for these miracle-working god-men. People of all hues and class flock to these god-men for spirituality, connection and advice. There seems to be no trouble for people to reconcile science and technology with the miracle-touting god-men. In fact, access to god-men is often through latest technologies—phones, tablets, computers and TV—for a large fraction of followers.

Paradoxical Existence of Pseudoscience

While people have a choice to their beliefs, some beliefs, such as astrology, coexist paradoxically with technological advancement.

Astrology is deeply ingrained in Indian life. Astrologists are often consulted before naming an infant, deciding on who and when to marry, starting a new home or a business, or even organizing the calendar.

While scientific consensus exists about astrology being a pseudoscience and perhaps not being anything more than storytelling, there are several universities in India which offer advanced degrees in astrology. In fact, in a widely publicized case from 2001, Andhra Pradesh High Court allowed India's University Grants Commission (UGC), which argued that 'Vedic astrology is not only one of the main subjects of our traditional and classical knowledge but this is the discipline, which lets us know the events happening in human life and in universe on time scale,' to offer courses and degrees in astrology. A petition challenging astrology's status as a science was subsequently sent to the Supreme Court of India, stating that the introduction of astrology to university curricula is 'a giant leap backwards, undermining whatever scientific credibility the country has achieved so far', was dismissed by the Supreme Court. This Supreme Court decision has been continually referred to by lower courts, subsequently allowing continued teaching of astrology in Indian universities.

The popularity of astrology in India continues in spite of high-profile excoriation of astrologers as well as their well-publicized failures at predicting events accurately. In 1951, after some astrologer's prediction that Pakistan will attack India which will result in a full-blown war made it to the newspapers, the erstwhile Prime Minister of India Jawaharlal Nehru declared, 'I would like to pass a law against the practice of astrology and other forms of soothsaying.' He further went on to say, 'Are we going to be guided by what fools tell us because they looked up at the starry forecasts?' 'We are a decadent people waiting on the stars,' he added.

In 1963, astrologers predicted a global catastrophe. Business and travel slowed down in India. Maharaja of Sikkim Palden Thondup Namgyal postponed his marriage to American Hope Cooke. Mass prayer meetings were organized. Jawaharlal Nehru had to publicly term it 'a matter for laughter'.

In 1981, an astrologer was arrested when he made a prediction about the assassination of then Indian Prime Minister Indira Gandhi and her son Rajiv Gandhi, and subsequent prime ministership of H. N. Bahuguna.

The head of Indian Astrologers Federation predicted a war between India and Pakistan in 1982. Of course, that war did not happen.

When astrologers predicted in year 2000 that there would be catastrophes, volcanic eruptions and tidal waves, an entire sea-side village in Gujarat panicked and abandoned their houses. Not only did the predicted event not occur, but the vacant houses were also burgled.

These high-profile failures and denunciations of astrology notwithstanding, India's faith in astrology continues to be strong alongside its faith in technology in spite of the two being seemly antithetical. In fact, there are a large number of phone applications, e-commerce websites, and TV and web shows devoted wholly to promotion of astrology.

Vaastu shastra is often used to decide the design, layout and measurements of Indian houses. The system is based on ancient texts and beliefs and in many cases does not align with modern architectural concepts. Indeed, vaastu shastra is considered pseudoscience by many. In *Astronomy, Pseudoscience, and Rational Thinking*, famed scientist Jayant Narlikar highlights some illogical principles of vaastu: 'Sites shaped like a triangle ... will lead to government harassment ... parallelogram can lead to quarrels in the family.' Another quote about vaastu from the book says, 'If the boundary lines of the plot on which the house is built are not parallel to the magnetic axis, such land is poor for overall growth, peace, and happiness.'

This has not stopped high-profile adoption of vaastu even at the governmental level. Demolition of Telangana Secretariat to build a vaastu-compliant one (Chapter 2) is simply one example. An ex-chief minister of Andhra Pradesh, famously used to seek help from vaastu consultants to solve his political problems. In one instance, it was recommended to him to enter his office from an east-facing gate to ward off his political troubles. The problem was that there was a slum on the east-facing side of his office, which would have prevented his car from entering. Unfazed, he ordered the slum to be demolished, making way for his car's entrance.

Vaastu is also creeping into higher education. There are several institutions which now offer courses in vaastu shastra, alongside courses in technology and innovation.

A similar story plays out for numerology, palmistry and use of gemstones as well—these pseudosciences continue to be popular even among people who value innovation and technology.

Rampant superstition leads to occasional massive disinformation and hysteria among seemingly technology and innovation-loving people. The milk miracle (Chapter 1) was only one example.

On 5 March 2012, the feet of a statue of Jesus in Mumbai started weeping water. The priest and the Catholic laity organizations associated with the Our Lady of Velankanni Church started promoting the idea that it was a sign from the God. Hundreds of devotees flocked. Many started drinking the 'holy water'.

Sanal Edamaruku, a rationalist author, went to investigate and found that the source of the drip was a faulty sewage system which leaked water due to capillary action.[9]

Upon discovery, several Catholic organizations accused Edamaruku of blasphemy and threatened to call for his prosecution. Edamaruku left India and settled in Finland. It is important to do a double take here. Essentially, a simple, direct scientific explanation of a 'miracle' was not sufficient to satisfy the believers so much so that the person with the explanation was compelled to leave India. This is a great example of the constant undercurrent of tension between faith and science and technology in India.

Debunking Myths and Challenging Superstitions

There has been a small but influential group of people—scientists and technologists featuring prominently in this group—which has voiced frustration at the reach of

---

[9] Henry McDonald, 'Jesus Wept ... Oh, It's Bad Plumbing. Indian Rationalist Targets "Miracles"', *The Guardian*, 23 November 2012, https://www.theguardian.com/world/2012/nov/23/india-blasphemy-jesus-tears

superstitions in India.[10] Many organizations, including Indian Rationalist Association, organize travelling seminars to expose false claims of different god-men and astrologers, often by demonstrating tricks behind the claimed miracles.

God-men, astrologers and soothsayers also have been publicly challenged. In 1963, Abraham Kovoor[11] famously declared an award of 100,000 Sri Lankan rupees to anyone who could demonstrate supernatural powers under foolproof and fraud-proof conditions. The challenge went like this:

> I, Abraham T. Kovoor of 'Tiruvalla', Pamankada Lane, Colombo-6 do hereby state that I am prepared to pay an award of 100,000 Sri Lankan rupees to any one from any part of the world who can demonstrate supernatural or miraculous powers under fool-proof and fraud-proof conditions. This offer will remain open till my death or till I find the first winner.
>
> Godmen, saints, yogis, and siddhas who claim that they acquired miraculous powers through spiritual exercises and divine boons win this award if they can perform any of the following 'miracles'
>
> 1. Read the serial number of a sealed-up currency note.
> 2. Produce an exact replica of a currency note.
> 3. Stand stationary on burning cinders for half a minute without blistering the feet.
> 4. Materialise from nothing an object I ask.
> 5. Move or bend a solid object using psychokinetic power.
> 6. Read the thought of another person using telepathic powers.

---

[10] Johannes Quack, *Disenchanting India: Organized Rationalism and Criticism of Religion in India* (New York, NY: Oxford University Press, November 2011).

[11] Abraham Kovoor, *Begone Godmen* (Mumbai: Jaico, February 2013).

7. Make an amputated limb grow even one inch by prayer, spiritual or faith healing powers, Lourdes water, holy ash, blessing etc.
8. Levitate in the air by yogic power.
9. Stop the heart-beat for five minutes by yogi power.
10. Stop breathing for thirty minutes by yogi power.
11. Walk on water.
12. Leave the body in one place and reappear in another place.
13. Predict a future event.
14. Develop creative intelligence or get enlightened through transcendental or yogic meditation.
15. Speak or understand an unknown language as a result of rebirth or by being possessed by a spirit, holy or evil.
16. Produce a spirit or ghost to be photographed.
17. Disappear from the negative when photographed.
18. Get out of a locked room by spiritual power.
19. Increase the quantity by weight of a substance by divine power.
20. Detect a hidden object.
21. Convert water into petrol or wine.
22. Convert wine into blood.
23. Astrologers and palmists, who hoodwink the gullible by saying that astrology and palmistry are perfectly 'Scientific', can win my award if they can pick out correctly—within a margin of five percent error—those of males, females, and living and the dead from a set of ten palm prints or astrological charts giving the exact time of birth correct to the minute, and places of birth with their latitudes and longitudes.

I invite miracle performers like Satya Sai Baba, Pandrimalai Swamigal, Neelakanta Tathaji, Nirmala Devi Srivastava, Pujya Dadaji, Dattabal, Triprayar Yogini, Gtirudev Anandamurthi, Kamubhai, Chinmayanand, Acharya Rajneesh, Muktanand, Swami Rama, Swami Haridas, Sivabalayogi, Bhagavan Gnanananda, Gurumaharaj-ji, Maharishi Mahesh Yogi, Hazarath Ali, Dr. Vadlaimudi, C. S. Teerthangar, R.P. Tiwari, Uri Geller, Nelya Michailova, Jeane Dixon, Sybil Leek and the numerous 'professors' of astrology and palmistry, in India and numerous other gurus, swamijis, mahants, acharyas, andas, babas and bhagavans who have found fresh pastures and wealthier gullibles in Western Countries, to take up my challenge and prove to skeptics like me that they are not hoaxers.

Till Kovoor's death in 1978, to no one's surprise, none could claim the award amount. Similar challenges have been successfully continued by others.

Another well-publicized challenge was offered by Hossur Narasimhaiah, then vice chancellor of Bangalore University. Narasimhaiah formed a committee in 1976 'to rationally and scientifically investigate miracles and other verifiable superstitions' and wrote Sathya Sai Baba three widely publicized letters challenging him to perform his miracles under controlled conditions. The letters were ignored by Sai Baba. Sai Baba simply declared that

Science must confine its inquiry only to things belonging to the human senses, while spiritualism transcends the senses. If you want to understand the nature of spiritual power you can do so only through the path of spirituality and not science. What science has been able to unravel is merely a fraction of the cosmic phenomena....[12]

Sai Baba's refusal to accept Narasimhaiah's challenge led to widespread debate, but Sai Baba's popularity endured.

Popular documentaries such as UK Channel 4's *Guru Busters* have also exposed miracles by gurus as simply sleight of hand. But they do not seem to have affected the popularity of god-men.

There have been legal attempts to curb superstition. The 1954 Drugs and Magic Remedies (Objectionable

---

[12] Interview given by Sathya Sai Baba to the Senior Editor, Sri R.K. Karanjia of Blitz News Magazine, September, 1976. http://saibaba.ws/articles/interviewwithjournalistsept1976.htm

Advertisements) Act prohibits advertisements of magical remedies, like amulets or spells, for 56 listed diseases. It also curbs sales and promotion of so-called miracle drugs and cures. However, the law is rarely enforced, and several such products are freely available. The list of diseases is also severely outdated—14 of the diseases in the list are now curable, and newer diseases like AIDS are not on the list.

Article 51A (h) of the Constitution of India lists that it is a fundamental duty of every Indian citizen 'to develop the scientific temper, humanism and the spirit of inquiry and reform.' The Article was enshrined in the Constitution during Emergency. By most measures, the popularity of god-men has only increased since then.

Bihar passed the Prevention of Witch (Daain) Practices Act in 1999, which outlaws witch-hunting and carries a sentence of three months for accusing a woman of being a witch and six months for causing any physical or mental harm. The law was subsequently adopted by Jharkhand as well. Chhattisgarh passed in 2005 the Tonahi Pratadna Nivaran Act, which holds a sentence of three years for accusing a woman of being a witch and five years for causing her physical harm. Rajasthan's Women (Prevention of Atrocities) Bill also covers witch-hunting. Odisha passed in 2013 the Odisha Prevention of Witch-Hunting Act, which has a maximum penalty of seven years. In 2013, the Anti-Superstition and Black Magic Act was passed in Maharashtra. The Act criminalizes practices related to black magic, human sacrifices, use of magic remedies to cure ailments and other such acts which may exploit people's superstitions.

Lawsuits have been brought to prevent the spread of superstitions. In 2001, when UGC decided to allow introduction of astrology courses in universities, P. M.

Bhargava, founder of the Centre for Cellular and Molecular Biology, and others filed a petition in the Andhra Pradesh High Court against UGC's decision. The court dismissed the petition stating that it had no expertise on the subject and thus could not interfere unless UGC had clearly violated a law. The same group subsequently filed a petition in the Supreme Court of India. However, the case was dismissed there as well after the Government of India argued that the petitioner's concerns were unfounded since the courses would not be mandatory and that several Western universities also offer courses in astrology.[13]

Janhit Manch, a non-profit organization, filed a public interest litigation in the Bombay High Court in 2010, asking the court to use its power to direct a legislation to make teaching of scientific temper compulsory in schools under Article 51A (h) of the Constitution. It also sought that a disclaimer be added to advertisements about astrology, vaastu shastra, feng shui, tarot cards, etc., under the Drugs and Magic Remedies (Objectionable Advertisements) Act, 1954, stating that these products and practices are only for entertainment. It also wanted the court to dismiss the plea citing the *2004 Bhargava vs UGC, Supreme Court* case and stated that Article 51A (h) was too vague to be implemented using its powers.

There have also been several lawsuits seeking to invalidate Section 295A of the Indian Penal Code which criminalizes 'deliberate and malicious acts intended to outrage religious feelings of any class by insulting its religion or religious beliefs'; it includes 'words, either spoken or written, or by signs or by visible representations'. The offence holds a maximum penalty of three years of prison. Section 295A has been used previously to intimidate and prosecute critics of superstitions.

---

[13] *The Hindu*, 'Introduction of Vedic Astrology Courses in Varsities Upheld', 6 May 2004.

Attempts to debunk superstition have had serious consequences, as such attempts typically face a strong opposition from the general public. Finnish exile of Edamaruku was one extreme example. As another extreme example, Narendra Dabholkar, the founder and president of the Maharashtra Andhashraddha Nirmoolan Samiti (MANS; the Committee to Eradicate Superstition in Maharashtra), was gunned down in 2013.[14] Dabholkar had campaigned against superstitions and god-men and had made several attempts to get an anti-superstition law enacted in the state of Maharashtra. It was under his supervision that MANS had drafted the Anti-Jaadu Tona Bill. When accused of being anti-religion, he had said, 'In the whole of the bill, there's not a single word about God or religion. Nothing like that. The Indian constitution allows freedom of worship and nobody can take that away, this is about fraudulent and exploitative practices.'[15] The bill was cleared as the Anti-Superstition and Black Magic Ordinance the day after his assassination.

Cohabitation of Science and Superstitions

Despite all efforts, superstitions continue to be rooted, even among scientists and technologists.

Officials at the Indian Space Research Organisation (ISRO) famously place a replica of the rocket at god's feet at the famed Lord Venkateswara Temple in Tirumala

---

[14] Ellen Barry, 'Battling Superstition, Indian Paid with His Life', *The New York Times*, 25 August 2013, https://www.nytimes.com/2013/08/25/world/asia/battling-superstition-indian-paid-with-his-life.html

[15] Narendra Dabholkar, Govind Pansare, and M. M. Kalburgi, *The Republic of Reason: Words They Could Not Kill—Selected Writings of Dabholkar, Pansare and Kalburgi* (Delhi: Sahmat, January 2015).

before every rocket mission, seeking blessings for a successful flight.[16]

Similarly, no rocket countdown is started at ISRO at *Rahu Kaalam*. *Rahu* is considered an inauspicious planet in vedic astrology. Any time that falls under the influence of *Rahu*, *Rahu Kaalam*, is considered a bad time for starting any new work. Chances of attaining desired results are considered higher if the work starts outside *Rahu Kaalam*.

After launching PSLV-C12 rocket, ISRO skipped to PSLV-C14. There was no PSLV-C13 in the launch roster.

Pujas are conducted before starting the integration of different stages of a rocket.

As a former ISRO chief said, 'One cannot take chance with God and poison.'

There are other high-profile instances. In a well-publicized incident in 2019, India's defence minister went to France to take delivery of the 36 long-awaited Rafale aircrafts which were acquired from France by the Indian Air Force. On receipt of the first Rafale aircraft, to the amusement of the French audience, the minister cracked a coconut, placed flowers, tied mouli and applied Om tilak behind the cockpit, while tying chillies and lemons to the wheels of the aircraft.[17] In this ceremony, the minister was assisted by an Indian priest who had been arranged in advance by the Indian ambassador to France on instructions by the government. The minister promptly flew on a sortie as a passenger right after the ceremony.

---

[16] Indo-Asian News Service, 'Isro Scientists Superstitious, Follow Rahu Kaalam, Unlucky 13 before Rocket Launch: Former Official', *India Today*, 21 July 2019, https://www.indiatoday.in/science/chandrayaan-2-mission/story/isro-scientists-superstitious-follow-rahu-kaalam-unlucky-13-before-rocket-launch-former-official-1571882-2019-07-21

[17] NDTV, 'Rajnath Singh Performs "Shastra Puja" after Receiving First Rafale Jet', 19 October 2019, https://www.ndtv.com/india-news/rajnath-singh-to-perform-shastra-puja-after-receiving-rafale-jet-in-paris-2112754

A well-publicized survey called 'Worldviews and Opinions of Scientists in India' was conducted in 2007 by the Institute for the Study of Secularism in Society and Culture of the Trinity College with the help of the Center for Inquiry (India).[18] One thousand and one hundred doctorate degree-holding scientists from 130 institutes in India were surveyed. The results were striking. Forty-nine per cent scientists believed that prayers could be effective. Sixteen per cent believed in faith healing. Thirty-eight per cent believed that god could perform miracles. Twenty-four per cent believed that holy people could perform miracles. Twenty-nine per cent believed in sins and deeds of past life and in life after death. Seven per cent believed in ghosts, spirits, connection between comets and human events, and caste system. Fourteen per cent believed in Vaastu. Fourteen per cent believed in astrology. Sixty-nine per cent strongly approved introduction of astrology courses in universities. Sixty-seven per cent strongly approved the tradition of seeking blessings of Tirupati before rocket launches.

It should not be a surprise, therefore, that the general population continues to carry superstitions while embracing technology.

In fact, many have argued that there is no dichotomy between technology and superstitions or religiosity in the Indian context. One of the authors of the aforementioned survey noted, 'Secularism has a unique meaning in India.... A vast majority of scientists perceive secularism as tolerance for various religions and philosophies and this is reflect[ed] in their approach to scientific issues.'

Even in the above survey, for example, only eight per cent of the scientists said that they would not work on stem cell research because of their moral or religious

---

[18] Institute for the Study of Secularism in Society and Culture, 'Worldviews and Opinions of Scientists: India 2007–2008', June 2008, https://commons.trincoll.edu/worldview sofscientists/

beliefs. Forty-four per cent of the scientists were willing to criticize and confront religious practices if they contradicted accepted scientific theories. Thirty-three per cent agreed with occasional confrontation. They also did not differentiate much between doing research on cows (a holy animal for most Hindus) and pigs.

In 2020, Pew Research conducted an in-depth interview of some Hindus, Muslims and Buddhists to understand their view of the intersection between technology and faith.[19] A large fraction of the interviewed Muslims said that Islam and science were mostly compatible, with a small number of exceptions centred around human origins and evolution. Hindu interviews described science and religion as overlapping spheres, often pointing to instances where they claimed that science later discovered what their religion had already taught them—health benefits of turmeric and antimicrobial properties of copper were presented as examples. The theory of human evolution was not considered contrary to their religion. Buddhists described science and religion as two separate and unrelated spheres—religion offers guidance on how to love a moral life, while science describes observable phenomena. In fact, they were not able to identify any point of conflict between science and their religion. Gene editing and cloning were the only issues which raised religious concerns.

A Handyman of Growing Evangelism

Superstitions and god-men tap into the nagging feeling that many Indians have that globalization and consumerism are threatening Indian traditions. Old superstitions and new-age god-men allow the followers to feel both as a citizen of the world and the one steeped into tradition.

---

[19] Courtney Johnson, Cary Lynne Thigpen, and Cary Funk, 'On the Intersection of Science and Religion', Pew Research Center, 26 August 2020, https://www.pewforum.org/essay/on-the-intersection-of-science-and-religion/

This is especially true of the burgeoning middle class which continually suffers from a cultural and social crisis which it seeks to run away from.

Another possible reason for popularity of superstitions and god-men is the highly inequitable distribution of the spoils of economic development. While a section of the society prospered, rest sought solace in the alternate reality offered by the god-men.

Yet another reason is that the education system has not fulfilled its role of promoting rational thinking and scientific temper. The well-educated continue to embrace the irrational under the pretext of traditions and culture.

Also, there is continuous reinforcement from the media which promotes and celebrates these god-men and superstitions as well as from the celebrities who continue to embrace them. This creates a vicious cycle which is difficult to break.

In fact, one could argue that superstitions and god-men have thrived not in spite of technology, but because of technology. Technology is being successful as a tool to spread beliefs in all contexts, whether it is related to business, politics or religion. God-men are no different.

Gurmeet Ram Rahim Singh of Dera Sacha Sauda dramatically increased his popularity through his videos and films. Sri Sri Ravi Shankar and Baba Ramdev created and reached millions of followers through TV. TV evangelism on channels such as Aastha and Sanskar is at record high.

Many god-men and their organizations have strong online and social media presence.

Art of Living (AOL) founded by Ravi Shankar and worth hundreds of millions of dollars has a full-fledged 45-person digital team, the Art of Living Digital, which supports online payments, e-commerce, mobile application development, digital content and social media management. It's 'Art of Living' mobile app was the first subscription-based spiritual app in the country; devotees could pay for access to religious lyrics, talks, chants, videos and e-books. Ravi Shankar himself has over 4.2 million followers on Twitter.

In fact, the relationship between AOL and technology is particularly unique. The foundation has created a successful volunteer-run, for-profit company, Sumeru Software, which provides software, security and banking solutions to blue client such as Aditya Birla Finance, Axis Bank India and other MNCs, and invests its profits into social projects run by AOL. The Art of Living Digital is simply a part of the larger Sumeru Software team of 200 employees.

Sadhguru Jaggi Vasudev's Isha Foundation has over 100-strong digital team which creates and manages content for his millions of online followers. The Sadhguru app has been downloaded over 1 million times. Users can register and pay for programmes like Guru Pooja, Shoonya and Samyanma through the app. Sadhguru has over 3.5 million followers on Twitter, 6.2 million followers on YouTube and over 4.4 million followers on Instagram.

Ramdev has over 10 million followers on Facebook and millions of followers on other platforms. He also built Patanjali, a ₹10,000 crore fast-moving consumer goods (FMCG) business based on his brand. Patanjali's app, with close to a million downloads, allows one to discover and buy Patanjali's products. He also owns through Vedic Broadcasting several media channels, including Aastha TV. He has also built a messaging platform, Kimbho, to compete with the WhatsApps of the world. The platform had to be taken down due to security and privacy concerns.

Self-styled god-man and rape accused Nithyananda Paramashivam also successfully used his wide online presence to spread his claims, including that he could delay sunrise, see through smog and walls, cause cattle to speak in Tamil and Sanskrit and disprove that E is not equal to MC square. His NLighten mobile app discusses his secrets of opening the third eye, blindfolded body scanning, blood group scanning and family scanning. The app also allows users to register and pay for different sevas and workshops. There is even an app targeted at kids, 'NLighten for kids', which covers topics such as clairvoyance, mind reading, remote view and body scan. Nithyananda reportedly fled India at the end of 2019 and founded his own self-proclaimed island nation, Kailaasa. Kailaasa has an exhaustive website to connect to the followers, a set of e-embassies to process visas and two online knowledge repositories—Nithyanandpedia and Kailasapedia—for controlled information dissemination.

In fact, India's technology industry now clearly recognizes the need to cater to India's religiosity. Religious and spirituality market is estimated at 40 billion dollars. Several technology entrepreneurs have started getting into this market.

OnlinePrasad.com was founded by Goonjan Mall, a senior analyst at Bain & Company, after discovering that difficulty of getting prasad at a temple ruined the experience of many devotees. The company backed by luminaries such as former MD of Microsoft India and founder of Sify allows one to order 'authentic' prasad from a temple of choice. It has also diversified into organizing pujas (or religious ceremonies) and feasts at temples of choice as well as online ordering of devotion-related items.

Companies such as ePuja have similarly raised millions of dollars to serve the prasad and puja market.

There are companies such as ProudUmmah.com, focusing on Islamic pilgrimages to Mecca.

Shubhpuja.com, in addition to puja and prasad, also offers astrology, numerology and vaastu consultations.

Similarly Kalpnik offers 'immersive and interactive' experiences to devotees using virtual reality (VR).

Companies such as Mokshshil organize remote personalized funeral and post-death events.

Most Indian travel websites offer customized religious pilgrimage packages.

These initiatives simply mirror business in other societies which are focused on faith, religion or culture, and have been shown to be highly lucrative.

India's Modern Hesitancy against Technology and Innovation

The cultural and religious hesitation towards technology and change has also gotten routinely reinforced over time by the several adverse experiences India has gone through at different times that technology was blamed for.

For example, India had a rough interaction with technology and change during the Industrial Revolution.[20] Cotton production shifted to the southern US devastating cotton growers in India. Similarly, the new textile machinery devastated the cloth weavers in India. In 1834, the governor of the British East India Company wrote, 'The misery hardly finds a parallel in the history of commerce. The bones of the cotton-weavers are bleaching the plains of India.' When the British mill owners and the US slave owners discovered that India remained competitive due to the finer quality and lower price of the Indian cloth, impossible production quotas were set by the British agents, and the defaulting Indian weavers had their goods confiscated. After the Luddite rebellion ended, harsh restrictions were imposed on the export of India's finished cloth, eventually destroying the Indian textile industry and the lives and livelihood of its workers.

Such was the impact that country started seeing new technology and mechanization as agents of ruin.

---

[20] Shashi Tharoor, *Inglorious Empire: What the British Did to India* (London: Hurst, September 2017).

Understandably, Gandhi expressed strong opposition to machinery in Hind Swaraj (1909).[21] He said, 'I cannot recall a single good point in connection with machinery.... If, instead of welcoming machinery as a boon, we shall look upon it as an evil, it would ultimately go.' 'It is machinery that has impoverished India. It is difficult to measure the harm that Manchester has done to us. It is due to Manchester that Indian handicraft has all but disappeared,' he added.

Gandhi also held mechanization responsible for the poor condition of workers in India.

> The workers in the mills of Bombay have become slaves. The condition of the women working in the mills is shocking. When there were no mills, these women were not starving. If the machinery craze grows in our country, it will become an unhappy land.[22]

Furthermore, he made a case for physical labour over automation,

> Nations are tired of the worship of lifeless machines multiplied ad infinitum. We are destroying the matchless living machines, viz our own bodies, by leaving them to rust and trying to substitute machinery for them. It is a law of God that the body must be fully worked and utilized. We dare not ignore it. The spinning wheel is the auspicious symbol of Sharir Yajna—body labour. He who eats his food without offering this sacrifice steals it. By giving up this sacrifice we became traitors to the country and banged the door in the face of the Goddess of Fortune.[23]

---

21 Mohandas Karamchand Gandhi, *Hind Swaraj* (Ahmedabad: Navajivan Trust, June 2010).

22 See Note 21.

23 Mohandas Karamchand Gandhi. Presidential speech. Kathiawad Political Conference. 8 January 1925.

Similarly, India has had an unfortunate history with industrial disasters,[24] each making people recoil, at least temporarily, against industrialization and technology.

In 1944, 800 people died and 80,000 were made homeless when the SS Fort Stikine, a freighter carrying tons of explosives, caught fire and resulted in two massive explosions in the Victoria Dock of Bombay, leading to sinking of ships in the area of the explosion. In 1975, 372 miners were killed in the Chasnala colliery in Dhanbad (then under Bihar) due to a huge explosion caused by sparks from equipment igniting a pocket of flammable methane gas. The explosion caused flooding in the mine, drowning the miners trapped under the debris. In 1984, at least 5,295 people died and 527,894 affected after being exposed to 40 tonnes of methyl isocyanate gas that had leaked from a pesticide plant owned by the US multinational, Union Carbide Corp, in Bhopal. Some estimate around 20,000–25,000 deaths.[25]

In spite of a strong modern anti-technology strain of thought-from Gandhi's suspicion of modern technologies in Hind Swaraj to wariness of technology and change due to India's several adverse experiences, India and Indians have seen an enthusiastic adoption of the modern technological innovations. This apparent paradox—the coexistence of wariness and enthusiasm towards technology—along with the fact that superstitions and religiosity thrive alongside technology in India, serves as a great example of India's complicated relationship with technology.

---

[24] *Hindustan Times*, 'Accident at NTPC Plant: India's Worst Industrial Disasters, Bhopal to Korba', 1 November 2017, https://www.hindustantimes.com/india-news/boiler-explodes-at-ntpc-plant-india-s-worst-industrial-disasters-bhopal-to-korba/story-a60C113OGSSvbez8lDn7wM.html

[25] Dominique Lapierre and Javier Morro, *Five Past Midnight in Bhopal: The Epic Story of the World's Deadliest Industrial Disaster* (New York, NY: Grand Central Publishing, June 2002).

CHAPTER 4

THE MISGUIDED UTOPIANISM

Many have believed that technology cures all ills.

Ronald Reagan had famously declared of computer technology: 'The Goliath of totalitarianism will be brought down by the David of the microchip.' The assumption was that the Internet would give power to the people. H. G. Wells, in *The Shape of Things to Come* (1933), predicted a new World War, aerial destruction of Europe and weapons of mass destruction. He also predicted a new secular and egalitarian, if authoritarian, world order, where science would be the primary way to achieve progress. Karl Marx believed that science was crucial to move from 'the realm of necessity to the realm of freedom' and that science has the power to delegitimize the rule of the kings and the power of the Christian Church. Arthur C. Clarke's assertion about any sufficiently advanced technology being indistinguishable from magic also stemmed from a strong belief in the power of technology.

The optimism was not baseless. When the printing press was invented by Johannes Gutenberg, it was believed that mass printing would allow wide dissemination of knowledge which, in turn, would usher in a better society. By many measures, it did. One could trace the origin of the Reformation movement, the Age of Enlightenment, the invention of the steam engine and the Industrial Revolution, journalism, modern medicine and indeed modern democracy to the invention of the printing press.

This technological triumphalism continues to modern times.

Eric Schmidt, the former executive chairman of Google, and his co-author, Jared Cohen, wrote in *The New Digital Age*,[1] 'The best thing anyone can do to improve the quality of life around the world is to drive connectivity and technological opportunity.' Google ex-CEO Larry Page claimed, 'I think we need to be training people on how to change the world. Obviously, technologies are the way to do that ... that's what drives all the change.' Wael Ghonim, the former Google engineer who used Facebook to help organize the Arab Spring, claimed, 'If you want to liberate a society, just give them the Internet.'[2] *The New York Times* columnist Thomas Friedman famously claimed that technological innovation is creating a 'flatter' world, that people everywhere are 'on a more equal footing than at any previous time in the history of the world—using computers, e-mail, networks, teleconferencing, and dynamic new software.' Apple's Tim Cook once remarked that Steve Jobs 'convinced me that if we made great products, we too could change the world'.

Facebook founder Mark Zuckerberg declared, 'The richest 500 million [people in the world] have way more

---

[1] Eric Schmidt and Jared Cohen, *The New Digital Age: Reshaping the Future of People, Nations and Business* (New York, NY: Vintage, March 2014).

[2] Wael Ghonim, *Revolution 2.0: The Power of the People Is Greater Than the People in Power—A Memoir* (Boston, MA: Houghton Mifflin Harcourt, January 2012).

money than the next six billion combined. You solve that by getting everyone online.' In fact, Zuckerberg wrote an open letter in 2012 before Facebook's initial public offering (IPO)—the letter was a part of Facebook's official Securities and Exchange Commission (SEC) filings—where he compared his company's mission and potential impact to be no less nobler than printing press.

> We often talk about inventions like the printing press and the television—by simply making communication more efficient, they led to a complete transformation of many important parts of society.... They encouraged progress. They changed the way society was organized. They brought us closer together.[3]

Facebook's state mission is to 'give people the power to build community and bring the world closer together'.

The breathless optimism can be seen in persistent claims that the problems of the world, from 'inefficiency to inequality to morbidity and mortality', can be addressed through a computer code. There exists a technology company to address each problem with idealistic aims about how they can reshape the world. As Marc Andreessen says, 'Software is eating the world.' and that 'Every company needs to become a software company.'[4]

When Optimism Became Utopianism

Extreme optimism about technology has often been expressed in terms of technological utopianism. Technological

---

[3] SEC Form S-1, REGISTRATION STATEMENT. Facebook, Inc. Letter from Mark Zuckerbeg. https://www.sec.gov/Archives/edgar/data/1326801/000119312512034517/d287954ds1.htm.

[4] Marc Andreessen, 'Why Software Is Eating the World', *The Wall Street Journal*, 20 August 2011, https://www.wsj.com/articles/SB10001424053111903480904576512250915629460

utopianism has been described as an ideology which is based on the belief that technological progress will ultimately lead to utopia, a society with ideal living standards. Interestingly, the belief is that sufficient technological advancement can solve even social, economic, cultural and political problems. Bernard Gendron, a philosopher at the University of Wisconsin at Milwaukee and the author of *The Technology and Human Condition*, laid out the four principles of modern technological utopianism as follows[5]: (a) We are undergoing a technological revolution, (b) going forward, technological advancements will continue, (c) these advancements will lead to the end of economic scarcity, which, in turn, (d) will end all social evil. While this may sound extremely optimistic, there are others which are even more gung-ho about what technology can bring. In the essay *The Law of Accelerating Returns*, futurist Ray Kurzweil writes:

> An analysis of the history of technology shows that technological change is exponential[...]. So we won't experience 100 years of progress in the 21st century— it will be more like 20,000 years of progress (at today's rate).... Within a few decades, machine intelligence will surpass human intelligence, leading to The Singularity— technological change so rapid and profound it represents a rupture in the fabric of human history. The implications include the merger of biological and nonbiological intelligence, immortal software-based humans, and ultra-high levels of intelligence that expand outward in the universe at the speed of light.[6]

This utopianism about the power of technology has permeated through policy, governance and law. Governments

---

[5] Bernard Gendron, *The Technology and Human Condition* (New York, NY: St Martin's Press, January 1977).

[6] Ray Kurzweil, 'The Law of Accelerating Returns', in *Alan Turing: Life and Legacy of a Great Thinker*, ed. Christof Teuscher (Heidelberg: Springer, 2004), 381–416.

routinely attempt to address social, cultural, economic and political problems through the use of technology. To address education gap, give children free laptops. To address inequality, give people broadband access. To integrate people in the remotest corners of the world, launch balloons and satellites to improve digital connectivity. To decide the length of parole for an inmate, use AI. To decide how to allocate policing resources, use data analytics. To take care of the elderly, build and use robots. In fact, it would not be an exaggeration to say that technological utopianism implicitly guides today's technologists and policymakers who routinely throw technology at any problem that befalls them.

A Solution or Just a Mirage?

This techno utopianism starts getting exposed as a mirage once evidence and details start getting factored in.[7] Again, the printing press serves as a good cautionary tale. While printing press loosened the power of the rich, the church and the state, it created new gatekeepers of information—anyone who controlled access to this technology.

William Caxton[8] was an English merchant who is believed to be the first person to introduce printing press into England; he was also the first retailer of printed books. Many of these books were English translation of books in other languages. Caxton was once going through the manuscript of an English translation of the French version of *The Dictes* one day. He noticed that certain misogynistic passages ('He saw a woman sick, of whom he said that the

---

[7] Andrew Marantz, 'The Dark Side of Techno-utopianism', *The New Yorker*, 23 September 2019, https://www.newyorker.com/magazine/2019/09/30/the-dark-side-of-techno-utopianism

[8] Lotte Helinga, *William Caxton and Early Printing in England* (London: British Library, December 2010).

evil resteth and dwelleth with the evil' and 'he saw a young maid that learned to write, of whom he said that men multiplied evil upon evil.') in the original Socrates text were missing in the translation. He had a choice to make: Should he modify the manuscript to include original misogynistic text or publish only the 'clean' version? Ultimately, the printed book had the clean version, while the misogynistic text was reproduced in an epilogue that Caxton wrote. The epilogue also discussed Caxton's rationale for editorializing. He wrote how the translator 'hath left out certain and divers conclusions touching women', but how the readers must still get to see the passage. A reader offended by the passage could 'with a pen race it out, or else rend the leaf out of the book'.

The seemingly inconsequential story lays bare how misguided technological utopianism can be. The supposedly emancipating printing press was still producing information controlled by the powerful!

In fact, Caxton used his position of power (over technology) for a more directed purpose soon thereafter. In 1481, when the Ottomans were marching towards Jerusalem, Caxton published *Godeffroy of Boloyne*; or, *The Siege and Conqueste of Jerusalem*. The book was a tale of Godeffroy, an 11th-century crusader famed for slaughtering vast Muslim armies while leading Christian armies through Nicaea and Constantinople, and into Jerusalem. Caxton was a faithful Christian and disliked Muslims. His primary goal in publishing the book was to recount tales of the Christian victories in the First Crusade. He wanted to inspire the Christians 'with strong hand to expelle the Saracens and Turks out of the same, that our Lord might be there served & worshipped of his chosen Christian people'. He admitted in the epilogue that the book had been 'translated & reduced out of French into

English by me, symple persone Wylliam Caxton, to the end that every Christian man may be better encouraged to enterprise warre for the defense of Christendom'. Here was an example of a purported levelling technology being exploited for personal agenda by the person controlling the technology. Furthermore, it was done by controlling the information.

Another example of an early misuse of technology involved the great Martin Luther.[9] Martin Luther was a German theologian and a priest and a key figure in the Reformation movement. He took advantage of the advent of printing to publish *The Ninety-Five Theses*—a rejection of several teachings and practices of the Roman Catholic Church. He also directly challenged the authority of the pope by teaching that the Bible is the only source of divinely revealed knowledge. Furthermore, he took advantage of the new printing technology by translating the Bible into German and widely distributing it. Martin Luther greatly impacted religion, culture and human history through the power of the printing press.

However, at the same time, Martin Luther was virulently anti-Semitic. In his printed book *On the Jews and Their Lies*, he wrote, 'We are at fault in not slaying them.... I shall give you my sincere advice: first, to set fire to their synagogues or schools.... Second, I advise that their houses also be razed and destroyed.' He similarly published a pamphlet called 'Warning against the Jews'.[10]

As his books earned him power and influence, Luther 'got Jews expelled from Saxony in 1537, and in the 1540s he drove them from many German towns', writes Paul

---

[9] Eric Metaxas, *Martin Luther: The Man Who Rediscovered God and Changed the World* (New York, NY: Viking, October 2017).

[10] Eric Gritsch, *Martin Luther's Anti-Semitism: Against His Better Judgment* (Grand Rapids, MI: Eerdmans Publishing Company, January 2012).

Johnson in *A History of the Jews*. Luther's followers also 'sacked the Berlin synagogue in 1572 and the following year finally got' Jews banned from the entire region. Johnson says that *On the Jews and Their Lies* was 'the first work of modern anti-Semitism, and a giant step forward on the road to the Holocaust'.

This was an example of how a technology celebrated for disseminating information was used to disseminate hate speech and promote radicalization.

There are now routine examples of online platforms which were supposed to promote connectedness or community building being misused for ulterior reasons—disinformation, incitement, bullying and crime.[11] This came to head in 2019 when three separate terrorist incidents—attacks on two mosques in Christchurch in New Zealand, on a Walmart store in El Paso in Texas and on a synagogue in Poway in California—were traced to radicalization on 8chan, an online messaging board which promotes itself as a staunch defender of anonymity and free speech.

State actors can also routinely exploit technology for exerting and enhancing control. While the best of technology was perhaps exemplified during the Arab Spring when technology platforms were used to challenge dictatorships, the more common reality is 'smart repression'—the widespread use of technologies by authoritarian governments to surveil and manipulate their populations. China's massive surveillance system uses sophisticated tools to control access to information and monitor communication. Iran reportedly uses Internet slowdowns to control the content its citizens see. Russia is often accused of using technology for election meddling, defending aggression and striking up anti-American sentiments.

---

[11] Evegny Morozov, *The Net Delusion: The Dark Side of Internet Freedom* (New York, NY: PublicAffairs, February 2012).

In fact, Mark Zuckerberg, who took his company public with the flourish and ambition of a Gutenberg or a Caxton, was forced to set up 'an independent body' in 2019 for content moderation. In this announcement note, he said,

> The past two years have shown that without sufficient safeguards, people will misuse these tools to interfere in elections, spread misinformation, and incite violence.... One of the most painful lessons I've learned is that when you connect two billion people, you will see all the beauty and ugliness of humanity.[12]

The above examples are not aimed at showing the dual-edge nature of technology (which, of course, is true!), but that technology is often considered an omnipotent tool to solve a hard socio-economic problem or to achieve a social goal—for example, connected and free flow of information. The reality is that technology often does not do more than make a dent.

This technological triumphalism is routinely seen in India as well. It is perhaps most directly seen in India's attempts at tackling corruption.

Technology and Corruption

It is widely believed that technology can be a tool at targeting corruption. India has devoted considerable effort and resources at developing technology-based interventions to reduce corruption.[13]

---

[12] A Blueprint for Content Governance and Enforcement. Mark Zuckerberg. https://www.facebook.com/notes/mark-zuckerberg/a-blueprint-for-content-governance-and-enforcement/10156443129621634/

[13] Josy Joseph, *A Feast of Vultures: The Hidden Business of Democracy in India* (Noida: HarperCollins India, January 2016).

Examples of technology-based interventions which have been developed include government-enabled marketplaces (for procurement of common goods and services), direct benefit transfer (for transferring subsidies to citizen bank accounts), digitization of information (e.g., using DigiLocker) and automated processes in different programmes and services (including procurement, taxation, policing and judiciary). The assumption is that these interventions will improve transparency, eliminate discretion and reduce intermediaries, leading to a less corrupt society. Technology is also assumed to aid with detection of corrupt transactions and practices, thereby helping with deterrence.

What is not asked enough, however, is whether the assumptions underlying these interventions are sound; that is, does employment of technology really reduce corruption? The question is not simply academic either. Technology-based interventions soak up a lot of governmental resources. It is important to know whether these resources could be better targeted at other anti-corruption programmes and institutions which are currently being crowded out.[14]

Corruption Triangle[15]

There are three prerequisites for corruption: (a) motivation, the compulsion or the driving force to acquire material gain, (b) rationalization, the justification for acting on the motivation and (c) opportunity, the circumstances or the environment which allow the act to be committed. In the Indian context, motivation and justification for indulging in corruption have largely stemmed from some

---

[14] Kiran Batni, *The Pyramid of Corruption: India's Primitive Corruption and How to Deal with It* (Chennai: Notion Press, January 2014).

[15] Edwin Hardin Sutherland and Donald Ray Cressey, *Criminology* (Philadelphia, PA: Lippincott, 1978).

of the most fundamental issues in the society—deep inequality, salaries not commensurate with skill or effort, autarky, limited media freedom and poor education levels. However, the opportunity for graft has largely depended on the specifics of delivery of a programme or a service. So our earlier question boils down to: Does the opportunity for corruption always decrease when employing technological solutions?

There are several kinds of corruption. Perhaps the most common kind of corruption is 'petty corruption'. Here, low-level public officials extract services, favours or payments by exploiting the asymmetry of information and power. Examples of petty corruption include bribes paid at police stations, traffic stops, hospitals, government offices, licensing boards and government offices. Technology-based interventions can indeed be effective in reducing petty corruption by minimizing the interaction between the public and the public officials through automatic and direct delivery of programmes and services. However, the implementations of these technology-based interventions are often not foolproof. Flaws in implementation allow petty corruption to continue and, in some cases, enable new forms of corruption to take over. Consider direct benefit transfer, for example, which promises direct and instantaneous transfer of subsidies. A recent study pointed out several instances where a direct benefit transfer initiated by the government did not result in either direct or instantaneous transfer of payment. Several new intermediaries—banking correspondents, private payment agencies and bank staff—were needed to enable these payments, especially for the people living in remote areas with no local banking institutions. These new intermediaries increased the exposure to the officials and, therefore, could potentially lead to increased overall corruption. As another example of corruption in direct benefit transfer, there were documented cases in Afghanistan where a superior officer would register SIM cards in a subordinate's name and then collect direct benefit transfer in their name. Such flaws in the implementation of direct payment could undermine a lot of the benefit of direct payment.

Historically, petty corruption required in-person interactions between the public and the public officials. New forms of petty corruption which do not require in-person interaction emerge once processes move digital. For example, digital blackmail, extortion and bribery are now possible. Corrupt officials may have authorized and unauthorized access to digital information. This access can then be parlayed into material gains. Similarly, technology-based interventions often increase the complexity of systems and processes for the layperson, especially ones who are digitally illiterate. So those who are conversant with technology may exploit this knowledge asymmetry to commit graft. The increased complexity of different processes and systems may also make it difficult to detect corrupt transactions and practices using traditional techniques. This will encourage further corruption.

These arguments apply even to 'systemic (or endemic) corruption'. This second kind of corruption exists when the entire organization or the process is weak, and corruption is considered a way of life. Bad actors do not act individually but are simply widespread symptoms of the weakened institutions. For example, most institutions are dominated and used by corrupt individuals and groups in a systemically corrupt society. In such societies, not only is technology not effective at reducing corruption, but it can also be often used as a tool by the corrupt to 'facilitate' corruption. For example, technology can be used to commit financial graft. Imagine the corrupt using technologies such as cryptocurrencies to transfer money remotely (without physical presence), untraceably and anonymously from one account to another. These transfers can easily span national boundaries and hide corruption. Similarly, alternative banks such as Revolut and Monzo, which support cryptocurrency exchange and peer-to-peer payments, can be used for money laundering. Massive multiplayer online games and online gaming can also be used to launder money. Technology can also be employed by the corrupt to avoid detection. Technologies such as WhatsApp and Instagram which support end-to-end encrypted messaging make it difficult to detect corrupt dealings. Anonymous communication technologies such as Tor and darknet make detection and, therefore, deterrence even harder. One may think that technology-based tools can be used for detection and deterrence. However, tools such as data mining which are increasingly used by governments for detection have high false positive or false negative rates, limiting their effectiveness significantly. Furthermore, successful detection does not always lead to deterrence. Strong privacy laws and the cost and length of court cases in most jurisdictions make it very difficult to prosecute the corrupt solely based on technology-based detection of corruption.

Technology may be even less effective in reducing 'grand corruption'. This third kind of corruption occurs at the highest levels of the government where law, economy and politics are routinely subverted for material gains. For example, corrupt lawmakers can promote cronyism and benefit from it by creating laws favourable to the cronies. Similarly, new instruments and policies can be easily legislated to support existing corruption and enable its new forms. No application of technology can deter this behaviour. Initiating and approving projects to funnel resources to cronies are legal, if corrupt. These activities can also go unchecked by technology. Any technological intervention which may be useful can also be legislated against. Vested interests can both bend state laws and influence them in such settings.

Overall, technology has very limited effectiveness at checking corruption. While some forms of petty or systemic corruption may reduce when technology-based interventions are used, other forms may be unaffected.[16] In fact, in some cases, corruption may increase. Besides, technology may only impact 'vertical corruption'.[17] Vertical corruption is characterized by repeated, small-magnitude corrupt transactions with the public. Technology-based interventions can lead to deterrence and elimination of opportunity. On the other hand, 'horizontal corruption' may largely be unimpacted by technology. Horizontal corruption is characterized by infrequent, large-magnitude corrupt transactions with commercial or high-worth entities. If anything, technology may facilitate and magnify such corruption

Corruption is a socio-economic problem which requires a multipronged approach which targets the entire corruption triangle (motivation, justification and opportunity). This targeting needs a suite of programmes and institutions. Any technological utopianism which exaggerates the impact technology can have at reducing corruption is both wasteful and dangerous.

How Much to Depend on Technology?

A myriad of social and context-specific factors determines the effectiveness of a technological intervention.

---

16 N. Ram, *Why Scams Are Here to Stay: Understanding Political Corruption in India* (New Delhi: Aleph Book Company, July 2017).

17 Jennifer Bussell, *Corruption and Reform in India: Public Services in the Digital Age* (New York, NY: Cambridge University Press, August 2013).

Consider Pradhan Mantri Jan Dhan Yojana (PMJDY), a flagship financial inclusion programme of the Government of India launched with much fanfare in 2014 which aims to provide affordable access to banking and financial services, including card-based services, to Indian citizens. By many measures, it has been a success. By the end of 2020, there were over 400 million accounts with total deposits exceeding ₹1.30 lakh crore. This scheme also became the basis of direct benefit transfer to the poor with the end goal of plugging leaks in subsidy transfers.[18]

PMJDY is part of the JAM trinity—Jan Dhan, Aadhaar and mobile. The PMJDY bank accounts are linked with the user's mobile number as well as Aadhaar number (unique identification for Indian citizens). The linking allows individuals to perform cashless transactions using their phone. The technology-based vision was that all universal bank accounts directly linked to mobile phones would eventually allow all financial transactions to become cashless, leading to convenience, efficiency, reduced leaks and formalization of the economy which, in turn, would lead to greater revenues and better targeting. In January 2017, NITI Aayog CEO Amitabh Kant predicted the imminent demise of cash transfers:

My view is that in the next two-and-a-half years, India will make all its debit cards, credit cards, all ATM machines all POS machines totally irrelevant.... India will make this jump because every Indian will be doing his transaction just by using his thumb in thirty seconds....[19]

---

[18] Samrat Sharma, 'Modi's Jan Dhan Yojana Reaches New Height; 40 Crore Bank Accounts Added under PMJDY in 6 Years', *Financial Express*, 3 August 2020, https://www.financialexpress.com/economy/modis-jan-dhan-yojana-reaches-new-height-40-crore-bank-accounts-added-under-pmjdy-in-6-years/2043276/

[19] Amitabh Kant. Youth Pravasi Bhartiya Diwas. 2017. Session: Start-ups and Innovations which had social impact in India.

However, India's unique social context has made the effectiveness of the programme limited.[20] Small merchants who dominate Indian business are wary of supporting cards—high transaction and one-time costs cut into already thin profit margins. Poor electricity, digital literacy and Internet infrastructure introduce additional friction. Cash-first mentality of citizens discourages initiative.

Particularly, for the poor and the underprivileged, even ones with a bank account, cash is almost exclusively the only way to perform financial transactions. This means that they must physically go to banks, often not easily accessible, to withdraw cash. A recent survey found that only 25 per cent respondents found it easy to access cash benefits.

The unique Indian context also affects this technology-based programme in other adverse ways.[21] Over 15 per cent of the accounts are inoperative—an account is considered inoperative if there are no customer-induced transactions in the account for over a period of two years. Most of the inoperative accounts belong to the poor and the underprivileged—the segment which did not use formal banking earlier and that the programme was trying to target. Essentially, this segment continues to shun formal banking due to both distrust and inconvenience.

The programme has had an unequal impact on different population groups. For example, women are disproportionately outside the financial inclusion programme. A Yale study showed that less than half of poor adult women have a PMJDY account. Only one-fifth know that that they have a PMJDY account.[22]

---

[20] Dipa Sinha and Rohit Azad, 'Can Jan Dhan Yojana Achieve Financial Inclusion?' *Economic & Political Weekly* 53, no. 13 (2018, 31 March), https://www.epw.in/journal/2018/13/money-banking-and-finance/can-jan-dhan-yojana-achieve-financial-inclusion.html

[21] Rohit Azad and Dipa Sinha, 'The Jan-Dhan Yojana, Four Years Later, *The Hindu*, 29 May 2018, thehindu.com/opinion/op-ed/the-jan-dhan-yojana-four-years-later/article24017333.ece

[22] Rohini Pande, Simone Schaner, Charity Troyer Moore, and Elena Stacy, 'A Majority of India's Poor Women May Miss Covid-19 PMJDY Cash Transfers' (policy brief, Yale

The limited effectiveness of the JAM trinity in spite of the best intentions and seemingly careful implementation is a good reminder of the limitations of technology at solving hard socio-economic problems. Limits of technology can also be seen when considering BharatNet, India's ambitious programme to connect rural India to the Internet.

India ranks along with Tanzania at the bottom in Internet usage-to-population ratio, with only one out of four Indians using the Internet. The vast fraction of the unconnected resides in rural India. BharatNet is an National Optical Fibre Network being built by the Government of India to provide a minimum of 100 Mbps broadband connectivity to all 250,000 gram panchayats in the country, covering nearly 625,000 villages. The vision is that improved digital connectivity would promote 'inclusion, empowerment, innovation and efficiency'.

The project started in 2011 and has already seen an outlay of tens of thousands of crores. However, even government admits that it has not made a serious dent in rural connectivity.[23]

The reasons, again, are due to unique socio-economic factors. What constitutes connectivity? Connecting a gram panchayat office with broadband does not entail that people in that panchayat are connected. The last-mile connectivity needs to be made (to the potential users). The huge size and population of India makes it prohibitive to guarantee that last-mile connectivity. Similarly, once the broadband connectivity has been established, the corresponding equipment

University, the Center for Economic and Social Research), 17 April 2020, https://www.findevgateway.org/paper/2020/04/majority-indias-poor-women-may-miss-covid-19-pmjdy-cash-transfers

[23] Ananya Bhattacharya, 'Charted: India's Much-hyped BharatNet Project Is Falling Short', Quartz India, 7 February 2020, https://qz.com/india/1798873/indias-bharatnet-is-falling-short-admits-ravi-shankar-prasad/

needs repair and maintenance. Lack of skilled staff (due to generally poorly trained workforce) means that any technical snag remains unattended for long periods (or sometimes permanently). Also, even if a gram panchayat is physically connected, unreliable electricity can cause unreliable connections. Inadequate space to secure equipment can lead to vandalism and theft. A memo sent at the end of 2018 by the then telecom secretary acknowledged that networking equipment in over half of the connected gram panchayats was non-functional. In addition, there is limited awareness of the benefits of broadband connectivity among the general population. Unsurprisingly, the existing BharatNet infrastructure sees limited utilization. A recent committee for evaluating BharatNet noted:

> The lessons of the pilot project implemented under NOFN indicate that there was almost no utilization of bandwidth by three prominent service providers—the telecom service providers, the cable T.V providers and Internet service providers. The cited reasons ranged from poor return on investment for rural service provision, lack of market volumes and lack of assured service levels. Service provision in the pilot projects had to be sustained entirely by Government expenditure which makes the entire investment case uneconomic when scaled up across the country.[24]

Digital connectivity in India also has a gender problem.[25] Women constitute less than 30 per cent of Internet users in India. Significantly, fewer women in India own cell phones

[24] DoT Report of the Committee on National Optical Fibre Network (NOFN). https://smartnet.niua.org/sites/default/files/resources/DoT%20Report%20of%20the%20Committee%20on%20National%20Optical%20Fibre%20Network%20(NoFN).pdf

[25] Archana Datta, 'Internet & the Big Indian Gender Divide', *The Tribune*, 3 March 2019, https://www.tribuneindia.com/news/archive/features/internet-the-big-indian-gender-divide-737100

than men. Less than half of the women in India who owned phones know how to use them. In some khap panchayats, women have gotten fined if they were seen using mobile phones outside their homes. There have been reports of women not using gram panchayat BharatNet Wi-Fi because of social taboos and limitations on mobility.[26]

Essentially, deep-rooted societal problems such as patriarchy, gender-biased belief and values systems, and sexism continue to determine both access to technology and capacity to use it. After all, literacy rates for women in India are much lower (65% vs 80% for men according to 2011 census). A quarter of girls drop out of school before reaching puberty. Patriarchal attitudes limit access to mobile phones since 'by creating all these new possibilities, and especially by creating spaces for privacy that were previously not available to young women in these communities, mobiles have disrupted the existing patriarchal regimes of control and surveillance.' It is the same attitude which restricts women's access to public spaces, education, training and employment.

Again, this shows that technological utopianism can be blunted by socio-economic ground realities. Also, these realities may not change simply with application of technology.

Investing in Technology to Solve Social Problems

Another example of misguided utopianism in India has been the huge technology-based investments, which have been made into improving educational outcomes.

---

[26] Urvashi Aneja and Vidisha Mishra, 'Digital India Is No Country for Women. Here's Why', The Wire, 25 May 2017, https://thewire.in/economy/digital-india-women-technology

Technology has been explored exhaustively in India to improve literacy and educational outcomes in rural India. However, for the most past, these technology-based initiatives have failed to achieve desired outcomes.

The first visible technology-based education initiative for rural India was SITE, a joint project between NASA and ISRO.[27] A NASA ATS-6 satellite broadcasted agriculture-focused educational content produced by All India Radio from 1 August 1975 to 31 July 1976 to 2,400 villages in 20 districts across the states of Andhra Pradesh, Bihar, Karnataka, Madhya Pradesh, Orissa and Rajasthan. At its peak, 200–600 people thronged each TV set. The number subsequently declined to 60–80 people per TV once the novelty wore off.[28]

Simple, Inexpensive and Multilingual People's Computer, or Simputer, introduced in 2001, was arguably the first visible Indian project for Internet-based learning. Designed to address 'digital divide, social welfare and contribute to human development in India', the Simputer was a sharable device designed at the IISc. Every user stored their data on a removable memory card—the card was plugged by the user to personalize the device and use it. A touchscreen interface, handwriting-based input and text-to-speech synthesis features were supported for improved accessibility. The device was named as one of the top technological advancements of 2001 by *The New York Times*.[29]

Unfortunately, Simputer started hitting ground realties right after it launch. The initial price of ₹9,000 was too

---

[27] Romesh Chander and Kiran Karnik, *Planning for Satellite Broadcasting: The Indian Instructional TV Experiment* (Paris: UNESCO Press, 1976).

[28] Planning Commission, India, *Evaluation Report on Satellite Instructional Television Experiment (SITE)—1981* (New Delhi: Planning Commission, 1981).

[29] *The New York Times*, 'The Year in Ideas: A to Z', 9 December 2001, https://www.nytimes.com/2001/12/09/magazine/the-year-in-ideas-a-to-z.html

high for the individual users among the poor and the underprivileged which it wanted to target. Efforts to introduce Simputer into schools also did not succeed. Electricity supply was a concern. So was the fear of theft and loss. In fact, many schools who bought Simputers kept them locked in cupboards! There were also concerns related to lack of training, especially related to technical support, repair and maintenance. Any hardware device needs a software and application ecosystem—there wasn't any incentive for many programmers to generate user content for the Simputer. Struggles with initial adoption also discouraged public funding for the effort. The device was finally shelved. PicoPeta Simputers Private Limited and Encore Software, the two licensees for the Simputer, declined to renew their licence in 2006.[30]

Another project which caught imagination was the 'Hole in the Wall' project initiated by Sugata Mitra.[31] The project involved setting up stand-alone computer kiosks in poor localities. Anyone was free to walk up and use the kiosk. The vision was that the self-guided experimentation with technology would foment curiosity and learning among the most marginalized. More than 300 such kiosks were set up covering, it was claimed, over 30,000 children. The project received wide acclaim. Sugata Mitra received the TED Prize. However, it was not clear if it made a dent. It mostly attracted boys. The kiosks eventually fell into disrepair and disuse.

Another technology-based initiative was EDUSAT, a satellite dedicated to education for the disadvantaged

[30] *The Economic Times*, 'Why Did the Simputer Flop?' 23 July 2015, https://economictimes.indiatimes.com/news/science/why-did-the-simputer-flop/articleshow/48180974.cms

[31] Peter Wilby, 'Sugata Mitra—the Professor with His Head in the Cloud', *The Guardian*, 7 June 2016, https://www.theguardian.com/education/2016/jun/07/sugata-mitra-professor-school-in-cloud

launched in 2004 by ISRO in collaboration with the Ministry of Human Resource Development (MHRD). The satellite supported education-based programming till 2010. However, again, the lack of the technical and social infrastructure to translate EDUSAT's capabilities into meaningful and sustained improvement meant that the programme had limited educational impact. A Department of Space audit report from 2013 said, 'EDUSAT failed to effectively achieve its objectives due to deficiencies in planning for the network connectivity, content generation and failure to have a robust management structure.'[32]

Perhaps the most widely publicized project was the Aakash tablet.[33] In 2010, the MHRD declared its intent to support the development of a 35-dollar tablet to enable the vision of bringing high-quality education to the underprivileged in India by 'providing high-quality, personalized and interactive knowledge modules over the internet in an any-time-any-where mode'. The development of Aakash as a government project was also supposed to showcase India's technological might, especially at 'frugal innovation'. In fact, the tablet was unveiled with much fanfare as 'world's cheapest tablet' at the UN headquarters when India assumed rotating presidency of UN Security Council.

The announcement of Aakash was followed by announcement of a subsidized distribution policy aimed at college and university students all over India. MHRD declared that they 'wish to develop a technically and financially sustainable model to ensure that Aakash reaches every household in the country and every

[32] *Business Standard*, 'EDUSAT Failed due to Deficiencies in Actual Implementation: CAG', 6 September 2013, https://www.business-standard.com/article/pti-stories/edusat-failed-due-to-deficiencies-in-actual-implementation-cag-113090600803_1.html

[33] Josh Halliday, 'India Unveils World's Cheapest Laptop', *The Guardian*, 23 July 2010, https://www.theguardian.com/world/2010/jul/23/india-unveils-cheapest-laptop

Indian is empowered and connected to the twenty-first century world through Information and Communication Technologies'.

The project went through several iterations between 2010 and 2014, with increasingly messy challenges related to failures to meet deadlines, costs and acceptable standards. The stewardship of the project had to be transferred midway from IIT Jodhpur to IIT Bombay. Colleges and universities were wary to buy in due to the same issues which affected the Simputer project. Also, criticism mounted about investment into computer-aided learning when the markers for human-based education were still poor. When a new government took power in 2014, the project was unceremoniously dropped.[34]

The failure of these projects is again a stark reminder that hard challenges such as education see limited progress from even a careful application of technology.

DigiLocker is a flagship project of the Government of India where every Aadhaar holder is provided an online account to access authentic documents such as driving licence, vehicle registration and academic mark sheets in electronic format from the original issuers of these documents. It also provides each user 1 GB of storage space to upload scanned copies of legacy documents. Features include ability to e-sign documents. DigiLocker is also supported by a law requiring that the documents provided and shared through DigiLocker be treated at par with the corresponding physical certificates.

The vision is that the use of DigiLocker will minimize the use of physical documents, reduce administrative expenses, provide authenticity of e-documents, provide

---

[34] Seema Singh, 'What Went Wrong with the Aakash Tablet', *Forbes India*, 25 June 2012, https://www.forbesindia.com/article/real-issue/what-went-wrong-with-the-aakash-tablet/33218/1

secure access to government-issued documents and make it easy for the residents to receive services. A press release, put out by the government when the locker reached 1 lakh users in the first 100 days of its launch, had said, 'In effect Digital Locker will touch every citizen's life by bringing in lot of convenience and therefore fulfilling the government's vision of a citizen centric governance model of providing services at the door-step of citizens.'

DigiLocker currently has 38 million accounts—less than 3 per cent of country's population. So while it may have reduced friction for some users, it has not practically affected administrative ease. The reasons for the low use of DigiLocker, despite clear appeal, are many, including the different socio-economic reasons that affected the success of Aakash, BharatNet, JAM trinity or other digital anti-corruption mechanisms. In addition, there are concerns about the security and privacy implications storing all important and private documents in a central repository. These concerns have been justified. In 2020, a security vulnerability was discovered which would have allowed anybody to set up and access DigiLocker accounts without a password.[35] Previous widespread leaks of Aadhaar information did not help. Finally, does DigiLocker mean that physical papers are not needed anymore? No. Policing, for example, is a state subject. A state's police can simply refuse to accept electronic documents. In fact, most states in India refuse to accept electronic driver's licence, again showing how the use of technology can only carry so far.

To be clear, it is not that a scheme such as DigiLocker is not a worthwhile effort or that it cannot eventually

[35] HT Tech, 'DigiLocker Bug Risked Info of Over 38m Accounts', *Hindustan Times*, 2 June 2020, https://tech.hindustantimes.com/tech/news/digilocker-bug-risked-info-of-over-38m-accounts-71591106298225.html

succeed. It is simply that these technology-based schemes run into stubborn societal problems which impede their progress and limit impact.

Kentaro Toyama, a Microsoft computer scientist, moved to India in 2004 to start a new research group focusing on technological solutions to problems unique to developing countries like India. Over multiple years, this group invented a wide array of technologies. Many technologies worked well in controlled settings. For example, the educational technologies worked well in well-funded demonstration schools. But the same technologies showed poor adoption and outcomes when applied more broadly. For example, he saw poor adoption of technologies in underfunded government schools. He writes in his book *Geek Heresy* how poor outcomes were primarily due to social factors—poorly trained teachers, disengaged administrators and lack of infrastructure.[36] He also cites examples where ingrained societal attitudes and realities led to unequal outcomes. In one case, girls of the village were forbidden from experiencing technology due to the fear of this driving dowry prices up! Toyama writes, 'Technology—even when it's equally distributed—isn't a bridge, but a jack. It widens existing disparities.'

Evgeny Morozov defines techno utopianism as 'Recasting all complex social situations either as neat problems with definite, computable solutions or as transparent and self-evident processes that can be easily optimized—if only the right algorithms are in place.'[37] As results bear out, this solutionism does not work, at least in the Indian context. Social factors often decide success.

---

[36] Kentaro Toyama, *Geek Heresy: Rescuing Social Change from the Cult of Technology* (New York, NY: PublicAffairs, May 2015).

[37] Evgeny Morozov, *To Save Everything, Click Here: Technology, Solutionism, and the Urge to Fix Problems That Don't Exist* (London: Penguin, March 2013).

Efficiency Myth

A relentless focus on solving problems with technology also warps how we think about a problem. For example, many socio-economic problems are often reduced to problems of waste and inefficiency, not the least because technology-based optimizations are often effective only when the target problem is expressed as an efficiency problem. This shoehorning often prevents a holistic examination of the nature and the magnitude of the target problem.

Consider, for example, the common refrain in India about the lack of efficiency in all aspects of Indian life. It often takes two to three times longer to travel between two cities in India than an equivalent journey in most Western countries. Only 60 per cent of the fruits which are produced can be sold—over 40 per cent fruits rot before they reach the market. It takes weeks to get a driver's licence. Agriculture produces less than 20 per cent of the economic output in spite of employing over half of the country's workforce. Infrastructure projects see huge cost overruns due to delays. Planes and trains are routinely late.

This chronic inefficiency is well-recognized as a big drain on the economy. Unsurprisingly, enormous effort and resources have been directed towards improving efficiency of processes and institutions. Automation has seen widespread deployment. Information and records are being digitized. Disinvestment in public sector industries and institutions has reached a fever pitch. Technology-based professions and industries—especially electronics and the software industry—are being incentivized.

Amid all this activity, one would be inclined to think that efficiency is an unquestionable goal and that devoting effort and resources towards attainment of efficiency is an unquestionable strategy. However, is efficiency really what it is made out to be?

Excessive efficiency brings with it several perils.[38] For example, efficiency increases fragility and reduces robustness. Since an efficient system is optimized for a particular goal in a given environment, it is necessarily more fragile. The system can collapse in the case of natural or man-made disruptions, since the goal or the environment changes suddenly during such disruptions. An inefficient system, on the other hand, is likely to be more resilient to sudden changes in the goal or the environment. The economic crisis of 2008 provided a good example of the benefits of inefficiency. Western economies were reputed as efficient economies. The distribution of resources and the supply chains in these economies were optimized to maximize benefits to customers and economic output. However, once the stock markets crashed, these economies collapsed as well due to a direct and streamlined relationship of these economies to the stock market. Countries like India had inefficient economies. In fact, a vast fraction of the economy was not even formal (the parallel economy). These economies withstood the stock market collapse well due to, among other things, the informality of their economies—their often-ridiculed inefficiency became their saviour!

A blind pursuit of efficiency also adversely impacts jobs and employment. For example, Western economies have heavily relied on outsourcing to increase the efficiency of their economy. They have also relied on automation to streamline systems and processes. However, outsourcing and automation may eliminate jobs and reduce motivation to support public well-being, skilling and labour rights. In an agricultural setting, for example, mechanized farming

---

[38] Peter Wenz, *Functional Inefficiency: The Unexpected Benefits of Wasting Time and Money* (Buffalo, NY: Prometheus Books, June 2015).

and irrigation may be more efficient, but they may worsen rural employment and social equilibrium. The trade-off between efficiency and employment and labour rights is becoming even more acute with the emergence of robots and AI.

Another interesting impact of efficiency-driven outsourcing is that erstwhile in-house knowledge and skills may get lost. A good example is how the USA has discovered over last few years that it has lost key knowledge and skills for mass manufacturing. During the COVID-19 crisis, it found it particularly hard to quickly scale up manufacturing and supply capabilities for vaccines, ventilators, masks and other medical equipment.

An endless quest of efficiency also increases social and economic inequality in the long term and creates monopolies.[39] Efficient organizations acquire more resources than organizations which are less efficient. The less efficient organizations, therefore, lose resources which could have otherwise been used to increase their efficiency. This leads to a widening gap between the organizations ultimately making it impossible for most organizations to compete against the leader. One only has to look around to see the near-annihilation of small, family-owned businesses in several sectors in efficient societies. These businesses were pushed out by the more efficient corporations. The same dynamic is currently in play in India. Corporate and more efficient organizations have started eliminating less-efficient competition. A recent example is the current near-total dominance of Reliance in the telecom market. Till very recently, telecom industry was one of the most competitive industries in India with a large number of viable players.

---

[39] Roger Martin, 'The High Price of Efficiency', *Harvard Business Review*, January–February 2019, https://hbr.org/2019/01/the-high-price-of-efficiency

An excessive focus on efficiency also discourages innovation and risk-taking. One of the requirements of efficiency is centralization, where the different system components may explore solutions independently but perform a quick and coordinated communication of the solution as soon as one is found. This encourages hasty and sometimes premature convergence to a single solution. On the other hand, an inefficient system can be considered a decentralized system with poorly communicating components. There is a much higher likelihood for such a system to come up with a set of very different, especially out-of-box, solutions. This is often seen in a variety of industries where disruptive innovations are often made by inefficient and disorganized start-ups, as opposed to well-oiled corporations.

Inefficiency may also be beneficial for democracy.[40] Several studies have shown that there is greater political knowledge and participation in inefficient media markets, where the number of entertainment options is limited. Similarly, it has been shown that investments in education, healthcare and skilling are higher in inefficient labour markets.

The above is indeed an argument that efficiency should not be an automatic goal. There are, of course, clear instances where efficiency is preferable. Shorter trips are better. It would be good for fewer fruits to rot. There is no reason for drivers' licences to take weeks to be delivered. Agricultural productivity should be enhanced. Projects, planes, trains and automobiles must be characterized by punctuality. However, systemic policy interventions which prevent excessive efficiency may be useful in other contexts.

---

40 Markus Prior, 'Efficient Choice, Inefficient Democracy? The Implications of Cable and Internet Access for Political Knowledge and Voter Turnout' (29th TPRC Conference), 2001.

For example, tariffs and other forms of productive friction which reduce efficiency, when introduced selectively, can build resilience and protect jobs. Anti-trust policies also introduce inefficiency but increase competition. Carrots and sticks which encourage businesses to create good jobs and better work environment may not optimize for efficiency but ensure general welfare. Incentivizing long-term investments over short-term capital may not be efficient in the short term but may encourage innovation and risk-taking.

More generally, a key premise of technological utopianism is that all problems can recast into problems such as waste and inefficiency which technology can solve. However, reducing waste or inefficiency does not automatically solve hard problems and can sometimes be counterproductive.

One needs to be careful when estimating the power of technology in the Indian context. Mountain of evidence now exists which suggests that techno-utopian thought, especially strong in the Indian policymaking circles, which believes that technology can be used to solve the society's hard problems, will keep hitting the brick wall of reality. Technology has limited effectiveness in solving these problems. Furthermore, deep-rooted societal problems such as inequality, patriarchy, sexism and corruption determine who has access to technology and, therefore, who can benefit from the opportunities any such access enables.

CHAPTER 5

THE UNEQUAL OPPORTUNITY

C. V. Raman was arguably the greatest scientist India has produced. He made pioneering contributions in the field of light scattering and was awarded the 1930 Nobel Prize in physics. He was the first person from Asia to be awarded a Nobel Prize in any branch of science.

India celebrates National Science Day every year on 28 February to mark C. V. Raman's discovery of scattering of light. Each year, there is a theme around which different outreach programmes are organized. The theme in 2020 was 'Women in Science'. It was ironic considering that C. V. Raman held strong anti-women views when it came to science.[1]

Kamala Sohonie[2] had just graduated in 1933 with BSc degrees in chemistry and physics from Bombay University and had applied to IISc for a research fellowship. C. V. Raman, who was then director of IISc, summarily rejected

---

[1] Abha Sur, *Dispersed Radiance: Caste, Gender, and Modern Science in India* (New Delhi: Navayana, August 2011).

[2] Anirban Mitra, 'The Life and Times of Kamala Bhagvat Sohonie: The Unsung Hero of Science in India', *Resonance* 21, no. 4 (April 2016): 301–314.

her application as he believed that women were not competent enough to do research. 'I am not going to take any girls in my institute,' Raman told her directly. In fact, IISc had already been around for 20 years and had admitted only 2 female students till then. Appalled, Sohonie travelled to Bangalore, sat on a Satyagraha outside Raman's office and forced him to relent. However, she was granted admission only on three conditions: she would be on probation for the first year to ascertain her suitability for research; would have to prove that she could work late nights and, most astonishingly, would have to guarantee that she would not be a 'distraction' to the male researchers in her lab!

Sohonie accepted the humiliating conditions and became the first Indian woman to get a PhD degree in a scientific discipline. She later remarked,

> Though Raman was a great scientist, he was very narrow-minded. I can never forget the way he treated me just because I was a woman. Even then, Raman didn't admit me as a regular student. This was a great insult to me. The bias against women was so bad at that time. What can one expect if even a Nobel Laureate behaves in such a way?[3]

Women Science and Technology Pioneers Faced Discrimination

Anandibai Joshi[4] was the first Indian woman to go abroad and get a medical degree. She studied at the Women's Medical College in Philadelphia from 1883 to 1886 and received her MD degree for her thesis 'Obstetrics among

---

[3] Dhrubajyoti Chattopadhyay, *Kamala Sohonie: First Indian woman PhD in science, Science and Culture*, Vol. 81 (2015): 128–130.

[4] Caroline Healey Dall, *The Life of Dr. Anandabai Joshee* (Boston, MA: Roberts Brothers, 1888).

Aryan Hindoos'. She was only 19 when she began her medical training. The trailblazing nature of her graduation received instant recognition. *The Philadelphia Post* wrote, 'Little Mrs Joshee who graduated with high honours in her class, received quite an ovation.' Among other people, she received a congratulatory message from Queen Victoria when she graduated.[5]

Unfortunately, Joshi had gotten sick during her training and contracted tuberculosis. When she returned to India, she could not receive any treatment. Western doctors refused treatment because she was brown. Indian doctors refused treatment since she had broken a large number of societal rules in both travelling overseas and getting a degree. Joshi died in 1887 at 22. Her ashes were placed in a cemetery in New York. The inscription states, 'First Brahmin Woman to Leave India to Obtain an Education'. A crater on Venus has been named after her.

Anna Mani[6] graduated in 1939 with a degree in physics from Madras University and received a scholarship in 1940 to perform research in C. V. Raman's team at the IISc. She soon discovered that being a woman in C. V. Raman's lab meant that she was not allowed to talk to her male colleagues. She would also later recall Raman muttering 'Scandalous!' every time he would see a man and a woman walk together in the hallway by his window. She lived through this discrimination and still managed to publish five single-author papers on her research by 1945. In spite of her prolific research, Madras University declined to grant her a PhD degree on the grounds that she did not have an MSc degree (many universities today allow a

---

[5] Leila McNeill, 'This 19th Century 'Lady Doctor' Helped Usher Indian Women into Medicine', *Smithsonian Magazine*, 24 August 2017, https://www.smithsonianmag.com/science-nature/19th-century-lady-doctor-ushered-indian-women-medicine-180964613/

[6] Abha Sur, 'The Life and Times of a Pioneer', *The Hindu*, 14 October 2001.

direct PhD degree after BSc). While Mani continued her career (and thrived as a meteorologist) without a PhD degree, her fellow researcher in the Raman lab, Sunanda Bai, committed suicide under the same circumstances. According to Mani, Sunanda's last wish was being conferred a PhD degree which she rightfully deserved.

Kadambini Ganguly[7] was the first woman to pass the University of Calcutta entrance examination. This was in 1878. In 1883, she graduated from Bethune College and became the first female graduate in India and in the entire British Empire. After graduation, Ganguly joined the medical college. Widespread criticism ensued, since medicine was considered exclusively the domain of men. In 1886, she was awarded the medical degree. This made her the first Indian woman as well as the first South Asian woman trained in Western medicine to graduate in South Asia. In 1893, she travelled to Edinburgh and was awarded several licentiates, further increasing heartburn among those opposed to her medical education and degrees. Once she returned to India, she was criticized ceaselessly. A popular magazine Bangabashi called her a whore only to be sued by her husband. The editor of the magazine was sentenced to six months of imprisonment for defamation and slander.

There are countless such stories of Indian women in science and technology being discriminated against. In fact, stories of discrimination against women span generations and continents.

Marie Curie[8] was a Nobel Prize winner in physics when she applied for membership to the French Academy of Sciences in 1911. However, despite her fame, she was

[7] Mousumi Bandyopadhyay, *Kadambini Ganguly: The Archetypal Woman of Nineteenth Century Bengal* (London: The Women's Press, January 2011).

[8] Barbara Goldsmith, *Obsessive Genius: The Inner World of Marie Curie* (New York, NY: W. W. Norton, October 2005).

rejected by two votes. Her fault was that she was Polish, non-Church-going and a woman. An academy member Emile Hilaire Amagat put it bluntly, 'Women cannot be part of the Institute of France.' Instead, they picked a much less accomplished or famous Edouard Branly. Branly was a devout Catholic, had blessings of the Pope and was a man. Also, as opposed to Curie who was constantly covered by the French press for her personal affairs and romances at least much as her scientific accomplishments, particularly after the death of her husband in an accident in 2006, Branly was considered a family man with high morals—a direct, sexist judgement on Curie's personal life.

Of course, Marie Curie went on to win her second Nobel Prize in the same year and is till date the only person to win a Nobel Prize in two different branches of science. She is also till date not a member of the French Academy of Sciences.

Tim Hunt, a British biochemist and Nobel Laureate, was invited to Seoul, South Korea, to deliver a keynote address at 2015 World Conference of Science Journalists. He infamously professed to the gathering that he preferred single-sex labs. 'Let me tell you about my trouble with girls.... Three things happen when they are in the lab.... You fall in love with them, they fall in love with you and when you criticise them, they cry,' he said.[9] This led to a global hue and cry. Female scientists all over the world took to Twitter to express their outrage—the hashtag #distractinglysexy trended.

The gender bias in science and technology in India can be easily seen in numbers.[10] Women comprise less than

[9] Dan Bilefsky, 'Women Respond to Nobel Laureate's "Trouble With Girls", The New York Times, 11 June 2015, https://www.nytimes.com/2015/06/12/world/europe/tim-hunt-nobel-laureate-resigns-sexist-women-female-scientists.html

[10] Aashima Dogra and Nandita Jayaraj, 'Indian Science and Gender Bias, Nothing Scientific Here', The Indian Express, 14 March 2018, https://indianexpress.com/article/gender/indian-science-and-gender-bias-nothing-scientific-here-5097171/

15 per cent of the R&D workforce in science and technology in India. For context, this is less than 40 per cent for Sudan, 37 per cent for Sri Lanka, 26 per cent for Iran and 20 per cent for Pakistan. While almost 40 per cent of India's science undergraduates and graduates are female, women comprise less than 12 per cent of the faculty in research institutions. Percentages are worse when going up the hierarchy. Among the four major government agencies which fund basic research in science and technology—CSIR, DST, Department of Earth Sciences and DBT—there has been only one female secretary till date in the four government agencies 'combined'. Only 10 per cent of the fellows in the three Indian science academies are women. Only 3 per cent of Shanti Swarup Bhatnagar awardees, the highest science award in India, have been women. Despite the large number of women in the field of medicine, both Indian Council of Medical Research (ICMR) and the All India Institute of Medical Science (AIIMS) have had one female director each. Even among undergraduates and graduates, numbers are worse for more selective institutions. For example, the number of female students studying at the 23 IITs has registered a steady drop.

There are several possible explanations for the numbers. Surveys have shown that four out of five women in the science, technology, engineering and mathematics (STEM) field experience bias in recruitment, promotion, retention, compensation and evaluation, often driving them away from a career in science and technology.[11] There is also often lack of support from families and institutions. Mentorship is rare.

[11] *Hindustan Times*, 'There Is an Inherent Gender Bias in India's Scientific Community', 11 January 2019, https://www.hindustantimes.com/editorials/there-is-an-inherent-gender-bias-in-india-s-scientific-community/story-Cb0lrJeJo16hulDc7yBorM.html

Gender Biases and Cultural Stereotypes

Women also experience stereotypes and biases right from their early childhood. Several studies have found that girls grow up believing that they are inferior to boys in STEM fields, even when they are capable of doing at least as well. Similarly, STEM subjects are often viewed by both women and society as masculine, while the humanities and the arts are often viewed as feminine. So women and girls experience 'disidentification'; that is, they lose aspiration for the subjects they are stereotyped against. Another effect is the 'geek culture' driven by men and boys which discourages anyone who may feel anything less than extreme enthusiasm for a subject. In an interesting study, researchers showed that many of these cultural stereotypes might be rooted in language.[12] They studied what words co-occur next to each other most often and found that words 'man' and 'career' tend to co-occur much more frequently than 'woman' and 'career'. Similarly, 'woman' was often associated with 'home', 'children' and 'family'. The researchers believe that a high gender bias in language both leads to and is reflective of a high gender bias in culture. Girls also routinely have more limited access to technology than boys (Chapter 4).

More generally, disparity in STEM is simply reflective of the wider gender disparity in the society. The 2020 Global Gender Gap Index studied gender disparity in 153 countries. India was placed 112th on the list—four spots worse than where it was in 2018. The report predicted that it would take India nearly 100 years to close the gender gap.

---

[12] Caroline Perez, *Invisible Women: Data Bias in a World Designed for Men* (New York, NY: Harry N. Abrams, March 2019).

Women have started from a very poor baseline in India.[13] Modern education for women began in Indian in the early 19th century. Calcutta University was the first university to open their doors to women in 1877–1878. Bombay University began admitting women students in 1883. Sexism was rooted even in these reforms. The British needed nurses and doctors to look after the Indian colony's population. Since it was considered improper for male doctors to treat women, special amendments were passed to incorporate women into higher education. Female literacy rose from 0.2 per cent in 1881 to 1.2 per cent in 1921. Progress was faster after 1921 and accelerated further after Independence. However, absolute progress was still slow. The 1959 report submitted by the National Committee on Women's Education expressed great concern at the slow pace of progress in women's education. Unfortunately, India's first five Five-Year Plans (ending in 1979) considered women as a subject of 'welfare'. Women's 'development' started being a goal only after the sixth Five-Year Plan (beginning in 1980). Gender parity was first stipulated as a stated goal only in 2013!

Interestingly, Indian women experience much less disparity and bias than many Western women when it comes to certain areas of engineering and technology.[14] For example, nearly half of the computer science undergraduates in India are women. Similarly, at least 30 per cent of programmers in Indian are women. The proportion is close to 20 per cent in the USA. Surveys also show that women in India do not view computer science as a masculine field. Rather, they consider it a pathway to socio-economic success. Indian women studying computer

13 T. V. Sekher and Neelamber Hatti, *Unwanted Daughters: Gender Discrimination in Modern India* (New Delhi: Rawat Publications, June 2010).

14 Vikram Chandra, 'What India Can Teach Silicon Valley about Its Gender Problem', *Wired*, 28 August 2014, https://www.wired.com/2014/08/silicon-valley-sexism/

science also tend to report high satisfaction with their academic performance.

This seeming contradiction, considering that India does poorly on most gender parity measures, can be explained by the fact that the number of career choices are limited for lower- and middle-class families in India. Therefore, Indian women are put under pressure by their parents to pursue computing due to socio-economic reasons. Computing is often viewed as both producing better career outcomes and better marriage prospects.

These exceptions notwithstanding, gender disparity and bias present a significant challenge in India. Reducing gender disparity in STEM will require effort on multiple fronts. Students should be given more exposure to female scientists and technologists. Incidentally, there have been several recent stories about involvement of female scientists in both Chandrayaan-2 and Perseverance projects. Gender bias should be erased from textbooks—in terms of both content and language. Applications for recruitment, promotion and retention should be anonymized to the extent possible. Women should be provided access to mentorship opportunities. Maternity and paternity leaves should become a norm. Institutions' structures must recognize the productivity impact of pregnancy and motherhood.

Caste and Creed Shaping Engineering and Technology Education

The caste hierarchy in India[15] which had ossified over centuries had an interesting implication for science and technology in India—technology and engineering ended up being a domain of the Shudras, the lowest rung in the case

---

[15] Ekta Singh, *Caste System in India: A Historical Perspective* (New Delhi: Kalpaz Publications, June 2005).

hierarchy, till the end of the 19th century. Shudras studied maths, science, art and architecture; produced builders, sculptors, architects and engineers; and built cities, temples, palaces and forts.[16] These professions required the kind of manual labour which Kshatriyas, Brahmins and Vaishayas detested. Since intermixing between castes was minimal and since Brahmins were responsible for dissemination of knowledge, all generated technology and engineering knowledge remained within the Shudras. In fact, generated knowledge often stayed within a hereditary guild. Even within a guild, a hierarchy often existed based on skill. Vaidagdhi Visvakarman were at the top of the hierarchy due to their skill and experience and were equivalent to modern-day chief architects and chief engineers.

Things started changing once engineering colleges and universities started being set up.[17] Modern engineering and technology education started in India towards the beginning of the 20th century. The British had a choice to make. Either make the education focus on building and developing hands-on skills (and, therefore, have the education be driven directly by the immediate needs of the society and economy) or focus on classroom-based theoretical knowledge. The danger with the first option was that it would grow the lower castes while alienating the higher castes (since higher castes largely disdained manual labour and considered it beneath them). The second option would necessarily exclude lower castes since neither the higher castes nor the British wanted intermingling. The British finally decided to go with the latter option to prevent social unrest, even if it meant wilful exclusion of lower castes.

---

[16] Nicholas Dirks, *Castes of Mind: Colonialism and the Making of Modern India* (Princeton, NJ: Princeton University Press, November 2001).

[17] Ajantha Subramanian, *The Caste of Merit: Engineering Education in India* (Cambridge, MA: Harvard University Press, December 2019).

One key person in the transition of Indian engineering and technology from being a practical domain dominated by lower castes to a classroom-based pursuit primarily for upper castes was Sir Alfred Chatterton. Chatterton was a British civil servant and a civil engineer who began his career in 1889 as a professor in Madras Civil Engineering College. He later became a member of the Indian Industrial Commission and advised the government on industrial development and engineering and technology matters, including education.

While Chatterton largely admired the science and technology accomplishments of Indians, he was one of the proponents of focusing modern Indian engineering education on classroom-based theoretical knowledge and the upper castes. He believed that the 'subtle mind of the Hindu [which] delights in philosophic speculations' was ill-suited for hands-on engineering and that modern engineering education in India could not be made practical 'largely due to the characteristics of the people themselves'. He also believed that Indians largely 'do not possess in any very large measure the grit and common sense which mark the engineer'.[18]

Furthermore, Chatterton believed that allowing castes to migrate across different industries would be detrimental to the society and economy.

For the indigenous industries [therefore] it seems inevitable that we must have recourse to industrial schools, but I would suggest that instruction in each industry should be confined to the sons and relatives of those actually engaged in the industry at the present time: that is to say, we should carry on the industrial schools on a caste basis. The indigenous industries have suffered very severely from foreign competition and it will not help the people still dependent on these industries for a livelihood to

---

[18] Alfred Chatterton, *Industrial Evolution in India* (Charleston, SC: Nabu Press, August 2010).

have added to their difficulties the competition of locally trained people belonging to the non-artisan castes.[19]

Such views meant that modern engineering education started being organized as a theoretical classroom-based pursuit focused on upper castes, while the lower castes were left to languish with existing skills and industries. This also meant that the demography of engineers and technologists started shifting. A domain which was dominated by lower castes started becoming dominated by the upper castes.

Other British engineering and technology policymakers also held views which stemmed from existing caste divisions and which ultimately changed the demography of engineers and technologists in India. Francis Spring, the president and chief engineer of the Madras Port Trust from 1904 to 1919, had scant respect for Indian engineers. He told the Indian Industrial Commission that Indian soul lacked the 'the intense internal desire for accuracy' and that only Indians studying engineering were 'young men who do not see much prospect of succeeding in law'. This and similar prejudices were mainly shaped by the existing stereotypes of Brahmins and other high-level castes focusing more on 'philosophic speculations', not practical hands-on work. The stereotypes were reinforced by the upper castes themselves who extolled the virtues of spiritualism over material vocations such as engineering and technology. A switch to theoretical classroom-based engineering nevertheless started attracting the upper castes to the field.

By 1921, 'Brahmins made up approximately 74 percent of engineering college students, despite being only 3 percent of the enumerated regional population'. This transformation continued with time and by the middle and the late

[19] Padmini Swaminathan, *Technical Education and Industrial Development in Madras Presidency: Illusions of a Policy in the Making*, Economic and Political Weekly, Vol. 27, No. 30, (25 July 1992), pp.1611-1622. https://www.jstor.org/stable/4398695

20th century, engineering and technology were dominated by Brahmins and the upper castes. Lower castes were largely shut out of pursuing science and engineering.

The wider caste dynamics and discrimination also started showing within engineering and technology institutions. Here's how IISc advertised its hostel when opening its door to students in 1911: 'There are 72 single rooms, and eight mess rooms, each with its own store and kitchen, so that members of different races and castes can form separate groups, each observing its own customs.'

Morris Travers[20] was the founding director of IISc. He recalled several years later how he felt compelled to support a caste-based organization of the hostel and the messes:

> When I first went to India one of the first things I did was to look into the question of housing and feeding students drawn from all over India. I came to the conclusion that I should have to have several messes. Then I was right, for when we opened I found that we had to have five. Then a Muslim student turned up, and as no mess would take him in, I had to make a one-man mess for him. I still wonder how fish-eating Bengalis get on with meat-eating Punjabis.
>
> If it should sound strange that five messes were necessary, here's something that will make it sound stranger: Classes began in 1911, and that academic year saw only about 20-odd students at IISc.[21]

In 1942, the institute had grown to over 200 students. The institute administration decided that a new common dining hall would be built and that the nine messes targeting different castes and groups would be shut down. When

---

20 Keith Kostecka, *Morris William Travers: A Lifetime of Achievement* (Bloomington, IN: Xlibris, February 2011).

21 Deepika S. Dining at IISc. Connect. https://connect.iisc.ac.in/2018/10/dining-at-iisc/

the plan became public, it set off widespread students' protests channelling the caste tensions that existed. More importantly, it demonstrated that overt caste discrimination was acceptable. Students were protesting, largely claiming the right to not eat with others with lower castes!

The caste tensions in engineering and technology only increased in the second half of the 20th century, as new laws mandated reservation of seats for lower castes in colleges. The tensions came to a boil in 1990 when the Mandal Commission recommended a 27 per cent reservation of public sector jobs for those belonging to Other Backward Castes (OBCs). A large number of upper-caste college students protested. Some committed self-immolation. They believed that an active increase in the number of low-caste students would lead to an end of merit. Many also believed that this would reduce the upper-caste students to 'low-caste jobs'. Indeed, many carried out protests, dressing up as sweepers, shoe shiners and vendors.

The protests against caste-based reservations were particularly strong in selective technology institutions. P. V. Indiresan was the director of IIT Madras in 1983 when it was decided to extend the 22.5 per cent reservation for Scheduled Castes and Scheduled Tribes to the IITs. In his annual director's report, he wrote:

> Some members of the [Parliamentary Committee on Scheduled Castes] have gone so far as to say that what we need is an Indian standard and not an international standard of instruction. Whether we need or need not be aware of the latest developments in technology, it is necessary to debate the fundamental question whether, just because a group of people cannot cope with a certain level of education, they should have the veto power to deny such an education to the rest; whether social justice should imply that there shall be no institution at all in

the country where merit shall be the criterion and also while the socially-deprived should have special privileges, the talented need have no rights of their own.[22]

Again, caste-based reservations were equated with the end of merit, implying somehow that lower-caste students could not be trained into good-quality engineers.

Similar protests were triggered in 2006 when the Supreme Court mandated implementation of 27 per cent reservation for OBCs in all central institutions, including IITs. Mass protests occurred within IITs. Pronouncements were made that meritocracy is dead, again implying that engineering and technology merit was somehow an upper-caste virtue.

The opportunity for lower castes in engineering and technology fields continues to be unequal today in both access and outcomes. Most students and faculty continue to be upper caste in spite of caste-based reservations. Similarly, there continue to be stories about caste-based discrimination at schools, universities and workplaces. Lower-caste students are often treated as trespassers or usurpers.[23]

Caste Politics in Indian Diaspora

B. R. Ambedkar, widely acknowledged as the architect of India's Constitution, wrote in an 1916 essay:

[22] Ajantha Subramanian, *The Caste of Merit: Engineering Education in India* (Cambridge, MA: Harvard University Press, December 2019).

[23] Renny Thomas, 'Brahmins as Scientists and Science as Brahmins' Calling: Caste in an Indian Scientific Research Institute', *Public Understanding of Science* 29, no. 3 (2020), https://doi.org/10.1177/0963662520903690

The caste problem is a vast one [...] It is a local problem, but one capable of much wider mischief, for 'as long as caste in India does exist, Hindus will hardly intermarry or have any social intercourse with outsiders; and if Hindus migrate to other regions on earth, Indian caste would become a world problem'.[24]

Indeed, the inequality of opportunity as well as caste discrimination have followed Indians in engineering and technology fields even outside India.

Indian immigrants into the USA before 1965 mostly consisted of peasants and farmers from the Punjab region. These farmers often made their way to America either directly or through the Caribbean or the East or South Africa. The USA passed the Immigration and Nationality Act of 1965, creating H-1B visas for foreigners working in specialty professions. The primary beneficiaries of these visas were the well-educated, often engineers and technologists, who mostly belonged to upper castes. The educational requirements for H-1B visas were tightened even further, leading to a large influx of upper-caste technologists and engineers. A 2003 study by the University of Pennsylvania found that Dalits (or the oppressed castes) constituted only 1.5 per cent of the Indian immigrants in the USA. The influx has continued till today. Current estimates suggest that 90 per cent of Indian immigrant population belongs to upper castes.

At least in some cases this has translated to caste-based discrimination even in the USA.[25] In 2020, the State of

---

[24] CASTES IN INDIA: Their Mechanism, Genesis and Development. B. R. Ambedkar. Paper presented at an Anthropology Seminar taught by Dr. A. A. Goldenweiser Columbia University 9th May 1916. http://www.columbia.edu/itc/mealac/pritchett/00ambedkar/txt_ambedkar_castes.html

[25] Yashica Dutt, 'The Specter of Caste in Silicon Valley', The New York Times, 14 July 2020, https://www.nytimes.com/2020/07/14/opinion/caste-cisco-indian-americans-discrimination.html

California's Department of Fair Employment and Housing sued Cisco, world's largest computer networking company, and its two upper-caste, Brahmin Indian employees, on behalf of John Doe, a Dalit Cisco employee for caste-based discrimination under the Equal Protection Clause.[26] Doe alleged that he was discriminated against in terms of compensation, opportunities and workplace conditions due to his caste. Similarly, a 2018 caste-based survey of 1,200 South Asian participants found that 59 per cent of the participants had experienced caste-based insults, 25 per cent had witnessed caste-based physical assault and 50 per cent were scared of being outed as belonging to a lower caste. South Asian workers in some of the biggest technology companies in the USA, such as Facebook, Google, Microsoft and IBM, have reported caste-based discrimination. Similar to India, the South Asian technology leaders in the USA largely belong to upper castes. The awareness about caste-based discrimination in the USA has been increasing. Brandeis University officially added caste to its non-discrimination policy at the end of 2019.

India's Crony Capitalism

Unequal opportunities exist not only for individuals in India but businesses as well due to cronyism. The word 'cronyism' comes from the Greek word khronios, meaning 'long-standing' and first appeared in the literature around 1840 to mean 'the ability or desire to make friends'. Crony capitalism refers to a scenario where a large fraction of a country's economy is controlled by a small number of families or institutions due to selective political patronage

---

26 Saritha Rai, 'How Big Tech Is Importing India's Caste Legacy to Silicon Valley', *Bloomberg*, 11 March 2021, https://www.bloomberg.com/news/features/2021-03-11/how-big-tech-is-importing-india-s-caste-legacy-to-silicon-valley

which favours them and aims to eliminate any competition. From the perspective of a future business owner, this discourages initiatives and saps motivation. From the perspective of an existing business owner, this prevents growth and success.

The history of cronyism in modern India[27] is as long as the nation's history. In 1600, Queen Victoria granted British East India Company the royal charter which gave the company monopoly over Indian trade. By the 18th century, the company had displaced other European mercantile companies, conquered territories and established a government. The company-run government, in turn, allowed the company officials and friends to amass huge personal fortunes and snuff out any possible competition. No other existing or future businesses stood a chance.

Even the end of the monopoly on trade in 1813 was a case of cronyism. A new industrial capitalist class had emerged in Britain which wanted to share the spoils of colonialism. It also wanted to destroy any competition. Through the powerful Lancashire lobby in the British Parliament, this class controlled Indian trade policy for over a century, leading to India's de-industrialization and, in particular, destruction of India's textile industry. This wilful destruction of the British textile industry's most formidable competition was arguably responsible for the rise and spread of the British colonial empire.

Unequal opportunities persisted for Indian businesses as railways construction began and modern industry and capitalism started being defined. Expatriate Europeans controlled private railway construction, shipping, banking, international trade and government business due to an

---

[27] James Crabtree, *The Billionaire Raj: A Journey through India's New Gilded Age* (New York, NY: Tim Duggan Books, July 2018).

open preference by the government and its institutions for European business houses over native Indian counterparts. This unequal opportunity continued till at least the First World War.

In the period after the First World War, native Indian business started aligning with the national movement due to shared economic policy goals. This led to both connections between businesses and the future political establishment as well as some patronage, since many national movement leaders had already started influencing economic policies. When India became independent, the existing connections between the businesses and the political establishment were leveraged into explicit patronage and cultivation of these businesses by the Indian government, and native Indian crony capitalism was born.

Large family-based businesses dominated the Indian economy even in 1947. For example, family businesses, such as Jain, Tata, Sahu, Walchand, Birla and Thapar, controlled most of the Indian manufacturing sector. This only worsened after Independence. Over next several decades, Indian economic system was based on routine interactions with the state for capital issue controls, foreign collaboration approvals, land ownership, import and industrial licensing (Licence Raj), etc. This compelled businesses to cosy up further with the political establishment, often through political donations, bribes and kickbacks. In return, the political patronage was granted which enabled both growth and boxing out of the competition. For example, governments' regulatory, executive and legislative actions were designed and manipulated to support the cronies, thereby undermining competition. This collusion between the political establishment and the chosen few also entailed that the spoils of businesses were available only to the few. For example, of all the licensed industrial investment approved by the government between 1957 and 1966, the Birla Group alone received 20 per cent! This disbursement of scarce resources only to a few large business houses with close connection to the government meant that these houses further extended their influence on governance and policy at the expense of other smaller or upcoming businesses.

Interestingly, India's decision to adopt a socialist economic model only increased the footprint of cronyism. Once the scope of private activities was restricted by legislations such as the Industrial Policy Resolution of 1948 and 1956 and the monopoly legislation of 1969 to make way for state-owned and state-run enterprise, the crony family-owned businesses diversified considerably and entered all sectors they could get licences in. So the breathing space for new and upcoming businesses shrank even further.

While the economic liberalization of 1991 led to loosening of the Licence Raj and the state controls, it did not end or, for that matter, reduce crony capitalism. Indeed, around 90 per cent of businesses in India today are still family owned. The non-family-owned businesses also largely depend on family-owned ones for their survival and growth. Similarly, the top family-owned groups still own a large fraction of India's total market capitalization.

As another metric, India has world's second largest number of billionaires per trillions of dollars of national output. This is only second to Russia where most of the large number of billionaires are oligarchs who stole national wealth during the hasty privatizations during the Boris Yeltsin era. Many Indian billionaires in competitive industries such as software have been self-made. However, a vast fraction of the billionaires still attribute their wealth directly or indirectly to government licences, land and natural resources. They have often benefited from political patronage to get sweet deals in oil, telecom, mining and real estate.

An interesting recent study looked at the contributions that India's political parties received from different industries.[28] The study found that the biggest donors were involved in sectors such as mining and power which require government to access natural resources. Regulated sectors such as real estate were the next level of contributors. Companies in sectors as technology and services businesses which require minimal government interaction contributed almost nothing!

Raghuram Rajan, former governor of the Reserve Bank of India, once remarked frustratedly, 'With the right policies and some luck, we will become a middle-income constitutional democracy in my lifetime. But inaction, coupled with bad luck, could make us an unequal oligarchy or worse—perhaps far sooner than we think.'

Monopoly in Technology Sector

The technology sector has also seen its share of family-owned businesses. Some of the largest technology-based businesses in the country are family-owned businesses.

Tata Consultancy Services (TCS), headquartered in Mumbai, is the largest IT company in the world with a market capitalization of 170 billion dollars. It was one of the first homegrown computer companies in India. However, it is also a subsidiary of Tata Group, which is largely owned by the Tata and Pallonji Mistry families. Tata Group was founded in 1868 by Jamsetji Tata as a textile company and over the years moved into sectors as diverse as iron and steel, power, chemicals, airlines, automobiles, fast-moving consumer durables (FMCD),

[28] Naresh Khatri and Abhoy Ojha, *Crony Capitalism in India: Establishing Robust Counteractive Institutional Frameworks* (London: Palgrave Macmillan, February 2016).

engineering, hospitality and tea. Essentially, ownership has passed within the same family, always connected with the political establishment, for over 150 years!

Reliance Jio is the largest telecommunication company in India and the second largest telecommunication company in the world. It is a subsidiary of Jio Platforms, which, in turn, is a subsidiary of Reliance Industries Limited. Reliance started in 1960 by Dhirubhai Ambani as a textile company and over the years ventured into sectors as diverse as oil, gas, petrochemicals, retail and media. The Ambani family still holds at least 45 per cent of the equity in Reliance.

Tech Mahindra is often ranked as one of the top five IT companies in India with over 5 billion dollar valuation and with over 125,000 employees spread over 90 countries. It is a subsidiary of the Mahindra Group. Mahindra Group was founded in 1945 by Mahindra brothers as a steel company and then subsequently diversified into sectors such as automobiles, farm equipment, infrastructure, and trade and financial services. Mahindra family continues to be the biggest shareholders.

Wipro was founded in 1945 by M.H. Hasham Premji as a manufacturer of vegetable and refined oils, 'Western India Palm Refined Oils Limited', and over the years moved into sectors as diverse as lighting, furniture, consumer care and infrastructure. It moved into IT during the 1970s and 1980s. Over 70 per cent of the ownership still rests with the Premji family.

While family ownership of the largest technology businesses is not a concern by itself, both optics of unequal opportunity and reality this represents are disturbing. A budding technology entrepreneur sees a tilted playing field at best and a plutocracy at worst. A small and medium-sized technology company sees the government's regulatory, executive and legislative actions to be favouring the chosen few. The discouraged businessman sees an oligarchy where corruption and cosying up to political establishment are prerequisites for success. New and upcoming businesses as well as businesses without the deep links to the political establishment which many of the large family-based businesses employ find it difficult to compete.

Success Overseas Suggests Problems at Home

An indirect metric of the unequal opportunity in the technology field in India is also suggested by the successes Indians have had in developing, monetizing and driving technology outside India. Indian technology community in the USA, in particular, serves as a great example.[29]

Almost one-third of the technology companies founded in the USA by immigrants have Indian founders. Some of the highest-impact technologies and technology companies in the world—Sun Microsystems, SanDisk, Bose Corporation, Hotmail, HDTV, USB, etc.—were built by an Indian in the USA. Almost 30 Indian-founded technology companies in the USA have seen exits worth over half a billion dollars just in last 8 years. Some of world's largest companies—including Google, Microsoft, IBM and Adobe—are being run by Indians. Even in academe, Indian professors dominate the technological landscape developing some of the most innovative technologies today. To top it all, most of these successes have been achieved by Indians which grew in lower- or middle-class Indian families. It is not a surprise that Indians are often discussed as the model immigrant community, especially in terms of technological and entrepreneurial successes.

---

[29] Monica Biradavolu, *Indian Entrepreneurs in Silicon Valley: The Making of a Transnational Techno-capitalist Class* (Amherst, NY: Cambria Press, September 2008).

While not to the same degree as in the USA, Indian technology-based expatriates have enjoyed disproportionate success, especially in academia and industry, in other countries as well, including Canada, the UK and Australia, and parts of Europe.

One could argue that the high rate of technological success Indians enjoy outside India is due to the fact that an already-selective set emigrates, but it still poses some hard questions. Why did the set emigrate in the first place? Why do people with identical education and background see much less success at developing, monetizing and driving technologies inside India? Why are there many more success stories in technology involving women, minorities, lower castes and those born in lower-class or lower-middle-class Indian families outside India than within India? Why do the people who achieve a lot of success outside India do not exhibit comparable success when they move back to India?

To be clear, discrimination and inequality of opportunity exist almost everywhere—even outside India. In the USA, for example, blacks and Hispanics see many fewer opportunities to succeed than their white counterparts. Women often report discrimination. Sexual orientation and preferences affect opinions and prospects. A large fraction of wealth is still inherited. Discrimination based on language, politics and property also exists. In fact, Indian immigrants in the USA also see discrimination.

However, that does not absolve the need to address the problems in India. We cannot afford whataboutism. The inequality of opportunity in India must be addressed for true technological progress.

CHAPTER 6

THE LEGITIMATE FEAR

While on the one hand, we appear to be overly sensitive to real and perceived slights on and by Twitter, WhatsApp or Facebook (Chapter 1), on the other hand, we appear to be relatively unprepared for the several challenges technology does present, such as magnifying existent biases due to increasingly algorithmic decision-making, exacerbating social and economic inequality due to progressive automation of jobs, impact of technology on environment and health, and increased hate speech and extremism due to unregulated online content.

Jobs at Risk

The impact of technology, specifically automation, on jobs and inequality is one legitimate fear almost as old as human civilization.[1] Ancient Greeks worried about labourers getting unemployed due to different labour-saving technologies which were developed at that time (e.g., gears, screws,

---

[1] Erik Brynjolfsson and Andrew McAfee, *The Second Machine Age: Work, Progress, and Prosperity in a Time of Brilliant Technologies* (New York, NY: W. W. Norton, January 2016).

catapults and torsion). Aristotle worried in his book *Politics* that there would be no need for manual labour once technology became sufficiently advanced. In fact, several labour-saving innovations were banned. Emperor Vespasian of Rome famously disallowed to a new method of low-cost transportation of heavy goods, declaring 'You must allow my poor haulers to earn their bread.'

There was plenty of concern in the Middle Ages as well. There have been records of people getting executed for selling forbidden goods, including ones which were put on the list for their potential of destroying jobs.

Perhaps the most famous example of the concern about technology's potential impact on jobs affecting history relates to William Lee.[2] He was a priest's assistant in England. He invented a labour-saving knitting machine purportedly because the woman he was courting seemed more interested in knitting than him. He invited Queen Elizabeth I to view his machine which produced wool for stockings. However, the Queen refused to issue him a patent for the machine, since she was concerned that the machine would snatch the livelihoods of the many knitters in the kingdom. She is said to have remarked to Lee, 'Thou aimest high, Master Lee. Consider thou what the invention could do to my poor subjects. It would assuredly bring to them ruin by depriving them of employment, thus making them beggars.' Unfazed, Lee built another version of the machine which could produce silk of finer texture. However, he was denied patent on the same grounds. He moved to France where his machine was widely accepted. Upon the death of Queen Elizabeth I, Lee returned to England. However, he was refused again by the new King James I, for the same the reason.

---

[2] *Scientific American*, 'Origin of the Stocking Frame', 13 (14 August 1858): 387.

Lee's knitting machines were eventually adopted in England and became quite popular. In the early 19th century, during the harsh economic realities of the Napoleonic Wars, they caused quite a stir among a group of textile workers who were later referred to as Luddites.[3] This group of skilled artisan workers, first in Nottingham and then the entire region, started destroying knitting machines in different textile factories, as they feared that the machines would eventually replace them. These machines needed only less-skilled, low-waged workers to operate. In the short term, these machines weakened their bargaining position with their employers. The movement which started in early 1811 spread throughout England over next two years. A combination of shooting by mill and factory owners and use of military and legal force finally brought the movement to rest in 1816.[4] One of the outcomes was the Parliament making industrial sabotage a capital crime with the Frame-Breaking Act of 1812.

Then were Swing Riots as well.[5] In 1830, agricultural workers in eastern and southern England destroyed hundreds of threshing machines to protest agricultural mechanization. Almost 2,000 were tried for the riots, 644 were imprisoned and 19 were hanged to death.

India's Devastating First Interaction with Automation and Mechanization

Till the middle of the 18th century, India was a manufacturing power producing around 25 per cent of the

---

[3] Daron Acemoglu and James A. Robinson, *Why Nations Fail: The Origins of Power, Prosperity, and Poverty* (Redfern: Currency, September 2013).

[4] Kirkpatrick Sale, *Rebels against the Future: The Luddites and Their War on the Industrial Revolution—Lessons for the Computer Age* (New York, NY: Basic Books, April 1996).

[5] Eric Hobsbawm and George Rude, *Captain Swing* (Brooklyn, NY: Verso Books, August 2014).

world's industrial output. India particularly dominated the textiles market.[6] However, things turned with the advent of the Industrial Revolution. India's economy—based on the export of handloom textiles—started becoming decimated due to cheap machine-produced textiles manufactured by Britain. These machines, export-controlled by Britain, could produce textiles much faster and much cheaper than what weavers in India could produce. India's textile industry collapsed, and millions lost their jobs. In around 100 years (i.e., by the middle of the 19th century), textile production had shifted to Britain, and India was left with producing cotton to export to Britain for its textile machines. A raw material (cotton) did not fetch the same profits as a finished product (textiles). So even the ones in India with jobs barely made living. The shift in agriculture from producing food crops to cash crops (e.g., cotton) led to widespread famines and deaths in India.

The British need for cotton to feed their textile machines also ultimately led to India's colonization.[7] Through wins in the Battle of Plassey in 1757 and the Battle of Buxar in 1764, the British East India Company acquired Bengal and secured cheap production and supply of cotton.

Short-term vs Long-term Job Losses

Almost everyone agrees that technology can lead to short-term job losses. A common modern example is the replacement of cashiers in retail stores by self-checkout machines. During the Second World War, Alan Turing, the famed computer scientist, invented bombe—an electromechanical

---

[6] Giorgio Riello, *How India Clothed the World: The World of South Asian Textiles, 1500–1850* (Leiden: Brill Publishers, August 2013).

[7] Virginia Postrel, *The Fabric of Civilization: How Textiles Made the World* (New York, NY: Basic Books, November 2020).

machine which could decrypt German Enigma-machine-encrypted messages. Bombe could compress and decrypt thousands of man-years of encrypted data in a matter of few man-hours dramatically reducing the need for human code-breakers.

However, the long-term impact of technology on the number of net jobs is less clear. In fact, for much of the 20th century and second half of the 19th century, the common belief was that technology brings several compensation effects which ensure that there is never a long-term negative impact on jobs. The term 'Luddite fallacy' became popular to describe the seemingly erroneous thinking that technology leads to lasting harm in terms of employment.

The second decade of the 21st century has started seeing both popular and expert opinions swing the other way. An increasing fraction of economists and policymakers is getting concerned about the impact of technology on jobs. A fascinating book *A World without Work*[8] from Daniel Susskind argues that 1987 was when the job-creating effects of technology started getting outweighed by the job-displacing effects of technology. According to the Susskind's study, the average displacement (or job loss) from technology was 17 per cent during 1947–1987. The average reinstatement (or job gain) was 19 per cent during the same period. Essentially, technology freed up people to perform more complex tasks. However, the same figures were 16 per cent and 10 per cent, respectively, during 1987–2016. That is, more jobs were getting lost than were being created by technology. Furthermore, Susskind argues that the new job opportunities benefited low-skilled workers during the1960s–1980s timeframe. However, most

[8] Daniel Susskind, *A World without Work: Technology, Automation, and How We Should Respond* (New York, NY: Metropolitan Books, January 2020).

new opportunities created since then disproportionately benefit high-skill workers. They also do not often match in terms of location and skills.[9]

There is a widespread concern that this gap may only widen with increasing use of automation technologies which may take up even greater fraction of jobs currently performed by humans. For a country like India, where a large fraction of the population is young and job-seeking, the impact of automation can be concerning.

Not All Jobs Can Be Easily Displaced

Consider the impact of automation on the IT job market in India. There are plenty of headlines warning about projected and actual job losses in the IT industry. Both media and policymakers are operating under the premise that technology and automation will eliminate a large fraction of the Indian IT jobs. Is this premise sound?

A vast fraction of the India's IT professionals are software programmers or program testers. The above premise would be sound if and only if it were possible to automatically generate or test software.

Interestingly, program synthesis—automatically generate software from a high-level specification (i.e., what you want a program to be able to accomplish)—is very hard. For last 60 years, program synthesis tools have struggled to automatically generate software more complex than what can be easily written by a programmer with someone with less than a month of training. Even in those instances, the automatically generated software is much slower than handwritten programs. So there is no threat of computer programmers getting replaced anytime soon.

---

[9] Virginia Eubanks, *Automating Inequality: How High-tech Tools Profile, Police, and Punish the Poor* (New York, NY: St Martin's Press, January 2018).

Automated testing is much easier. However, it works only when the software being tested does not keep changing. Today's software keeps changing till the last release and often updated after release. Manual testing is needed in these cases. For some software where the output is interactive or visual, humans need to be in the loop. Even in cases where automated testing works, it is unclear if there is a net job loss. The cost of developing and maintaining automated testing infrastructure sometimes outweighs the labour costs of manual testing.

Automation has not led to previously expected widespread job losses in other domains as well.

There was a big concern about autonomous vehicles leading to enormous job losses. The hype was overwhelming. (Elon Musk famously said in 2015: 'I view it as a solved problem. We know exactly what to do and we will be there in a few years.') However, it has been more than a decade (and over hundred billion dollars of investment) since the beginning of the Google's self-driving car project in 2009, and we still do not have self-driving cars on roads anywhere (Google's Waymo provides limited number of self-driving rides in Arizona in constrained settings). Building a vehicle which drives itself is a very hard problem, since the vehicle must be capable of handling an extremely large number of 'edge cases', that is, unusual circumstances. Similarly, the vehicle must meet the rigorous safety standards such as ones for aviation. Unsurprisingly, focus has now shifted from self-driving personal cars (or robotaxis) to much more limited application settings such grocery delivery, warehouse automation and driver assistance on highways. Self-driving car companies such as Zoox are running out of cash; other companies such as Cruise have pivoted to goods delivery.

Similarly, consider jobs which require social intelligence and face-to-face interaction—therapists, nurses, teachers, receptionists, sales, artists, writers, managers, social workers, etc. Such jobs are unlikely to be displaced by technology. In fact, these jobs grew 12 per cent as a share of the US workforce during 1980–2012. There have attempts at automation in some of these spaces. For example, there has been a lot of recent work on caregiving robots. However, results and adoption have far lagged expectations.

Technology May Also Impact Economic Inequality

Economic inequality in India has been increasing.[10] Studies suggest that 35–60 per cent of India's wealth is held by the nation's top 1 per cent. Almost 70–80 per cent wealth is held by the top 10 per cent. For context, only around 25–35 per cent was held by the top 1 per cent 20 years ago. Only around 55–65 per cent was held by the top 20 per cent. Several rankings of countries based on economic inequality conclude that no more than a couple of countries in the world are more unequal than India.

Many experts blame the increased adoption of technology as being responsible for the increased inequality, especially over the last 20 years.[11] Their argument is that technology has a 'skill bias'. Those who can use technology experience an increase in productivity and wages. Those who cannot use technology see their productivity and wages (relatively) stagnate. The increased productivity leads to further penetration of technology, which, in turn, creates an even higher demand for technology-savvy workers. This self-perpetuating cycle exacerbates wealth

---

[10] Harsh Mander, *Looking Away: Inequality, Prejudice and Indifference in New India* (New Delhi: Speaking Tiger Books, June 2015).

[11] Jonathan P. Allen, *Technology and Inequality: Concentrated Wealth in a Digital World* (Cham: Palgrave Macmillan, July 2017).

and income inequality. Technology-based automation also leads to elimination of the medium-skill jobs, further increasing the wage gap.

Experts also argue that another reason why technology increases inequality is that technology has a 'capital bias'. Technology-based automation reduces the role of labour in the capital-creation process. This allows most gains from the increased productivity from technology to be delivered directly to the capital providers, instead of labour. This lopsided delivery of returns exacerbates the wealth and income gap.

However, there is some evidence that technology may have played only a minimal role in the burgeoning economic inequality in India. The key reason for inequality in India may be the large fraction of the labour force working in sectors with low productivity. Agriculture is a prime example. It contributes only 17 per cent to the GDP but supports 53 per cent of India's workforce. Another key reason may be the weakening of the labour movement. Studies have shown a strong link between the strength of labour unions and labour's share of income. This link has been repeatedly shown to be much stronger than the relationship between use of automation and technology and labour's share of income.

Skill-bias effects also do not seem to be at play in India, at least not just yet. It appears that there is not an excess demand for high-skill workers in India as is evident from the fact that an increasing fraction of tech-literate college graduates are unable to find employment.

In fact, one could argue that the wages of the medium skilled and the unskilled may have increased in the last few years, at least in the services sector, due to the use of technology. A large fraction of the workforce in the services sector which contributes over 50 per cent to India's GDP is medium skilled and low skilled. Increasing popularity of technology-based service companies such as Ola, Zomato, Flipkart and OYO has created significant employment opportunities for the medium skilled and the unskilled. Similarly, digitization of goods and services has enabled Indian businesses to sell directly to foreign customers, creating even a bigger employment market for medium-skilled and low-skilled workers.

While the dire predictions of large-scale job losses and gaping inequality due to increased use of technology and automation have not come true, at least not just yet, automation has already led to, at the least, a redistribution of jobs. The use of robots in Indian factories has replaced a lot of workers, and many cases obviated the need to hire workers. Popularity of Ola and Uber has led to considerable competition and hardships for professional drivers. Many fewer travel agents are needed. Many bank workers live in the fear of their jobs, as people switch to online banking.

Similarly, as the experience of more industrialized countries shows, entire segments of the traditional workforce—in manufacturing, mining, retail, services, etc.—may lose jobs or require reskilling in near to medium future. Large-scale loss of coal mining and steel manufacturing jobs has led to social, political and economic unrest in the USA, for example. India must also be prepared for the upheaval.

Technology Also Impacts Environment Adversely

First, it pollutes air and water.[12] Fossil fuels, power stations, factories, vehicles, and mass agriculture and transportation produce gases such as carbon dioxide,

---

[12] Edward Golding, *A History of Technology and Environment* (Oxfordshire: Routledge, December 2016).

carbon monoxide, methane, nitric oxide and sulphur dioxide, which go into the atmosphere causing global warming as well as health impacts for humans, animals and plants. Similarly, industrial and vehicular effluents, insecticides and pesticides, and domestic and animal waste contaminate water bodies such as oceans, lakes, rivers and groundwater, which can eutrophy and degrade aquatic ecosystem (negatively affecting the food chain) and produce diseases such as typhoid and cholera.

Second, it depletes natural resources.[13] Activities such as mining, agriculture, construction, transportation and electricity generation use water, timber and fossil fuels and can lead to deforestation, soil erosion, aquifer depletion, etc. Deforestation, for example, has caused loss of 1.5 million sq. km of forests in last 30 years alone, causing climate change and loss of habitat for plants and animals.

White collar industries have similar effect. Consider IT, for example. Over 35 precious metals and other natural resources drawn from all over the world are used to build a smartphone, leading to severe environmental and human toll. Servers and data centres now consume almost 1 per cent of world's electricity. We throw out almost 65 billion dollars' worth of electronic waste every year, a vast of majority of which is burnt in dumps or ends up in a landfill site in a poor country, endangering local health.

India has long been bearing the brunt of the environmental impact of technology. This impact must be managed for continued technological progress.

Curious Case of Electronic Waste

Consider electronic waste as a specific example. Vast quantities of electronic items end up in India as waste every

---

[13] Elizabeth Kolbert, *Sixth Extinction* (London: Picador Paper, January 2015).

year.[14] An estimate from 2016 put the amount of annual electronic waste just produced in India to be over 2 million metric tons. As the use of electronics increases in India, this number is increasing rapidly. In addition, a huge amount of electronics produced elsewhere ends up in India. Studies have estimated that electronic waste produced in other countries constitutes almost 70 per cent of the electronic waste handled in India. This is in spite of an import ban on electronic waste instituted in India in 2010.

Unfortunately, of the electronic waste India handles, it is able to recycle only 1 or 2 per cent. Over 98 per cent of the electronic waste—which tends to be toxic—ends up in some landfill or an informal dump. In fact, most of the toxic waste in a landfill in India is electronic. Toxic electronic waste in India's landfills leads to serious health and environmental concerns due to direct contamination of ground and surface water, stormwater run-off contamination, contamination during waste transport, and secondary contamination due to birds and other animals which landfills attract.

To make matters worse, the informal sector handles over 90 per cent of the recycling, for the 1 or 2 per cent electronic waste which does get recycled. The informal sector is over 1 million strong with over 50 per cent children. The lack of tools, training and resources makes this sector particularly vulnerable to health and environmental effects.

There have been attempts by the government to address the electronic waste issue in the last few years. Regulations for the formal sector were introduced in 2008 and 2011. An import ban on electronic waste was instituted in 2010. To increase recycling and reduce the production of electronic waste, electronic waste management rules were notified in 2016. Electronics producers were made liable to

---

[14] Rakesh Johri, *E-waste: Implications, Regulations and Management in India and Current Global Best Practices* (New Delhi: The Energy and Resources Institute, January 2009).

collect the waste when extended producer responsibility was introduced.

Participation by the private sector has also increased in recent times, with an increasing number of electronic recycling companies and electronics companies offering collection centres. More collection mechanisms are available than before.

Why does India still recycle only 1 or 2 per cent of the electronic waste? First, the government has been primarily focused on the formal sector in spite of the recycling being mostly handled in India by the informal sector. Second, the focus has not been on economic incentives. Rather, it has been on regulations. Informal recyclers do not have an economic incentive to either formalize (since the formalization process currently costs almost ₹10 lakh) or sell to the formal recyclers (since hand processing is currently more profitable). Similarly, formal recyclers do not have an economic incentive to perform full recycling. It is more profitable to perform partial recycling and either route the remains to the informal sector or dump the remains (in a landfill, for example). Since there is not much public awareness about electronic waste, electronics producers also do not have an economic incentive to invest in recycling. Third, given the lack of formal collection and recycling infrastructure in the country, current regulations and collection targets are practically unenforceable.

We must rethink solutions considering that the problem will keep getting worse. For more effective recycling, economic incentives will need to be created. For example, to encourage the informal sector to deliver electronic waste to the recycling centres, formal recycling centres could pay a delivery fee higher than the value of hand processing. Recycling centres, in turn, could be compensated for recycling: This compensation must be higher than the cost of component materials. The compensation money for the recycling centres can be raised from the recycling fee which electronics producers could be mandated to put into the price.

The government must also directly address the needs of the informal sector beyond providing economic incentives. The cost of formalization must be lowered. Training must be provided for safety and efficiency as well as to impart knowledge and skills. To enable safer recycling and the growth of the formal sector, R&D should be supported for lower-cost recycling technologies. The use of environment-friendly material in electronics should be encouraged through a mixture of incentives and regulations. To prevent smuggling of electronic waste from developed countries, border control should be better enforced. To set up collection and distribution logistics and incentives, lessons from successful public–private partnerships should be applied. Last-mile collection should leverage the vastness of the informal sector network. Most formal recycling centres in India currently send electronic waste to smelters overseas to recover precious metals. Support for construction and maintenance of recycling smelters in India should be provided.

India must attempt to meet the aspirations of its citizens, but not at the expense of health and environment. The problem of environmental impact of technology needs constant attention.

Increasing Biases and Prejudices

Increased penetration of technology also increases concerns about the automation and magnification of different prejudices and biases.[15]

Envision the following disturbing scenarios. A Muslim man with a solid economic background is denied by the

---

[15] Cathy O'Neil, *Weapons of Math Destruction: How Big Data Increases Inequality and Threatens Democracy* (New York, NY: Penguin, September 2016).

lending company every time he applies for a personal loan. A Dalit who committed an infraction gets a longer sentence than his non-Dalit accomplice. Young men from a minority community or a poor neighbourhood keep getting wrongly convicted for crimes. A job search website keep's preferring a man's resume over resumes of women with better qualifications. A housing society dominated by a community never approves housing applications from a different community. Amazon, Flipkart or Ola do not service certain neighbourhoods or communities.

These scenarios of religious, ethnic, gender or sexual discrimination are not unheard of in India. With the increasing use of computer technology for making decisions about law enforcement, judiciary, recruitment and lending, these scenarios may become even more common in future if we are not vigilant against 'algorithmic bias'.[16]

Biased Data Produce Biased Algorithms

Automated decision-making in the above scenarios relies on a technology called machine learning. In machine learning, past data is used to construct computer models, which can then be used to make decisions. One would be inclined to assume that human prejudices and biases are eliminated when computers are used to make decisions. However, nothing is further from truth. Computer-based decision-making can be biased as well and, in many scenarios, have more widespread and devastating consequences. Pre-existing human biases may get introduced into computer models for decision-making at different stages of development and deployment. Biases may get introduced either intentionally or unintentionally during

[16] Sara Wachter-Boettcher, *Technically Wrong: Sexist Apps, Biased Algorithms, and Other Threats of Toxic Tech* (New York, NY: W. W. Norton, October 2018).

the framing of the decision problem, selection of data to construct the models, tuning and optimization of the models, or interpretation of the model decisions.[17]

In the 1970s, Dr Geoffrey Franglen, vice dean of St George's Hospital in Britain, wrote a computer program to decide which of the roughly 2,500 applicants for admission should be shortlisted for the interview stage. Roughly 70 per cent of the applicants who made to the interview stage were granted admission; so the initial weeding out stage was crucial. Dr Franglen wanted to remove any inconsistency in the evaluation of the applications; he hoped that using a computer program for evaluation would make the system fair and efficient. His program analysed past admissions data to learn the characteristics of successful applications and was tuned in a manner that the decisions generated by his program matched the decisions made by human assessors. Initially, it seemed that he was right. In double tests which were performed over 3 years, his algorithm agreed with human assessors 90–95 per cent of time. In fact, by the early 1980s, all applications started getting screened by his program instead of human assessors.

Interestingly, after a few years, some staff members started noticing relative lack of diversity in successful applicants. An internal review found that the program was weighing applications based on seemingly non-relevant factors such as name and place of birth. A full enquiry was initiated which found that the program was discriminating against women and people of colour. Franglen's algorithm was classifying candidates as 'Caucasian' or 'non-Caucasian' on the basis of names and places of birth. A

[17] Frank Pasquale, *The Black Box Society: The Secret Algorithms That Control Money and Information* (Cambridge, MA: Harvard University Press, August 2016).

non-European (and, therefore, likely non-Caucasian name) would result in 15 points being docked off the applicant's score; female applicants were being docked 3 points. In fact, it was found that roughly 60 applicants were being denied admission based on this scoring system. Essentially, Franglen's program had learned the gender and racial biases which existed in the historical admissions data; women and men with 'foreign-sounding names' were being denied admission since the computer models tried to replicate historical trends in admission which were biased against women and men of non-European origin.

Considering how poor labour participation rate has been for women and minorities in India, there is a real danger of propagating, intentionally or unintentionally, biases against these communities when employing techno-logy for evaluating applications.[18]

A very similar incident played out in the 2010s. Amazon started building an automation tool in 2014 to review job applicants and assigning each application between one and five stars based on the estimated strength of the application. However, by 2015, it started realizing that the tool was not rating candidates in a gender-neutral way; it was discriminating against women. Upon investigation, it was found that the tool trained based on resumes received by Amazon over previous 10 years which, unsurprisingly, came mostly from men. Since it was men who were mostly applying and getting selection, the tool learned to penalize words such 'women's' as well as downgrade resumes from all-women colleges. Amazon had to shut down the project. Spotify's recommendation system was similarly found to be biased against female artists. Again, these serve as cautionary tales for India.

---

[18] Meredith Broussard, *Artificial Unintelligence: How Computers Misunderstand the World* (Cambridge, MA: MIT Press, April 2018).

Disproportionate Representation
Creates Data Bias

Perhaps a more shocking set of examples, with grave implications for India, is related to facial recognition. Researchers from MIT and Stanford analysed in 2018 three commercial face-recognition programs from big technology companies to look for biases. They found that all three programs demonstrated both racial and gender biases. For light-skinned men, the error rate of the three programs in identifying the gender was never worse than 0.8 per cent. On the other hand, the error rates in determining gender for dark-skinned women was more than 20 per cent for one of the programs and over 34 per cent for the other two programs. Interestingly, the error rate claimed by one of the programs was less than 3 per cent; unsurprisingly, this assessment was performed on data which was overwhelmingly male (>77%) and white (over 83%). Similar biases in face recognition have been observed by others. Google tagged a photo of two African-Americans as gorillas in 2015. iPhone X face unlock feature was failing to distinguish between different Asian women. Nikon's software would often mark an Asian face as blinking. In 2009, HP computers would have no trouble recognizing and tracking white faces but would often have trouble recognizing and tracking black faces.

One can imagine a similar problem in India, perhaps to a greater degree, where face-recognition software consistently mis-categorizes people belonging to disadvantaged communities (due to their likely poor representation in the training datasets), leading to amplification of social, economic or judicial injustice. Imagine, for example, someone wearing a skullcap wrongly marked as a suspect by the facial recognition software due to its inability to distinguish this person from the actual suspect. Or consider a dark-skinned person (typically belonging to poor strata of the society in northern and Central India) being marked as a suspect for a crime which someone light-skinned (or, for that matter, some other dark-skinned person) committed.

Disturbing examples abound even in other domains. A Carnegie Mellon University study found that men were shown advertisements for high-paying jobs far more frequently than women. Amazon same-day delivery services were excluding black neighbourhoods in several big cities in the USA. Apple's credit cards were giving higher credit limits to men than women. Black criminals were mistakenly flagged by predictive policing software as likely to recommit crimes at twice the rate of the white criminals, leading to over-policing of black neighbourhoods. Again, the implications for India can be dire where upward mobility of women and minorities can be threatened by indiscriminate application of technology.

Computer models may become biased not only due to a biased developer but also due to statistical bias stemming from incomplete or unrepresentative data used to construct models. A criminal database of images dominated by a certain gender is likely to provide false matches at a higher rate for a person of that gender. Similarly, an image database dominated by people with a certain kind of headgear, a certain set of facial features or a certain skin colour is biased against people of that kind. A canonical criminal image database in India is dominated by dark-skinned males with disproportionate representation from communities with specific accessory preferences. This database will produce false matches for this group of people with regularity.

This problem is not restricted to image-based decision-making. Misclassifications may be common for any computer model which has been constructed using data where a group (e.g., an ethnic, religious or caste group) is not represented proportionately. The misclassifications will create biases against groups which are overrepresented in existing databases.

Biased Computer Models May Be More Harmful than Biased Humans

Computer models also amplify human biases in addition to replicating them—computer models can make decisions at a scale humans do not. A software written by a single religious bigot for evaluating loan applications can discriminate against a vast number of applicants belonging to certain religions. A computer resume evaluation software carelessly fed past data on primarily male employees may be used by a large number of institutions where the software wrongly determines women to be un-hireable. A mass surveillance computer model systemically biased against a religious group may be far more devastating than a few bigoted individuals. Since reuse is quite common in software industry, the same computer model may be used in several applications, magnifying the impact of a bias.

Computer models can also lead to inadvertent propagation of biases. As one example, consider some law today which is discriminatory (e.g., laws against same-sex couples). A computer model may be developed to help conformation with the law, thereby replicating the societal discrimination. Let us say that the society evolves and decides to make the law more equitable in future. If the previous model continues to be used for decision-making, its decisions will continue to be discriminatory even though the society has made the law more equitable.

This is not an unlikely scenario either. There are several reasons why an older model may continue to get used. The model may be deeply embedded in an application. There may not be any way to understand and analyse the decision-making progress (due to trade secrets and other intellectual property protection reasons, for example). There may be lack of oversight, etc.

The problem may get exacerbated due to 'algorithmic authority'. Studies have shown that people put much more trust in computer-based decisions than human-based decisions. This trust may be exploited by the malicious and the mischievous to propagate and replicate intentional biases. The undue trust also discourages redressal requests from those victimized by the biases.

Concerns Are Already Real for India

Computer models are already being used in India much more than people realize. In a surprising admission, the Home Minister of India Amit Shah declared in the Parliament that 1,100 individuals were arrested for Delhi communal riots in February 2020 using a face-recognition system. Similarly, Uttar Pradesh's police has boasted about arresting hundreds of criminals using facial recognition. States such as Delhi and Telangana have admitted to using facial recognition for monitoring during public protests and rallies. India's NCRB is setting up nation's first centralized face-recognition-based surveillance system. It will be world's largest face-recognition system in the world where images will be pulled from a varied set of sources, including CCTV cameras, newspapers, social media accounts and criminal records. Face-recognition technology is already being used at several airports in India; railway also has plans to use such systems shortly to enhance safety.

Similarly, Indian fintech start-ups are already providing instant loans based on computer models. Fintech providers such as Capital Float, FlexiLoans and Lendingkart use computer models for risk analysis, wealth management advice, credit underwriting and fraud detection. mPokket uses computer models to assess students' creditworthiness based on demographic, social, behavioural, financial and transactional data. PaisaDukan similarly assesses credit-worthiness for rural users who may not have documents for traditional credit scoring. Shubh Loans uses computer models to provide credit to unserved or underserved user segments. Several similar start-ups use computer models for lending.

There are also Indian start-ups using computer models for hiring and retention. Belong, for example, uses computer models to find best candidates for a job by scouring different forums and networks, considering even people who are not actively looking for a job. Param.ai identifies links between skills to make better job recommendations.

Computer models are already being used for 'predictive policing'[19] where decisions about resource allocation, personnel movement and surveillance are made based on probability of a crime being committed.[20] NCRB has developed software for crime data analytics to enable predictive policing. Maharashtra government has a specific 'predictive policing policy' to spot people on social media who may fuel unrest. Jharkhand Police is working with data-mining software capable of scanning online records— such software can enable predictive policing. Delhi Police uses a software called Crime Mapping Analytics and Predictive System (CMAPS) to identify crime hotspots and perform mitigation.

---

[19] Sarah Brayne, *Predict and Surveil: Data, Discretion, and the Future of Policing* (Oxford: Oxford University Press, November 2020).

[20] Andrew Guthrie Ferguson, *The Rise of Big Data Policing: Surveillance, Race, and the Future of Law Enforcement* (New York, NY: New York University Press, October 2017).

Computer-based judicial decision-making has not yet started in India. Such models are already popular in several countries, to decide, for example, who should be granted parole and for what length. It is only a matter of time before Indian justice system starts using computer-based tools in different ways.

Judiciously Escaping Algorithmic Bias

It is inevitable that a lot of future decision-making will be computer-based. So what should be done to mitigate the impact of algorithmic bias?

EU put together a set of guidelines in 2019 to mitigate the potential impact of algorithmic bias.[21] The guidelines require that computer models must be lawful (i.e., they should comply with local laws and regulations), ethical (i.e., they should adhere to ethical principles and values—specifically 'respect for human autonomy, prevention of harm, fairness and explicability') and robust (from both technical and societal perspectives) to prevent unintentional harm. The corresponding framework lists 'seven requirements that computer models should meet. (1) human agency and oversight, (2) technical robustness and safety, (3) privacy and data governance, (4) transparency, (5) diversity, non-discrimination and fairness, (6) environmental and societal well-being and (7) accountability'. It also recommends having an assessment list to judge the trustworthiness of the models. Specifically, in any case where there could be significant or legal impact on the individual, Europe now prohibits solely automated decision-making. In all other cases, the individual has a right to human-in-the-loop. They also have a non-binding right to explanation of the decision.

---

[21] Bryce Goodman and Seth Flaxman, 'European Union Regulations on Algorithmic Decision Making and a "Right to Explanation"', *AI Magazine* Fall (2017).

Algorithmic Accountability Act introduced in the US Congress in April 2019 charges the Federal Trade Commission (FTC) with requiring entities which use 'high-risk' automated decision systems to conduct impact assessments.

India may need to bring an algorithm transparency bill modelled after these documents.

In addition, relevant existing laws should be amended to clarify how discrimination-related provisions apply in the digital space.

A careful regulation of computer-based decision-making may allow us to get the efficiency benefits of such decision-making without deepening the divisions in the society or increasing discrimination.

Concerning Case of Unregulated Online Content

Perhaps the most immediately visible technology-related concern is the enormous implication of unregulated online content.[22]

Mehdi Masroor Biswas was an executive with a multi-national firm in Bengaluru during the day. He was also '@ShamiWitness' on Twitter, operating a pro-jihad account, masquerading as a Libyan living in the UK. Biswas had never been to Syria, had 11,700 followers and was outed by London's Channel 4, leading to eventual arrest in December 2014.

In 2017, 'love jihad' was a popular and divisive term on Indian social media, denoting an alleged conspiracy by Muslim men to marry Hindu women to force conversion and demonstrate power. Incendiary tweets exhorting

---

[22] P. W. Singer and Emerson T. Brooking, *LikeWar: The Weaponization of Social Media* (Boston, MA: Mariner Books, October 2018).

Hindus to do something about it flew thick fast. On 6 December, Shambhulal Regar, a Hindu, hacked Mohammed Afrazul, a Bengali Muslim migrant worker, to death with a meat cleaver and then burnt his body. He videotaped the entire attack, uploaded it on YouTube and bragged about his act as a retribution for 'love jihad'. The video was watched widely.

Four friends from Maharashtra left for pilgrimage to Haj in May 2014 and then disappeared. It was believed that they had travelled to Iraq to join Islamic State (IS). One of them eventually retuned and was arrested. He confessed to being indoctrinated through Internet chat rooms. An intermediary on Facebook had introduced him to a contact in Mosul in Iraq who guided him and his friends to join the IS camps in Iraq.

Certain online content (e.g., extremist propagandas, hateful speeches and threats) poses tremendous threats.[23] India is a signatory to the Christchurch Call to Action which aims to curb 'the posting and spread of extremist violence and hate speech on the Internet, looking to stop the use of social media as a tool for terrorism'. The question is: How does one perform these curbs?

India's approach seems to be based on regulating online content. India intends to increase the liability of online platforms for the content they host. It also intends to enforce content traceability. In a Supreme Court filing, the government envisions 'unimaginable disruption to the democratic polity' from unregulated online content.

---

23 Richard Stengel, *Information Wars: How We Lost the Global Battle against Disinformation and What We Can Do about It* (London: Grove Press UK, October 2019).

Regulation Is a Challenging Task

However, regulating content which is not obviously illegal is challenging.[24] Consider regulation to minimize disinformation or fake news. Determining whether content is fake is not always easy, especially for a platform with limited resources. Determining intent is even harder—fake content could simply be satire or not meant to create harm. Even if the content is harmful, where does one draw the line? Freedom of expression is valued after all. Making platforms liable for content is heavy-handed—disinformation has been around much before social media (Chapter 1).

Regulating defamatory, seditious or hateful speeches is also hard since the line between permitted and prohibited speech is unclear.[25] The right to freedom of speech in India as enshrined in Article 19 of the Constitution is not absolute. The freedom of expression can be limited 'in the interests of the sovereignty and integrity of India, the security of the State, friendly relations with foreign States, public order, decency or morality, or in relation to contempt of court, defamation or incitement to an offence'. A large number of sections of penal code provide the government teeth. Section 124 states:

> Whoever, by words, either spoken or written, or by signs, or by visible representation, or otherwise, brings or attempts to bring into hatred or contempt, or excites or attempts to excite disaffection towards the Government established by law in India shall be punished with imprisonment for life.

---

[24] Timothy Garton Ash, *Free Speech: Ten Principles for a Connected World* (New Haven, CT: Yale University Press, March 2017).

[25] Dawn C. Nunziato, *Virtual Freedom: Net Neutrality and Free Speech in the Internet Age* (Stanford, CA: Stanford Law Books, August 2009).

Section 153A criminalizes 'promoting enmity between different groups on grounds of religion, race, place of birth, residence, language, etc., and doing acts prejudicial to maintenance of harmony by words, either spoken or written, or by signs or by visible representations or otherwise'. Section 292 criminalizes obscenity. Section 295A criminalizes 'deliberate and malicious acts intended to outrage religious feelings of any class' of citizens. Section 298 criminalizes 'uttering any word or making any sound' with 'the deliberate intention of wounding the religious feelings of any person'.

Governments over the years have used these sections and many more to quash free speech, often arbitrarily. They have banned books (most famous recent examples being Salman Rushdie's novel *The Satanic Verses* and Wendy Doniger's book *The Hindus: An Alternative History*), movies and documentaries (examples include Anurag Kashyap's *Black Friday* on Mumbai riots and *India's Daughter*, a 2015 BBC documentary on the 2012 gang rape of a Delhi college student) and charged people for sedition and defamation on frivolous charges which do not stand scrutiny in court but cause immense hardships to the accused before and after acquittal. A 19-year-old woman was arrested and charged with sedition for shouting 'Hindustan zindabad (long live India), Pakistan zindabad (long live Pakistan)'. She spent three months in jail before being acquitted. Fifteen Muslim men were charged with sedition in Madhya Pradesh for cheering for Pakistan during a televised cricket match against India. The charges were dropped in two days. A 16-year-old Muslim boy was detained for expressing anger at Atal Bihari Vajpayee on his death for his alleged involvement in Babri Masjid demolition. He was kept in jail for 39 days before being acquitted. Two persons were imprisoned in Karnataka for allegedly making a video abusing former Prime Minister H. D. Deve Gowda and his family. Of course, famously press freedom was censored completely during the 21-month Emergency in the 1970s. Unsurprisingly, India ranks 142 out of 180 countries in World Press Freedom Index. Regulation of extremist content is also hard for similar reasons.[26] Recognizing such content automatically is hard. Even if such content is detected, does one simply ban the content? Today, the content generator will simply migrate to a different, less regulated, likely less-known platform, if they are banned or discouraged on one platform. Fractured extremist communication will be even harder to track and counter. This will defeat the higher-level goal of preventing and detecting radicalization.

Government's Role

There is a role for the government—requiring online platforms to develop, publish and periodically update content standards and enforcement guidelines and periodically make compliance data public for transparency and increased compliance. In addition, if obviously illegal content is not removed from an online platform within a certain period of being reported, the government should make the platform liable. A transparent and rapid redressal mechanism to be used in the cases of disagreements would also be useful. Such a mechanism should place the burden of proof on the government to ensure that content removal is not a norm but an exception.

While a healthy, thriving democracy needs freedom of expression, online content presents a significant concern. A vigorous debate and a nuanced, careful execution will be

---

[26] Abraham H. Foxman and Christopher Wolf, *Viral Hate: Containing Its Spread on the Internet* (New York, NY: St Martin's Press, June 2013).

needed to address the genuine challenges from unregulated online content.

Cyberattacks and Hackers[27]

Technology also presents a large number of other concerns. The leak of Aadhaar data and the leak of personal information in the Cambridge Analytica scandal (Chapter 1) illustrate the privacy concerns which technology presents. Technology also presents new security concerns. Cyberattacks are now common in India, routinely leading to monetary losses, data leakage, ransomware, spyware and phishing attacks. The 2020 data from National Cyber Security Coordinator's office says that over 4 lakh pieces of malware are found every day in India. Over 375 cyberattacks are observed every day.

The cybersecurity attacks have become increasingly audacious. A group of hackers named John Wick hacked the personal website of Prime Minister Narendra Modi in 2020. After the takeover of Modi's verified Twitter handle, the group left several messages including seeking donations for Prime Minister's COVID-19 relief fund, using Bitcoins and signing off by saying 'This account is hacked by John Wick (hckindia@tutanota.com). In 2020 alone, several large Indian companies faced cyberattacks. Grocery delivery platform Bigbasket was attacked by a group called 'Shinyhunters', which led to compromise data of over 20 million users. The popular snack and sweets chain Haldiram faced an attack where the attackers demanded a $750,000 ransom. Government websites also have been routinely compromised. According to government data, 336 websites belonging to state governments and

---

27 Julia Angwin, *Dragnet Nation: A Quest for Privacy, Security, and Freedom in a World of Relentless Surveillance* (New York, NY: St Martin's Griffin, February 2015).

Central ministries and departments were hacked during 2017–2019.

The cyberattacks could be even more severe in future.[28] Nuclear installations, infrastructure (e.g., electricity grids, oil and water supply), industry—including manufacturing—and public and political institutions could all be vulnerable to attacks from state and non-state actors and present a large concern.

Stuxnet, a computer worm widely believed to have been developed jointly by the USA and the Israeli governments caused substantial damage to Iran's nuclear program.[29] Shamoon, a computer virus developed by a hacker group 'Cutting Sword of Justice', brought Saudi national oil company, Aramco, and Qatar's RasGas to their knees for a day in what was then described as 'the biggest hack in history'. A massive set of cyberattacks knocked down the Internet in Burma, including that of all media, little less than two weeks before its first general election in 20 years. A massive infiltration into Democratic National Committee (DNC) computer network and Hillary Clinton's campaign allegedly by Russian hackers which led to data breach might have affected the outcome of US presidential election in 2016. Here at home, Shadow Network, a China-based cyber-spying operation, allegedly stole classified information from the offices of Dalai Lama as well as the Indian government. These incidents foretell the magnitude of concern we may have in future.

---

[28] Fred Kaplan, *Dark Territory: The Secret History of Cyber War* (New York, NY: Simon & Schuster, March 2017).

[29] Kim Zetter, *Countdown to Zero Day: Stuxnet and the Launch of the World's First Digital Weapon* (New York, NY: Crown, September 2015).

A Perplexing Situation

Technology also raises different kinds of ethical concerns related to individual autonomy, privacy and trust. For example, the ethics of cloning, gene editing and neuro-hacking (e.g., neural stimulation) are unclear. The ethics of behavioural profiling to enable different applications need to be sorted out.[30] AI-guided weaponry poses hard ethical questions. The ethics of mass surveillance and monitoring are complex. So are the ethical concerns surrounding deep-fakes and addictive user experiences. Challenging ethical issues related to algorithmic bias and online content were already discussed above. It is unclear what kinds of ethics and morals we should program into intelligent machines (e.g., robots and autonomous vehicles).[31] While most of these issues apply anywhere, their implications may be even more dire in a country like India where diversity and economic hardships magnify many of these issues and their consequences.

In all, technology raises a large number of concerns in the Indian context. Careful, and, in many cases, uniquely Indian steps may be needed to navigate these concerns.

---

[30] Peter-Paul Verbeek, *Moralizing Technology: Understanding and Designing the Morality of Things* (Chicago, IL: University of Chicago Press, November 2011).

[31] Sheila Jasanoff, *The Ethics of Invention: Technology and the Human Future* (New York, NY: W. W. Norton, August 2016).

CHAPTER 7

THE MOTIVE TO SUCCEED

Why is it important for a country like India to be a technological nation? In a country still struggling with poverty, inequality, hunger, homelessness, geopolitical disputes, energy starvation, and poor education and healthcare, why should its effort, resources and priorities be directed towards adopting, developing and disseminating new technologies?

Technological Advancements Strengthen Defence

India's slow adoption of military technologies throughout history often led to incomprehensible and humiliating defeats at the hands of better technologically equipped armies and set the course of its history.

Indian armies had been battling Turkic militaries for centuries. These militaries relied on swift cavalry charges. Militaries of the Indian subcontinent, on the other hand, were large infantry-based and often lost easily to these cavalry-based Turkic militaries. This refusal to adapt the tactics culminated in the defeat of Prithviraj Chauhan against Turkic king Mu'izz al-Din at the Second Battle of Tarain in 1192, which ultimately led to further Muslim conquests in India and set the foundation of Muslim rule in India,[1]

In the 15th century, Indian armies such as the Delhi Sultanate and Vijayanagara Empire were slow to adopt the use of gunpowder despite being introduced in large quantities by the Portuguese and the Mughals and paid price in terms of humiliating defeats.

India armies' insistence on using elephants made it easy for the enemy to target the generals (who often mounted the elephants), leading to quick defeat at the hands of more mobile armies. When Nader Shah, the Persian king, defeated the Mughals led by Muhammad Shah at Karnal in 1739 in only three hours and then ran over Delhi, he remarked, 'What strange practice is this that the rulers of Hind have adopted? In the day of battle, they ride on an elephant, and make themselves into a target for everybody!'[2]

The story was similar at the Battle of Plassey in 1757. Indian armies, including Mughals and Nawabs, did not change with times and were slow to adopt European-style training and weapons. This put them at a distinct disadvantage against well-trained, well-equipped European armies. Unsurprisingly, the British East India Company army, largely composed of 1,100 British infantry and 2,100 trained Hindu peasants and led by Robert Clive, defeated a 50,000 Mughal cavalry in less than 12 hours and led the foundation of Company rule over India for next 100 years.[3]

---

[1] Cynthis Talbot, *The Last Hindu Emperor: Prithviraj Chauhan and the Indian Past, 1200–2000* (Cambridge: Cambridge University Press, June 2017).

[2] Uday S. Kulkarni, *Solstice at Panipat, 14 January 1761: An Authentic Account of the Campaign of Panipat* (Pune: Mula Mutha Publishers, April 2012).

[3] Sudeep Chakravarti, *Plassey: The Battle That Changed the Course of Indian History* (New Delhi: Rupa Publications, January 2020).

Geopolitical Conflicts Are Now Technology-Based

Technological capabilities continue to impact the dynamics in India's geopolitical conflicts—this time with its neighbours.

In June 2020, several Indian and Chinese soldiers beat each other to death with clubs and rocks in Galwan Valley near the Indo-China border which began a stand-off between the two armies at the border which continues till the time of writing. In October 2020, there was a massive power outage in Mumbai which shut down trains, the stock market and the normal life. At first blush, these seem like unconnected events. However, a *The New York Times* report from February 2021 suggested that the two events may have been interlinked.[4] The outage may have been caused by a Chinese malware, inserted as a part of a concerted campaign by Chinese hackers against Indian critical infrastructure, which could be flowing in India's electricity grids, power plants and control stations for some time. The outage was timed, the report claimed, to signal to India that a vigorous pursuit of border claims by India may lead to lights in India turning out. The linkage was claimed based on a research by Recorded Future, a Massachusetts-based company which keeps track of Internet activity by state actors who found that the signatures of the malware in India's power infrastructure had resemblances to the signatures of the malware purportedly developed by Chinese state-sponsored hacker groups.

Irrespective of whether the report is true, we know that such a possibility exists.

---

4 David E. Sanger and Emily Schmall, 'China Appears to Warn India: Push Too Hard and the Lights Could Go Out', *The New York Times*, 28 February 2021, https://www.nytimes.com/2021/02/28/us/politics/china-india-hacking-electricity.html

According to multiple reports over the years, Russia had successfully disabled part of Ukraine's Central Election Commission's infrastructure right before Ukraine's presidential election in May 2014.[5] This was right after Russian tanks had rolled into eastern Ukraine and annexed Crimea. In 2016, a Russian malware was used to paralyse parts of Ukraine's electricity grid. Over 230,000 Ukrainians were without power for 6 hours. The year after that, in 2017, there was another cyberattack attributed to Russia, which turned off lights in large parts of Keiv, the capital of Ukraine. In 2017, there was another attack where the code used for the attacks on the power grid was combined with another malware to cripple banks, airports and government agencies in Ukraine, including multinationals such as Maersk, FedEx and Merck. The attack took over 10 billion dollars to clean up!

Similarly, the USA has both accused Russia of placing malware into its power grids and unofficially admitted to placing such code into Russia's power grids.

Therefore, it is entirely possible for an adversarial nation to bring down India's power infrastructure for geopolitical signalling or as a direct cyberattack, if it has not happened already.

Sinister Offenses in Future

Future military conflicts are likely going to be much more sinister and technology-oriented than past conventional conflicts due to the technology-based capabilities being developed.

For example, future missiles may be hypersonic, travelling multiple times faster than the speed of sound

---

[5] Andy Greenberg, *Sandworm: A New Era of Cyberwar and the Hunt for the Kremlin's Most Dangerous Hackers* (New York, NY: Doubleday, November 2019).

and avoiding most detection and interception. Soldiers may wear exoskeleton to increase mobility and strength. Bullets may self-steer and enemy shooters may be easy to locate. Drones and robots may at least partly replace submarines, ships, fighter planes and perhaps even armies. India will need to acquire these technological capabilities over time as both a deterrence against a conventional military conflict and an insurance in case such a conflict does happen.

In addition, considering that both India and its geopolitical adversaries are nuclear-capable, and that it is likely, therefore, that future conflicts are largely going to be based in the cyberspace, India will need to develop strong technological capabilities, if not edge, in the computing space. A key example of the required technological capability in the computing space may revolve around quantum computing.

Today's sensitive communication and data are encrypted using algorithms which rely on secret keys.[6] Those who know the secret key can decrypt communication and data at small-to-moderate overheads. Those who do not know the secrete key cannot decrypt in any practical time since any attempt to decrypt without knowing the key reduces to a brute force search where an extremely large space of possible secret keys is searched; each different key is tried till one is found that unlocks the encrypted data. The actual overhead of decryption depends on the length of the key—the longer the key is, the greater is the decryption overhead. While the increase in overhead with key size is small for those who know the key, increasing the size of the key makes the already hard task of decryption for those who

---

[6] David Kahn, *The Codebreakers: The Comprehensive History of Secret Communication from Ancient Times to the Internet* (New York, NY: Scribner, December 1996).

do not know the key exponentially harder (since search space increases exponentially with key length). In essence, encryption works by keeping this overhead gap between the key-haves and the key-have-nots very large by tuning the key length. In fact, encryption using 128-bit keys is considered unbreakable today by someone who does not know the key but is manageable to those who have the key (i.e., they can decrypt in acceptable time).

Unlike traditional computers which rely on bits which take on a value of zero or one, quantum computers represent information using quantum bits (or qubits) which can stand for both zero and one simultaneously with some probability. Because of their unique information encoding, they can perform some computations much faster than traditional computers, including brute force search through a space of secret keys. This makes it feasible for quantum computers to break today's 128-bit encryption.

It is not surprising, therefore, that large and powerful countries seeking geopolitical edge are currently in a mad sprint to build the first quantum computer. The winner(s) may be able to unlock secrets of their adversaries, leading to a clear strategic edge. Even if encryption is scaled up later (by increasing key length, for example) to counter the threat posed by quantum computers, these computers' ability to decrypt past (today's) encrypted data or communication (which may already be getting intercepted or collected) will provide geopolitical advantages. This should be a strong motive for India to succeed in the quantum technology space.

There are similar geopolitical reasons for India to succeed at several other technologies—for example, technologies related to AI (as it may underpin most future defence technologies), electronic chips (as access to cutting-edge chips may be used as leverage in future geopolitical games; current tensions between the USA and China centred around semiconductors is a prime example and portends the future) and additive manufacturing (as control over supply chains may lead to strategic leverage). Considering that these technologies also yield several non-geopolitical benefits, investment into these technologies should be a no-brainer.

Technological Innovation Can Revolutionize Healthcare

Healthcare system in India is routinely rated as one of the worst in the world.[7] While there are world-class facilities accessible to some, a vast fraction does not have access to basic quality care. While the publicly funded healthcare system is large, its quality is so poor that even the poorest in the country prefer to pay out of pocket to access private healthcare infrastructure instead. In fact, over 60 per cent of India's healthcare cost is paid out of pocket. Poor quality of healthcare is not surprising, since India typically spends less than 1.5 per cent of its GDP on healthcare. This is low even for middle-income countries. Other issues with healthcare in India include poor awareness of health and hygiene; poor physical accessibility to healthcare facilities in rural areas; limited, poorly trained and poorly distributed workforce; poor regulation and accountability measures; limited insurance (though Ayushman Bharat scheme attempts to provide free treatment to bottom 50% of the population in private hospitals); and added pressure on healthcare due to factors such as malnutrition, deficient dietary habits, lack of cleanliness and road accidents.[8]

---

[7] K. Sujatha Rao, *Do We Care? India's Health System* (New Delhi: Oxford University Press, May 2017).

[8] Arun Gadre and Abhay Shukla, *Dissenting Diagnosis* (Gurugram: Penguin, April 2016).

AI could help with early and accurate diagnosis of different diseases (e.g., eye disease, heart disease and breast/skin cancer) as well as medical events (e.g., strokes and epileptic seizures).[9] As an example, Google's DeepMind created an AI algorithm for breast cancer analysis which outperformed human radiologists on the breast cancer identification task by an average of 11.5 per cent! Similarly, AI algorithms can be used to discover new drugs. The process of discovering and developing a new drug today is long and expensive. AI can accelerate development of new drug candidates and novel therapeutic solutions through intelligent large-scale simulations. For example, Atomwise used AI-based drug discovery algorithms in 2015 to create two drugs through modifications to existing medicines which appear to be effective at treating Ebola virus disease. AI algorithms can also be used to design personalized treatment plans. These can also be used to quickly mine medical records to improve productivity and efficiency. On the whole, AI can help compensate for shortage of skilled workforce in India and improve patient outcomes.

In a vast country with healthcare accessibility issues, technology can also be used to support virtual healthcare (also known as telemedicine or telehealth). Patients can use sensors and wearables to monitor any changes to health. The recorded data can be shared with the doctors. If needed, consultations can take place remotely over videoconferencing. This approach to healthcare where patients become the point of care can lead to massive cost savings and free up doctors to address more targeted needs. In addition, the enhanced ability of individuals to make informed health and wellness decisions based on easily

---

[9] Eric Topol, *The Patient Will See You Now: The Future of Medicine Is in Your Hands* (New York, NY: Basic Books, January 2015).

accessible personal health data can reduce pressure on the already-stressed healthcare system.[10]

A related technology is point-of-care diagnostics. Instead of the rural patients coming to town hospitals (so that heavy and expensive equipment in the hospitals can be used for diagnostics), several tests and diagnostics can be performed at the patient's home through use of small, portable gadgets which measure blood pressure, temperature, ECG, heart rate, respiratory rate, oxygen saturation and more. Wearable patches and bands can similarly measure body position, activity levels, gait, sleep status and more. Some of these devices may have a camera to support telemedicine. Several diagnostic kits (e.g., portable high-power microscopes, electronic nose and biosensors) can be used in conjunction with a smartphone to analyse swab samples, body fluids, skin lesions and more.

Given the diverse population, India also has a particular need for personalized medicine. A key technology to enable personalized medicine is 3D printing. 3D bioprinters can be used to print personalized organs (for organ transplants), skin (e.g., for burn victims), biotissues (e.g., for tissue repair), artificial limbs (for prosthetics), pills (at a fraction of original cost), polypills (which contain several layers of drugs corresponding to the patient's therapeutic plan) and blood vessels.

Another key technology could be nanomedicine. The ability to control individual atoms and molecules at nanometre scales allows the development of precise targeting and delivery systems, making it much easier to fight diseases such as cancer. It also allows more effective diagnosis, treatment and prevention of other diseases through

---

[10] Robert Wachter, *The Digital Doctor: Hope, Hype, and Harm at the Dawn of Medicine's Computer Age* (New York, NY: McGraw-Hill Education, April 2015).

personalization. Possibilities are endless. Wirelessly controlled microbots and nanobots can be designed to swim through bodily fluids to provide video and other diagnostic feedback and release drugs at precise times and locations (perhaps as response to smartphone commands or its sensor readings). Remote-controlled capsules can act as nano-surgeons. Nanotechnology-enabled patches can enable wound monitoring and stimulate would healing.

VR and augmented reality (AR) techniques also hold promise to revolutionize therapy and training in India. For example, VR and AR can be used to train surgeons in a simulated, realistic but low-risk environment. A *Harvard Business Review* study found that VR-trained surgeons had 2.3 times higher overall performance than traditionally trained surgeons and were also more accurate and faster at performing surgeries. VR and AR can similarly be used to train medical students and other healthcare workers. Another interesting application of VR is as an aid for pain management. For example, VR headsets displaying soothing landscapes have been shown to help women get through labour pain. When using VR as a distraction, patients suffering from post-surgical, neurological, cardiac and gastrointestinal pain have reported decline in pain levels. Patients undergoing surgery have also reported less pain and anxiety when using VR.

Robots hold exciting possibilities for the healthcare industry.[11] Robots can be used to perform remote, delicate and complex surgical procedures. For example, surgeons have already started using surgical devices controllable with a mechanical arm and with a high-definition camera to improve precision and minimize

---

[11] Eric Topol, *Deep Medicine: How Artificial Intelligence Can Make Healthcare Human Again* (New York, NY: Basic Books, March 2019).

scarring and complications such as infections. Robots can also be used as companions to treat mental health disorders, help children with chronic health issues (e.g., through constant health monitoring) and alleviate loneliness. These can be used for safe disinfection without bringing humans in harm's way. Exoskeletons can allow the paralysed and the injured to achieve mobility and help nurses to lift elderly patients.

Low-cost genetic testing can also revolutionize healthcare in India. A genetic test can provide knowledge about family history, drug sensitivity and monogenic or multifactorial medical conditions. It can also help create personalized diets through identification of deficiencies, intolerances, allergies and risks.

Finally, clinical trials are ripe for technological disruption. Today, they take too long, are expensive and often do not fully explore all the variables. In silico drug trials promise to upend the current system by using individualized computer simulations instead of human-based trials. The ability to test a drug on billions of virtual patients within a minute will dramatically accelerate development and regulatory evaluation of medical products, devices and interventions.

Improving Transport and Connectivity

India's transport infrastructure is notoriously poor.[12] Consider roads. While the road density (i.e., length of roads per square kilometre) in India is similar to that of the USA and much better than China or Brazil, most roads are congested due to poor lane capacity (e.g., a majority of national highways are two lanes or less), and their surface

---

[12] Nikhil Bharadwaj Namburi, 'Transportation in India', Medium, 25 March 2019, https://medium.com/@namburinb/examining-the-role-of-transportation-in-the-development-of-india-89968c69b0e9

quality is poor. One-third of Indian villages do not have access to all-weather roads and are often cut off during the monsoon season. Accessibility is particularly bad in northern and northeastern India. Urban areas are severely congested, especially during rush hours, as vehicle ownership has soared. Accident and fatality rates are one of the highest in the world. India's railway network is the largest in the world. However, most high-density rail corridors face severe capacity constraints. Freight transportation costs are one of the highest in the world, as the freight tariffs are kept high to subsidize passenger movement. Trains routinely run late. Indian ports are similarly congested and inefficient. Inland water transportation is minimal in spite of 14,000 km of navigable canals and rivers. Airport infrastructure is under stress due to dramatic growth in air traffic over last few years. India's rank on the World Bank's Logistics Performance Index was 44th in 2018. It was 35th in 2016.

India's investment into transport infrastructure has hovered around 1 per cent. China invests close to 7 per cent into transport infrastructure. Perhaps the most important way to improve India's transport infrastructure is to increase investment by multiple factors. A big fraction of that additional investment should go into technology-based innovations since new forward-thinking technology can help transportation in multiple ways.

Connected vehicle technology, where vehicles can talk to other vehicles, pedestrians and infrastructure can improve safety (e.g., by alerting drivers to dangerous situations) and speed (e.g., by sharing information about speed, heading and direction with other vehicles).[13] Communication points

[13] Venkat Sumantran, Charles Fine, and David Gonsalvez, *Faster, Smarter, Greener: The Future of the Car and Urban Mobility* (Cambridge, MA: MIT Press, September 2017).

at intersections and hazardous road areas can reduce crashes by enabling automatic speed management and signal timing. Vehicles with autonomy features such as automatic parking, lane detection and adjustment of cruise control can improve the speed.[14] Fully autonomous vehicles, while not yet near, can improve safety and productivity dramatically and reduce the total cost of vehicle ownership by running vehicles close to their designed fuel economy. Sensor-based data collection and analysis can help understand, predict and optimize traffic flows. In-vehicle sensors can communicate with GPS services to plan the best route, alert drivers to dangerous situations and override controls for accident avoidance if needed, and monitor driver fatigue or physiological state (e.g., whether the driver is intoxicated) to determine the next set of actions for safety. Electric vehicles can reduce the environmental impact of transportation.

Technological innovation may also enable lightweight vehicle materials. Studies show that a 10 per cent reduction in weight of a vehicle can improve its fuel economy by over 6 per cent. A US federal government study estimated that the country would consume 5 billion fewer gallons of gas each year of a quarter of the cars used lighter-weight materials. India with its rich history of metallurgy may be a contributor to a move away from current cast iron and steel-based vehicles. Carbon fibre and magnesium–aluminium-based alloys appear promising.

High-speed rail networks based on the Japanese Shinkansen bullet train, for example, can significantly improve connectivity. Truly disruptive technologies such as hyperloop which uses a series of linear induction motors

---

[14] Atossa Araxia Abrahamian, Darren Andersen, Laura Bliss, Alison Griswold, Nick Van Mead, and Christopher Schaberg, *The Future of Transportation: SOM Thinkers Series* (New York, NY: Metropolis Books, November 2019).

and compressors to propel vehicles through a pneumatic tube at speeds exceeding 350 miles per hour can change the face of long-distance travel.

Fixing Housing Problems

Housing in India is a decidedly mixed bag.[15] While a lot of houses have recently been built by the government for the poor, over 1.5 million people are homeless in India. Over 50 per cent of these homeless live in urban areas. Almost 80 million people in India do not meet their needs for adequate housing. UN defines adequate housing as 'adequate privacy, adequate space, adequate security, adequate lighting and ventilation, adequate basic infrastructure and adequate location with regard to work and basic facilities—all at a reasonable cost'. For example, tens of millions of Indians live in unstable or unsafe houses with mud or unburnt floors and walls and bamboo or dried grass roofs. In a country with months-long monsoon seasons, hot summers, fire lantern-based lightning, and open-fire stove-based cooking, such houses can be downright dangerous. Over 15 per cent of world's slum dwellers live in India. India's slum population now exceeds the total population of Great Britain. Increase in home prices outpaces wage growth, making housing increasingly unaffordable.

Technology can help the housing industry in several ways.[16]

Technology can make it considerably cheaper to supply new housing. For example, parts of a house can be built in

---

[15] Padmini Ram and Malcolm Harper, *The Affordable Housing Market in India: Institutional Constraints, Informal Sector and Privatisation* (New York, NY: Routledge, November 2020).

[16] Graham Cairns, Rachel Isaac-Menard, and Graham Potts, eds., *Housing the Future: Alternative Approaches for Tomorrow* (Oxfordshire: Green Frigate Books, April 2016).

a factory in bulk using 3D printing and other modular housing construction technologies. These parts can then be shipped to the housing site for assembly. This will reduce the cost and time of construction by decreasing the amount of physical labour used, significantly controlling the construction environment and guaranteeing productivity regardless of the weather. In some cases, 3D printing can build an entire home in under a day. A careful design of the modules also reduces the cost to install plumbing and electric systems. It can also allow extensibility and customization in future where a room or a storey can be added or removed on demand. 3D printing also cuts down on waste, since only necessary materials are used while printing.

Drones can be useful in guiding heavy machinery during construction. They can also be used to survey construction sites (e.g., to assess progress) and inspect hard-to-reach areas for damages and needed repairs.

AR can be used by architects and engineers for better design (e.g., to reduce cost and improve energy efficiency). VR can be used by workers to better understand the construction goals and update the construction plan(s). Both AR and VR can be used by customers to improve decision-making related to buying, renting or modifying homes.

Smart devices (e.g., sensors and smart thermostats) can be used to improve home security, efficiency, comfort and energy costs.

Ride-hailing services and self-driving cars can reduce the amount of land used for highways, driveways and garages. This reduces the cost of land for home construction. Similarly, online platforms which encourage shared living help bring down the cost and increase the supply of housing. Platforms which allow easier access to capital and home loans enable greater access to home ownership. AI and blockchain technology can be used to improve risk prediction through more accurate and data-driven modelling. This in turn may allow a more equitable access to home credit. Blockchain technology can also be used to reduce the cost of loan administration by automating the process of originating a loan, collecting payments, searching titles and servicing defaults. This, in turn, reduces the cost of ownership. Platforms which use public data to grade buildings (e.g., based on complaints registered by tenants) can improve the bargaining power of prospective tenants. This could lower rental costs.

Farming Solutions

Agriculture in India generates around one-sixth of the national income and directly employs nearly half of the Indian workforce.[17] In addition to generating food for human and animal population, it serves demand for fuel, fibre and timber. Till the early 1960s, India was barely able to feed its population. Famines and similar stresses were common. Droughts in 1965 and 1966 had led to food production decrease by 20 per cent, and India had to rely on sparse US food aid to prevent mass starvation. The 'ship-to-mouth' existence started getting ameliorated with the advent of the Green Revolution. New rice and wheat strains were invented under the leadership of M. S. Swaminathan, and large-scale agricultural extension services were launched which doubled the wheat production within three years. India's grain output is now six times the output in 1950–1951, thanks to the use of high-yielding variety (HYV) seeds, use of fertilizers and better irrigation facilities.

However, for a country with fast increasing population which needs to be fed (and has much higher expectation

---

[17] Kartik Prasad Jena, *Agriculture in India: Institutional Structure and Reforms* (New Delhi: New Century Publications, January 2014).

than before about the quality of food) and industry whose need for agriculture-based products keeps expanding, the current agricultural productivity would not suffice (India's rice yield is one-third of China and half of Vietnam and Indonesia). A quantum increase in agricultural productivity is needed. Addressing agricultural productivity can also address poverty in India directly.[18] An estimate suggests that 65 per cent of poor working adults globally are employed in the agricultural sector. So improving agricultural productivity can directly improve lives of the poor. Another interesting study concludes that investing into agricultural sectors is up to four times effective at alleviating poverty than investing in other economic sectors. Again, this positions agriculture as a key target for poverty alleviation.

Novel technology-based solutions promise to meet the needs of the agricultural sector.[19]

A promising farming technique is indoor vertical farming, where the produce is grown on shelves mounted vertically in a closed and controlled environment (e.g., hydroponic or aeroponic growth with artificial lights).[20] This reduces the land and labour requirement for farming (since vertical stacking uses the z-dimension; also robots can be employed easily to handle harvesting, planting and logistics), increases yield (since variables such as light, water and humidity can be precisely measured and controlled), reduces environmental impact of farming (since distance travelled in the supply chain is cut down; also indoor vertical farms may need

[18] Yoginder K. Alagh, *The Future of Indian Agriculture* (New Delhi: National Book Trust, 2012).

[19] David Julian McClements, *Future Foods: How Modern Science Is Transforming the Way We Eat* (New York, NY: Springer, May 2019).

[20] Amanda Little, *The Fate of Food: What We'll Eat in a Bigger, Hotter, Smarter World* (London: Harmony, January 2021).

up to 70 per cent less water than traditional farming methods) and allows sustainable urban growth (since this allows farming to be done in limited-space urban environments). Farm automation can make farming more efficient by automating the crop or livestock production cycle using agricultural robots, especially autonomous tractors, robotic harvesters, drones and automatic watering, and seeding robots.

Livestock industry and management have been slow to change. However, genetics and new nutritional and digital technologies have the potential to revolutionize the industry. Sensors can be fitted to dairy herds for health and activity monitoring and generate data-driven insights. Genetic analysis of animals can help livestock producers understand health risks, predict future profitability for a given livestock, and improve decision-making regarding animal selection and breeding to optimize profitability and yield. For example, animal geneticists can identify gene elements which enhance health, growth and ability to utilize nutrients. The knowledge can then be used to increase production, for example, through selective embryo transfer or through artificial insemination of females with semen from males with the desired genetic characteristics. Robots can be employed for both care of livestock (e.g., automated feeders) and their management (e.g., robotic milking machines) to reduce labour costs. Wi-Fi, cameras and sensors can be used for remote or automatic climate control and monitoring of animals (e.g., monitoring of an animal in labour).

Plant genetics have been used to enhance crop yields for some time. New plant breeding methods such as marker-assisted breeding are being developed which accelerate the process of achieving target characteristics. Genetic engineering holds promise to increase a plant's resistance to diseases and insects and tolerance to herbicides and other chemicals. Some genetically modified variants may have much higher yield and much lower need for water, nutrients or pesticides. Some transgenic crops can also have improved flavour or nutritional quality. In India, Bt cotton is the only genetically modified crop allowed for commercial cultivation.

Greenhouses produce vegetables worth nearly US$350 billion every year. Automated control systems and smart lighting technologies can improve the yields further.

Precision farming technologies can allow farmers to control different variables such as microclimates, soil conditions, moisture levels and pest stress. This can improve yields, increase efficiency and manage costs. GPS tracking systems and satellite-generated imagery can be used to monitor weather patterns, soil levels and yield. Drones can locate damaged or diseased crops and provide focused attention.

Blockchain technology can enable fast, low-cost and reliable food traceability. When a food-borne infection, contamination or unexpected spoilage comes to light, it is important to be able to trace the source, both for accountability and to prevent or minimize such issues in the future. Blockchains use a distributed tamper-resistant ledger to record how food and its constituents flow from farm to table, sometimes in real time, along with the record of ownership and accountability at every stage of the journey. As a result, it is easy to analyse quickly and automatically, both post-facto and in transit, the performance and quality of the different components of the food supply chain for safety, fraud and inefficiency. The confidence in traceability of products and services also creates a market for premium food products. Blockchains can also be used to balance market pricing of agricultural products. Traditional pricing relies on the judgement of the involved parties, largely since the supply chain and associated costs are opaque. Blockchain allows transparency into the food supply chain by recording verified transactions and costs incurred along the chain as well as by providing a more holistic picture of supply and demand. This enables better pricing. For the same reason, blockchain can disrupt the traditional commodity training and hedging markets.

AI, in conjunction with sensing technologies, can revolutionize agriculture.[21] Sensors, drones and satellites can be used to monitor plant health, temperature, humidity, soil condition, etc., and generate data which can be analysed by the farmers and policymakers to improve decision-making.

Technology can also directly help the food industry. For example, robots can be used to replace the more dangerous jobs such as butchery. They can also be used in settings where requirements on volume and price are stringent. 3D printing of food can help food sustainability and innovation. Technologies which enable edible, decomposable, recyclable and feature-rich packaging can help sustainability. Online platforms which connect food-surplus businesses with food-needy organizations (e.g., after-school programmes, local shelters and non-profits) can reduce food waste.

Resolving Energy Problems and Revolutionizing Electricity

Electricity is a precious resource in India.[22] There are several points of concern. First, coal continues to be the dominant source of electricity and will likely dominate electricity production in foreseeable future. While the production of coal

---

[21] Robert D. Saik, *Food 5.0: How We Feed the Future* (Reno, NV: Lioncrest, August 2019).

[22] Sudeshna Ghosh Banerjee, Douglas Barnes, Bipul Singh, Kristy Mayer, and Hussain Samad, *Power for All: Electricity Access Challenge in India* (Washington, DC: World Bank Publications, November 2014).

has increased steadily, India continues to be an importer of coal due to a large and increasing demand. India's almost 250 million tons of coal import per year is second only to China. Second, India is one of the largest importers of oil and petroleum, most of it coming from the Middle East. Again, these imports have been increasing as the middle class continues to expand and India continues to urbanize. Third, access to natural gas has been challenging due to falling local production and geopolitical factors (as various plans for pipelines with Afghanistan, Iran, Myanmar, Pakistan and Turkmenistan have failed to materialize due to border disputes and other issues). With increasing reliance on natural gas for power, the scarcity of natural gas has become a major issue. Fourth, electricity demand is expected to far outpace supply, especially in the industrial sector. This threatens profits, productivity and overall economic growth. Fifth, there is considerable inequality in access to electricity. A large number of people still use kerosene for lighting in spite of mass electrification drives. Finally, there is considerable energy wastage and theft due to poor electricity infrastructure.

In addition to the above concerns, an overarching concern is the impact on environment since four-fifths of India's electricity is generated using non-renewable sources.[23]

Many of the above problems can be addressed using technology-based solutions.[24]

Novel energy storage solutions can help address local demands, improve efficiency reduce carbon footprint and lower costs. For example, fuel cells are promising. Unlike batteries which run down and need to be recharged, fuel

---

[23] Shree Raman Dubey, *Energy Crisis in India: A Commentary on India's Electricity Sector* (Bloomington, IN: Partridge India, October 2015).

[24] Bill Gates, *How to Avoid a Climate Disaster: The Solutions We Have and the Breakthroughs We Need* (New York, NY: Knopf, February 2021).

cells can continue producing electricity as long as sources of fuel and oxygen to 'burn' the fuel are available. They can be used as a replacement of turbines or as stationary power sources. Fuel cells are often much more efficient than conventional sources of energy and produce much smaller amounts of emission. Lithium–air batteries and other solid state battery technologies can provide multiple times higher energy density than traditional Li-ion batteries and can dramatically increase the range of electric vehicles. Hydrogen can be stored and transmitted over a power grid as an energy carrier and can be used as a source in a fuel cell. Thermal energy storage (TES) stocks heat from combined heat and power plants or active solar collectors into an insulated storage medium so that the stored energy can be used at a later time for heating and cooling applications and power generation. Surplus power can be used to pump water into abandoned oil and natural gas wells. The water can then be released and used to drive a turbine generator above ground during periods of high demand.

A smarter electricity grid can also help alleviate energy shortage. For example, real-time electric metering tools and sensors can be used by both utility companies and users to remotely turn off non-essential devices at peak usage for load balancing. AI-based prediction models can predict energy usage and avoid overproduction. Electricity could be generated using a decentralized architecture with a large number of small energy sources instead of using centralized facilities. This will minimize transmission losses and improve adaptation to fluctuating demand while sacrificing economies of scale. An Internet-like global energy and power infrastructure with interoperating standards, interfaces and protocols can significantly lower the cost of accessing heat, energy, natural gas and possibly hydrogen while allowing better availability.

Technology has the potential to revolutionize electricity generation itself.[25] Tidal turbines which convert tidal energy into electricity have significant potential. Stirling engines which convert heat energy into compression and expansion strokes which, in turn, can be used to generate electricity can be 3D printed at micrometre scale and cover large heat-generating surfaces to produce power. Small robots can be used to reorient solar panels as weather changes to maximize efficiency. This will be less expensive than attaching each panel to a motorized tracking assembly. Emerging biofuels can produce energy at low greenhouse gas emissions. Microalgae-based biodiesel and cellulosic ethanol are particularly promising. Similarly, organisms (e.g., algae) can be genetically engineered to produce biofuels such as hydrogen and furans. Carbon-based waste can be turned into oil through thermal depolymerization where the waste is put through extreme heat and pressure. Photovoltaic transparent glass can allow powering a building using electricity generated by its windows, roof and facades. Solar power can be collected in space (at a much higher rate than earth since transmission is unaffected by the atmosphere's filtering effects) and beamed back to earth as microwaves. Use of pumped pressurized liquid to widen fissures and improve permeability can enable greater exploitation of geothermal energy. Micro-nuclear reactors which are only a few tens of metres in length and which can be sealed and transported to point of use can allow ubiquitous and efficient use of nuclear power. Nuclear fusion continues to present a scintillating promise to address energy needs without pollution.

---

[25] J. C. MacKay, *Sustainable Energy: Without the Hot Air* (Cambridge: UIT Cambridge, January 2009).

The above technologies not only make energy access cheaper and easier, but they also protect the environment by lowering greenhouse gas emissions.[26] Technology broadly has an important role to play in saving the environment and slowing down climate change. Environmental issues have been front and centre in India for some time. Two-thirds of world's most polluted cities are in India. Half of that pollution is caused by industrial emissions. Vehicle exhausts are the second biggest contributor. More than 1.67 million people (18% of all deaths) and 116,000 infants died in India due to pollution just in 2019 according to an estimate. Air pollution is the fourth largest cause of death in India among all health risks. A Lancet report estimated the economic cost of the 2019 fatalities to be 36.8 billion dollars, or 1.36 per cent of India's GDP. A government report estimated that average temperature in India had increased by 0.7°C during the 1901–2018 period due to greenhouse gas emissions. The temperature is expected to rise by 4.4°C by 2100. The report also predicted that summer heat waves will be three to four times as frequent and twice as long by then. India has also seen a lot of deforestation due to urbanization, farming, mining, logging and dam building, further adding to its environmental woes.

Emerging Technologies Address Environmental Problems Directly

It is well known that excess carbon dioxide in the air causes greenhouse effect. Technologies which capture and sequester carbon dioxide can help reduce global warming. One class of carbon capture and storage technologies

---

[26] Oliver Morton, *The Planet Remade: How Geoengineering Could Change the World* (London: Granta Books, July 2016).

separates carbon dioxide from other gases produced during industrial processes and in electricity generation. The captured carbon is then transported using a pipeline and stored in abandoned oil wells, saline reservoirs or geological formations far below the ground. This captured carbon can be used, if needed, to make synthetic fuels or plastics such as polyurethane. Another class of technologies takes carbon dioxide collected from industrial emitters and injects it into the concrete production process. This reduces atmospheric carbon emissions, strengthens concrete and permanently stores the gas as mineral.

Nitrous oxide is 300 times more potent than carbon dioxide as a greenhouse gas. Thankfully, some soil-based bacteria can convert nitrogen in air into nutrients. These bacteria also happen to easily colonize roots of crops such as wheat and corn. Technologies which synthesize such bacteria can help reduce the greenhouse impact of nitrous oxide while generating much-needed fertilizer for crops. Similarly, bioremediation technologies use plants and microbes for decontamination. For example, microbes can help clean up nitrates in contaminated water, while plants can be used to absorb arsenic from contaminated soil. Genetical engineering of plants to increase their absorption of contaminants as well as increase the likelihood of transmission of these contaminants all the way to the leaves (for ease of harvesting) can further increase the impact of phytoremediation (bioremediation using plants).

Technologies which can extract water from air (e.g., using a desiccant) and store it (e.g., by using a solar panel-mounted fan to evaporate the absorbed water and collect it) can reduce the carbon footprint of treating and transporting water to dry regions. Desalination technologies which remove salt and minerals out of seawater to make it potable can also help. Example includes evaporating water using inexpensive fuels and then running it through membranes with microscopic pores for filtration.

Smart home devices and sensors can use AI technologies to turn off a device not in use, control devices to optimize energy efficiency and resource usage, provide energy and resource usage analysis, identify energy and resource bottlenecks, and send notifications. Green buildings and homes with LED lights, energy-efficient appliances, smart heating, cooling, lighting, and in-house solar power generation can reduce environmental impact. Digitization eliminates need for paper and packaging. Innovations which reduce food waste (e.g., biofuel digesters which convert food waste to create energy) reduce the carbon footprint of food production. Electric vehicles and sharing economy (e.g., Airbnb, Uber and Netflix) can have significant positive environmental impact.

Graphene-based technologies can be used to build more efficient solar cells and water filtration systems. Graphene also promises superconductors which may be used to transmit electricity at minimal losses. Biodegradable plant-based plastics may replace today's packaging. Technologies such as pyrolysis which reconvert plastic waste back into liquid feedstock using heat and the absence of oxygen can extend the life of today's plastic while reducing environmental impact.

Eating meats has an immense impact on environment. A UN report estimates that livestock is responsible for over one-sixth of the anthropogenic greenhouse gas emissions. Run-off from industrial livestock operations contaminates local waterways, while livestock also has large freshwater needs. Fake meat technologies can help address these concerns.

Networked sensors for monitoring air, water, pollutants, acidification, deforestation, predators, poachers and natural distress can help manage the environment and wild-life. Drones, Wi-Fi and cameras can be used to track forests for deforestation and wildfires and patrol and enforce poacher exclusion zones. Smart collars can be used to track endangered wildlife, while SIM-based animal wearables can minimize conflicts with humans. AI can be used for reforestation where forests are planted to maximize carbon sequestration.

Uplifting Economy

Ultimately, for a developing country with a large and growing young population, the strongest motive to adopt and develop technology is that technology can help drive the economy and lift people out of poverty. As Peter Diamandis and Steven Kotler wrote in *Abundance: The Future Is Better than You Think*,[27] the cost of technology keeps falling with time, improving productivity and making the fruits of innovation available to an ever-increasing number of people. This leads to an increasing number of people climbing out of poverty. A World Bank report from a few years back had indeed concluded that technological progress is the most important driver of income and growth in developing countries. In fact, the benefits of technology (in terms of income growth, improvement in living standards, etc.) tend to be higher in emerging economies than rich nations.

E-commerce serves as a good example. E-commerce platforms allow online trading opportunities for micro, small and medium-sized businesses, including businesses which were typically marginalized due to their development capabilities, access to information or geographical location. By

---

[27] Peter H. Diamandis and Steven Kotler, *Abundance: The Future Is Better than You Think* (New York, NY: Free Press, February 2012).

connecting producers in rural areas, including those from the most poverty-stricken regions to large markets, their income is increased. Second, e-commerce encourages development of industrial chains and division of labour to maximize efficiency. This creates a diverse set of job opportunities—for example, processing, logistics, packaging, customer service—for the poor along each chain, including jobs for disadvantaged groups such as the elderly and women with children. Third, involvement with e-commerce transforms mindsets and encourages learning (e.g., further training and online classes), ultimately making the involved poor more entrepreneurial.

Similarly, digital technology can promote inclusive finance which, in turn, can reduce poverty. The poor and the micro and small businesses have always struggled to get access to easy and low-cost financing, often threatening their survival and development. The UN introduced in 2005 the concept of 'financial inclusion' where the goal is to provide appropriate and affordable financial services to the poor and the most disadvantaged groups. However, loans continued to be hard to come by due to high cost and credit gap. Digital technology can promote inclusive finance in three ways. First, traditional banks can use digital technologies to improve the convenience and availability of financial services for the disadvantaged groups. India has experienced this with the PMJDY, where the poor are encouraged to open online accounts, perform online payments, conduct cashless transactions during bulk sale of agricultural produce such as grains, and accept medical insurance, pension and agricultural subsidies online. Second, Internet companies can use digital technology to invent new credit evaluation mechanisms as well as sustainable mechanisms for digital credit, mobile payment and insurance for the poor in spite of insufficient mortgage. For example, electronic transactions data from e-commerce platforms can be analysed to deliver appropriate financial services without requiring a physical collateral. Similarly, quantitative model and historical data of agricultural production can be used to grant credit to farmers without collaterals. Third, traditional banks can collaborate with these Internet companies to further expand the coverage of their financial services. For example, banks can use electronic receipts and online ordering data to provide financing.

Also, big data technologies can be used for comprehensive and accurate identification of poor households. This information can be used for targeted and fair application of poverty alleviation programmes. Analysis of the underlying causes (e.g., healthcare vs education expenses, impact of climate, landform, personal capabilities, family population, economic and financial conditions) can enable high-quality delivery of these programmes at multiple levels (household vs village vs district). Big data can also be used to track and improve progress and efficiency of these programmes and promote evidence-based decision-making. Data sharing on outcomes, best practices, etc., can improve utilization of funds, help select the best poverty alleviation project in each situation and guide setting up of poverty standards.

Of course, there is no silver bullet to alleviating poverty. Health, farming, financial, inclusion, education, disaster and response, and social harmony are all important. As discussed in this book, technology should be able to address each of those, at least partly, one way or the other.

CHAPTER 8

THE CAVALIER ATTITUDE

For a country which believes that the use of technology can solve many of its deep-rooted problems, we have been surprisingly cavalier in nurturing technology throughout our history. The history of technology in modern India has been characterized by internal conflicts, turf wars, contradictions, tokenism, inconsistency, lack of immediacy, oversight, accountability, and occasionally misleading and often wrong road mapping and planning.

A Sputtering Start[1]

Signs of incoherence started appearing in the pre-Independence era. The British made scientific research exclusively the domain of the state-owned, specialized research institutions. Public universities were only expected to focus on generating trained workforce. The stated

---

[1] Arun Mohan Sukumar, *Midnight's Machines: A Political History of Technology in India* (Gurugram: Viking, December 2019).

rationale was that universities were too poorly funded to support and drive a fundamental but specialist venture such as modern science and technology. This separation of concerns made it difficult to keep university education relevant to practise and made it difficult for the research institutions to find well-trained researchers.

The cleavage between research institutions and universities notwithstanding, there was considerable optimism about the role of science and technology in the making of modern India. As India inched closer to Independence, this optimism only increased. The Congress party 1945 resolution had declared:

> Science, in its instrumental field of activity, has played an ever-increasing part in influencing and molding human life and will do so in even greater measure in the future. Industrial, agricultural and cultural advance, as well as national defense, depends upon it. Scientific research is, therefore, a basic and essential activity of the State and should be organized and encouraged on the widest scale.[2]

When India became independent, it was widely assumed that this optimism would lead to an ambitious and coherent plan for promoting science and technology. However, right at the outset, there was a conflict between two different visions to support science.[3] The first vision intended to continue and expand the pre-colonial structure that placed research within the confines of the government-run institutions, while universities focused solely on creating scientific manpower. The proponents of this vision argued that the separation of roles would help both research

---

[2] Manifesto of The Congress Party. 1945.

[3] B. V. Subbarayappa, *Science in India: A Historical Perspective* (New Delhi: Rupa, November 2014).

institutions and universities thrive in their specialized roles. This vision would entail almost all government funding for research in science and technology to go to these institutions, instead of the universities. The second vision—the Vannevar Bush model which was being created and refined in the USA—advocated universities as centres of scientific research with administration by scientists and only minimal involvement of government officials. Universities would receive much of the governmental funding for research. The proponents of this vision believed that an organic linkage between education and research will benefit both. They also worried that research institutions would cause the universities to wither away. Meghnad Saha, a noted physicist, arguing for this vision had said, 'National laboratories will drain the universities and compete for scarce resources. We must seriously consider the impact of independent stand alone publicly funded research laboratories on our universities.'

After much debate, and reportedly due to the close proximity of several scientists who personally wanted to start government-funded laboratories to Nehru, the Indian prime minister, the second vision won out, much to the consternation of the big university-based scientific community. The CSIR, which was established in 1942 to perform science planning, was now tasked with the creation and management of a large chain of government-funded laboratories.[4]

The CSIR reported directly to the prime minister which made oversight of its functioning difficult. Funding for a particular field depended on the proximity of the top scientists in the field to the political and administrative

---

[4] N. R. Rajagopal, *The CSIR Saga: A Concise History of Its Evolution* (Dehradun: Council of Scientific and Industrial Research, Publications and Information Directorate, 1991).

establishment instead of being based on a coherent strategy. The ones with Nehru's ears were particularly rewarded. This led to widespread resentment among academe-based researchers who felt that certain research areas were unduly preferred at the expense of other areas. Frustrated, J. B. S. Haldane, a noted British-Indian scientist, had remarked, 'The Council of Scientific and industrial research must be renamed as the Council of Suppression of Independent Research.' Distrust of the CSIR institutions among university researchers extended even to the quality of research these institutions were performing. Nobel Prize winner in physics in 1930, Sir C. V. Raman, opined, 'Shah Jahan built the Taj Mahal to bury one of his favorite women. The National laboratories were built to bury scientific instruments.'

To make matters worse, CSIR's new role in research administration did not include planning. Planning was now performed by the Planning Commission. There was not much coordination or dialogue between the institutions. This led to further weakening of oversight of CSIR's functioning, which showed in the lack of a coherent science and technology strategy.

John Desmond Bernal, a British physicist and Marxist, was invited in 1954 to Beijing by the Chinese Academy of Sciences to participate in the 5th anniversary of the founding of the People's Republic of China and also conduct an extensive review of China's scientific institutions. In Beijing he met Jawaharlal Nehru, Indian prime minister, who had also been invited to Beijing for the festivities. Interestingly, Bernal knew Nehru from his Cambridge days. Nehru, upon meeting Bernal, invited him to visit India to review India's scientific progress. Bernal agreed and visited India. At the end of his India visit, Bernal was asked to compare the status of science in India and China. Bernal responded,

'Science progress in India, though good, was not fast enough as compared to China.' When asked for a reason, he remarked, 'In China the government was in control while it was not clear who was in control in India.'

Nebulous Policymaking

India's public science and technology policy was also characterized by lack of consistency and a series of missteps, flip-flops and delays. Even the beginning, in the first decade after India became a Republic, was not auspicious.

In 1956, China released its science and technology plan.[5] The plan called for modernization of science, technology and education, with emphasis on practical and national defence-related technological developments. It also had a call for urgent implementation. A 1958 front-page editorial of the official newspaper of the Chinese Communist Party entitled 'March on a Technological Revolution' talked about how the Chinese revolution had entered 'a new historical epoch' marked by 'a technological revolution and cultural revolution' and called for the building of 'a great socialist country with modern industry, agriculture and science and culture'. It envisioned an industrialized China 'with chimneys of factories dotting towns and cities, big and small, all over the country'.

In contrast, the Indian Parliament passed a Scientific Policy Resolution in 1958. The resolution was, at best, a vague, philosophical statement on science's cultural and spiritual values and its industrial applications. It outlined the state's goals to be: 'pursuit of science as a tool to realize the objective of a welfare state; foster, promote and sustain the cultivation of science and scientific research; to

---

[5] Jahnavi Phalkey and Zuoyue Wang, 'Planning for Science and Technology in China and India', *BJHS Themes* 1 (May 2016): 1–31.

encourage individual initiative for the acquisition and for the discovery of new knowledge'. It also vaguely talked about the ability of science and technology to provide substitutes for the raw materials the country is deficient in as well as to allow corresponding skills to be exported in return for raw materials. These high-level goals roughly encapsulated Nehru's prior pronouncements about the value of science. He had said at the Indian Science Congress in 1938,

> I realized that science was not only a pleasant diversion and abstraction, but was of the very texture of life, without which our modern world would vanish away.... It was science alone that could solve these problems of hunger and poverty, of insanitation and illiteracy, of superstition and deadening custom and tradition, of vast resources running to waste, of a rich country inhabited by starving people.[6]

They also aimed to address Nehru's personal peeve about Indians' supposed lack of scientific temper. He said in his inaugural speech at the opening of the National Physical Laboratory in 1950,

> Large numbers of people talk glibly about science today and yet in their lives or actions do not exhibit a trace of science.... But science is something more. It is a way of training the mind to look at life and the whole social structure.... So I stress the need for the development of a scientific mind and temper which is more important than actual discovery as it is out of this temper and method that many more discoveries will come.[7]

---

[6] Jawarharlal Nehru. Message for the silver jubilee celebrations of the Indian Science Congress at Calcutta, 3-9 January 1938. The Hindustan Times, 8 January 1938.

[7] Jairam Ramesh, *Nehru's Scientific Temper Recalled*, Science and Culture. Vol.27. No.7. (2011) Retrieved from: http://www.scienceandculture-isna.org/July-aug-2011/01%20 Jairam%20Ramesh.pdf

The lack of specifics, ambition or immediacy of the resolution (simply mandating the adoption of a new scientific outlook by the entire population!) showed in the extremely slow process of carrying out the resolution. India's first science and technology plan was formulated in 1973—15 years after the resolution was carried out. Considering the lofty rhetoric from the topmost echelons of the government and the scientific community about the importance of science and technology in nation building as well as a rather vigorous pursuit of planning-related goals at the time, one would have expected a much quicker formulation of a detailed first science and technology plan. The long delay, among other things, demonstrated the limited priority India truly placed on science and technology in its early days.

A Reactive Attitude

The 1960s and 1970s did not see any consistency either and saw India's science and technology policies being largely dictated by internal and external events.

People often forget that India was wholly dependent on foreign food aid to feed its population in the 1960s. Even in good monsoon years, food aid was at least 10 per cent of the overall food production. It was widely known that India could not feed itself. In fact, in a highly controversial bestselling 1967 book *Famine 1975!*,[8] William and Paul Paddock argued that high-population countries such as India are incapable of being saved and should be left to starve since food aid givers would not be able to meet the needs of these countries.

---

8 William Paddock, *Famine, 1975! America's Decision: Who Will Survive?* (Boston, MA: Little, Brown and Company, January 1967).

In these circumstances, India was hit by two droughts in 1965 and 1966. The grain production declined by over one-fifth. This brought India to its knees—over 10 million tons of food aid (over 20% of the need!) was given by other nations just to feed the hungry. The biggest traditional food donor was the USA. However, the erstwhile US President Lyndon placed limitations on US aid to punish India for its criticism of war in Vietnam. The aid which was released came only after repeated begging by politicians and officials.

The humiliating experience led to a significant reorientation of India's research efforts. A significant fraction of the research budget was reallocated to the Indian Council of Agricultural Research (ICAR). Also, there was increased focus on technological self-reliance. 'Recent events have compelled us to explore the fullest possibilities of technological reliance', said Indira Gandhi, the then prime minister.

> It is now our endeavor to rationalize the structure of Indian science and to relate it more closely with the process of planning and development.... Growth cannot be sustained on borrowed or even adapted technology. True self-reliance can come only as we develop the ability to solve our technological problems.[9]

Gandhi's Congress party officially evoked technological reliance as a goal and in 1967 approved a resolution calling for setting up a Ministry of Science and Technology. The resolution also called for mandating 1 per cent of the gross national product to be devoted to R&D. It also called for increased participation of scientists in decision-making

---

[9] Indira Gandhi Abhinandan Samiti, *The Spirit of India*, vol. 1, Bombay: Asia Publishing House, 1975, pp. 205–206.

and for making R&D budgets mandatory for both public and private sectors.

At the same time, armed conflicts with China and Pakistan exposed India's poor preparedness and technological capabilities. This made the government question significant expenditures on science, especially in areas such as defence and atomic energy. Indira Gandhi declared, 'The nation had not secured sufficient returns from the quantitative expansion of scientific research.' In 1971, for the first time since Independence, the R&D expenditure in agriculture was higher than that in atomic energy. The Fifth Five-Year Plan allocations in 1972 saw a greater increase in expenditure for agriculture than on defence and atomic energy. US alignment with Pakistan during the 1965 war had also led to a fear that other powers could not be relied upon, 'We feel that a country as large as ours, with its rich and variegated technical talent, should work progressively towards self-reliance. Our past experience has been that aid can be stopped at crucial moments,' Gandhi had remarked.

Turf Wars and the Lack of Coordination

While these events steeled the government's resolve to create a concrete science and technology plan, the process of formulation of the plan was characterized by contradictions and turf wars. There were two camps which differed fundamentally in the purpose of the science and technology plan. One camp, led by Parmeshwar Narayan Haksar,[10] principal secretary to the prime minister (and

---

[10] Jairam Ramesh, *Intertwined Lives: P.N. Haksar & Indira Gandhi* (Noida: Simon and Schuster India, 2018).

later deputy chair, Planning Commission), believed that the government should identify a small number of sectors to focus on and aim at excellence in those sectors. The other camp, led by Ashok Parthasarathi,[11] special assistant for science in the prime minister's secretariat, believed that India should not pre-decide 'winners' and focus on science and technology comprehensively instead.

Similarly, there was significant tension between the National Committee on Science and Technology (NCST), which was tasked to identify science and technology projects that the government could focus on, and the Planning Commission, which would ultimately allocate resources for these projects in the Fifth Five-Year Plan. At one point, the commission officials refused to integrate NCST recommendations into the plan, accusing the NCST of plagiarizing the commission's own approach paper to the Five-Year Plan! Incredulous at the plagiarism accusation, when NCST pushed back and asked for an explanation, the Planning Commission officials asserted that NCST's paper was a 'large-scale reproduction' of another science plan document produced abroad and that if NCST wanted even a partial adoption of its plan, it must adapt its science planning philosophy to local socio-economic conditions first.

Beyond internecine conflicts, there was also lack of clarity about the roles of the different units participating in the formulation of the science and technology plan. Different ministries had temporary planning units set up to identify research priorities in their ministry. However, their status in relation to the NCST was unclear. Were

---

[11] Ashok Parthasarathi, *Technology at the Core: Science & Technology with Indira Gandhi* (Boston, MA: Addison-Wesley Professional, October 2008).

they partners, subordinates or service units? This lack of clarity also prevented dialogue between the units belonging to different ministries. Furthermore, only the Planning Commission held the purse strings anyway.

The turf wars and the lack of coordination between different institutions meant that the planning exercise often devolved into an exercise in self-preservation and budget-making instead of a strategic attempt at establishing national research and science and technology priorities. Unsurprisingly, the plan ended up being a motley collection of projects 'rather than a product of rigorous and integrated planning'. Furthermore, the plan mostly covered government-based research institutions. The role of the private sector was ignored. Important sectors such as agriculture, atomic energy, defence, electronics and space were also largely ignored in this exercise.

The science and technology plan, along with the Fifth Five-Year Plan, took off in 1974. However, the Emergency was declared less than a year later. Ironically, the biggest policy advancement related to science and technology during the Emergency, when questioning order was being criminalized, was incorporating Nehru's vision about inculcating scientific temper into the Constitution. The newly passed 42nd Amendment Part IVA Article 51A on Fundamental Duties to the Constitution of India stated that it shall be the duty of every citizen of India 'to develop the scientific temper, humanism and the spirit of inquiry and reform'. Indira Gandhi lost elections after the withdrawal of the Emergency, and the incoming government promptly decided to drop the science and technology plan.

The cavalier attitude to science and technology at the macro level could be seen even more clearly when zooming into specific sectors.

Insistence on Becoming a Nuclear Power

Nuclear power programme in India is a prime example where an off-hand approach led to ill thought-out conception, misleading and disingenuous promotion, and poor management of perhaps the most expensive single science and technology-based programme in the country.[12]

India's investment into nuclear power began right after Independence. The Atomic Energy Commission was established in 1948, only a year after India gained independence. For a country which had just become independent and faced enormous scarcity of resources, setting up of an expensive nuclear programme was surprising and arguably grotesque. Nuclear physicist Homi Bhabha, who was close to Nehru, was able to convince Nehru about the urgency of setting up such a programme. The primary purported benefit was dramatically lowering the cost of electricity. However, there was no evidence that nuclear power would dramatically reduce the cost of electricity. In fact, no comprehensive estimation was performed of the actual cost of nuclear power before India's nuclear power programme was set up! The uncertainties involved with assessing the actual cost of nuclear power were not communicated or factored in either before setting India on this path.

Furthermore, the true goal of the nuclear power programme was unclear. The outsized role planned for nuclear power did not seem justifiable only based on the claims of cheap electricity generation. Publicly, the goal was to build a seemingly 'limitless source of energy'. However, at least subtext suggested that India was really developing the

---

[12] M. V. Ramana, *The Power of Promise, Examining Nuclear Energy in India* (Gurugram: Penguin Books, February 2013).

ability to produce nuclear weapons. This was evident from the way the Atomic Energy Commission was set up. The corresponding bill was modelled after the British Atomic Energy Act and made pursuit of nuclear power generation exclusively the right of the government—the private sector was disbarred from participating. Also, the secrecy requirements surrounding R&D were made more stringent than the corresponding American and British legislations. When pressed about the secrecy provisions, given that the public goal of the programme was simply electricity generation and not enabling military nuclear technologies, Nehru said: 'I do not know how to distinguish the two.' In fact, while introducing the bill in the Parliament, while Nehru stated, 'I think we must develop it for peaceful purposes,' he also added, 'Of course, if we are compelled as a nation to use it for other purposes, possibly no pious sentiments will stop the nation from using it that way.'

The implied, but not explicit, duality of purpose led to a set of questionable decisions right at the beginning of the nuclear programme.

First, an administrative structure was set up, where, in the name of secrecy, there was little accountability and oversight. The Department of Atomic Energy was set up in 1954, six years after the founding of the Atomic Energy Commission. The head of the new department was Homi Bhabha, the same person who had helped architect the nuclear programme with minimal justification. As the head of the department, Bhabha reported directly and only to the prime minister (not even to the cabinet!). There was no oversight mechanism. The department's authority, opaqueness and centralization only increased in 1962 with a revised Atomic Energy Act which tightened secrecy provisions and vested in the department the sole power 'to produce, develop, use and dispose of atomic energy ... and carry out research into any matters connected therewith'. This made it almost impossible for politicians, bureaucrats and the public to scrutinize or challenge the department's policies or practices. It even made it difficult for the Comptroller and Auditor General (CAG), who performs external appraisal of public sector organizations and reports to the parliament, to get the Department of Atomic Energy to open its accounts for scrutiny. Whenever such scrutiny was possible, the department simply stonewalled investigations in the name of secrecy. In one instance, when the department was reprimanded by the parliamentary Public Accounts Committee for its 'disregard of accountability' while examining the cost of producing heavy water at department's facilities based on a CAG report, the department simply responded that 'Heavy Water being strategic material, it is not advisable to divulge information relating to its production and cost to functionaries at all levels.' Huge cost overruns were similarly explained. To make matters worse, there was little expertise on nuclear matters outside the department. Few universities offered nuclear engineering courses, and their graduates were often employed by the department (since there was no private nuclear industry in India). This forced the government to consult the department on all nuclear matters, even when it came to the department's own scrutiny!

Second, the lack of oversight meant that there were no checks on the scope of the programme. India, for example, decided to have an overly ambitious nuclear programme from the beginning to cover the entire nuclear cycle. In addition, India decided to invest in uranium mining and enrichment, fuel fabrication and heavy water manufacturing, and spent fuel reprocessing to extract plutonium. A programme this ambitious required enormous investment, especially for a country like India which had meagre resources. However, the political establishment gave it a greenlight in the name of self-reliance, a popular theme at that time. Of course, this came at the expense of other priorities.

Similarly, India decided to have a grand three-stage plan for nuclear power. India has a small deposit of uranium but large deposits of thorium. So a three-stage plan was crafted which would allow India to build significant nuclear capacity despite uranium limitations. In the first stage, uranium would be used as fuel in heavy water reactors. Spent fuel would then be used to extract plutonium. In the second stage, plutonium would be used in the core of fast breeder reactors. These nuclear cores would be surrounded by either a blanket of uranium to produce more plutonium or a blanket of thorium to produce uranium (uranium-233, to be specific). Finally, breeder reactors would be built that use uranium-233-based cores and thorium-based blankets. While the plan made sense on paper, it led to hugely uneconomical decisions, considering the circumstances. For example, India spent considerable resources on early acquisition of the reprocessing technology to produce plutonium for the second stage. Similarly, there was constant investment by the Department of Atomic Energy to build first-stage reactors so that enough plutonium could be produced to power the second stage. Those decisions led to a significant drain on India's resources. Nuclear power received a vast fraction of government's R&D funding during the 1950–1970 period at the expense of other areas of science and technology, essentially rendering India uncompetitive in many of these other areas.

Overpromise and Underdelivery

The issues with the nuclear programme continued much after its birth, often stemming from the flawed foundations the programme was built on.

Perhaps the biggest issue was that of overpromise and underdelivery, especially when considering the budget of the programme.[13]

Even in the early days, Bhabha declared that India would produce 8,000 MW of nuclear power by 1980. His predictions became more optimistic with time. A 1962 prediction stated that India would generate 20,000–25,000 MW by 1987. A 1969 Atomic Energy Commission prediction declared that India would produce 43,500 MW of nuclear power by year 2000. All these predictions were made even before a single unit of nuclear power was produced by the country!

When India did start producing nuclear power, it was nowhere close to even the conservative predictions. Only 600 MW was being produced around 1980—over 13 times lower than the prediction. Only 950 MW was being produced in 1987—25 times lower than what was predicted. Only 2,720 MW was being produced in 2000—16 times lower than what was predicted. In fact, nuclear power is still less than 3 per cent of India's electricity generation capacity.

This lack of output was despite the country devoting enormous resources to nuclear power. Until the mid-1960s, the Department of Atomic Energy's budget was over one-fourth of the country's overall science and technology budget! The fraction dipped a bit by the 1970s due to increased allocation to the space programme. However, even in its worst times—during the early 1990s when there were spending cutbacks to support economic liberalization—nuclear energy received at least 15 per cent of the overall budget (this was termed as 'a period of total dryness and stagnation', by the Department of Atomic Energy!). To keep this in perspective, renewables often receive less than 1 per cent of India's science and technology budget (over an

---

[13] N. Sharma and B. Banerjee, *Nuclear Power in India* (New Delhi: Rupa, July 2008).

order of magnitude lower than nuclear power) but produce over 20 per cent of India's electricity.

The slippages have been sometimes blamed on the international sanctions which were placed after India's nuclear tests.[14] However, ISRO achieved world-class launch and satellite capability during the same period, at lower or comparable budgets, despite similar embargoes.

India's nuclear programme is still firmly in the first stage of the three-stage plan—70 years after the start of the nuclear programme. We will be lucky if we get to the third stage in another 30 years.

The lack of oversight and accountability has also led to misleading claims about self-reliance and cost of nuclear power.

Cost and Foreign Help

From the beginning of the nuclear programme right after Independence till 1974, when India conducted its first nuclear test, the country received significant foreign help. In fact, the first two decades were marked by a flurry of acquisitions of technologies related to the entire nuclear cycle from different countries. The first important acquisition was the Canada–India Reactor US (CIRUS). The reactor was acquired from Canada, while the USA provided the heavy water for its operation. The construction of the reactor was financed by Canada. CIRUS ended up producing the plutonium which was used for the 1974 nuclear test. India similarly acquired from the USA the technology used to separate plutonium from the spent fuel rods in CIRUS. This technology formed the basis of India's first reprocessing plant at Trombay.

---

[14] George Perkovich, *India's Nuclear Bomb: The Impact on Global Proliferation* (Berkeley, CA: University of California Press, November 2001).

Subsequently, there were several other reactors which began construction in India with US and Canadian help. France helped with the design of a fast breeder reactor and trained personnel. Most of the foreign collaboration and help ceased after the 1974 tests. This led to large delays in completion of different ongoing projects. Reactors which were being built with Canadian help saw 8–16-year delay. The fast breeder reactor which was being built with French help saw a nine-year delay. Interestingly, delays and cost over-runs have continued even decades later.

Similarly, the primary argument which has been made right from the beginning for funding a nuclear pro-gramme in India, is that nuclear power is, or will be, cheaper than other forms of electricity. Seventy years later, this assertion still has not been proven true. Bhabha declared in 1958 that 'the costs of [nuclear] power [would] compare very favorably with the cost of power from conventional sources in many areas' in 10–15 years. He was specifically referring to regions which were far (>600 km) from coalfields. Larger distances mean higher transportation costs for coal and, therefore, higher cost of thermal power. In the 1980s, once it was clear that nuclear power was considerably more expensive than thermal power, the department of atomic energy revised its claim. In the revised claim, the cost of nuclear power 'compares quite favorably with coal fired stations located 800 km away from the pithead and in the 1990s would be even cheaper than coal fired stations at pithead'. Even this projection did not hold, and nuclear power continued to be more expensive than thermal power. So, in 1999, Nuclear Power Corporation (NPC) concluded that the 'cost of nuclear electricity generation in India remains competitive with thermal [electricity] for plants located about 1,200 km away from coal pit head, when full credit is given to long term operating cost especially in respect of fuel prices'.

This has not been surprising. Studies have repeatedly shown that nuclear power is more expensive than conventional sources under reasonable assumptions. A 2003 MIT study declared, 'Today, nuclear power is not an economically competitive choice' due to the capital-intensive nature of the nuclear enterprise. So, essentially, the purported premise upon which India's nuclear programme was set up has still not been shown to be true and is likely never going to hold.

Toning Down Safety Concerns

Finally, the lack of accountability and oversight has led to poor safety standards. Operations of civilian nuclear facilities are supposed to be overseen by the Atomic Energy Regulatory Board (AERB). However, AERB is not independent of the Department of Atomic Energy, as the department operates the facilities. Also, AERB lacks adequately trained staff and sophisticated testing facilities. So, again, there is reliance on the department. According to A. Gopalakrishnan, a former chairman of the AERB,

> 95 per cent of the members of the AERB's evaluation committees are scientists and engineers on the payrolls of the DAE. This dependency is deliberately exploited by the DAE management to influence, directly and indirectly, the AERB's safety evaluations and decisions. The interference has manifested itself in the AERB toning down the seriousness of safety concerns, agreeing to the postponement of essential repairs to suit the DAE's time schedules, and allowing continued operation of

installations when public safety considerations would warrant their immediate shutdown and repair.[15] 🙚🙚

This lack of independence has led to documented reports of interference into AERB functioning as well as routine neglect of safety recommendations. In one instance, AERB produced in 1995 a detailed report which identified 134 safety issues, 95 of which were marked as 'top priority'. Interestingly, many of these issues had been discovered even during 1979 and 1987 evaluations and had been marked as items requiring 'urgent action'. However, they had simply been ignored resulting in their rediscovery in 1995. Similarly, the 1993 accident in the Narora Atomic Power Station where two blades in a turbine generator snapped under accumulated stress leading to a major fire in the turbine room was entirely avoidable. The department had been warned earlier by the turbine blade manufacturer about the susceptibility of the blades to fatigue failure. However, the warning was simply ignored.

The numerous above examples illustrate India's cavalier approach to technology. India's nuclear energy programme has continued for over 70 years without compelling justification, professional management, or necessary accountability and oversight.

Stumbling through the Computer Industry

Another example which demonstrates India's inconsistent approach to technology is the computer industry. The present-day successes in the computer industry have largely happened *in spite of* significant roadblocks and stumbles

---

[15] A Gopalakrishnan, *Issues of Nuclear Safety*, Frontline. March 13, 1999. https://frontline. thehindu.com/other/article30256875.ece

along the way, stemming from an inconsistent and often-contradictory approach.

Unlike the nuclear programme, computing started in India on a solid and promising note. The beginning of computing in India could be traced to the eminent statistician P. C. Mahalanobis.[16]

Mahalanobis was the founder of the Indian Statistical Institute (ISI)—then India's top institute for statistical research. He also founded the globally popular statistics journal, *Sankhya*, and performed pioneering work on design of surveys, etc. ISI, his brainchild, performed several projects for the government in the 1930s and 1940s related to measurement and forecasting. When India became independent, the government came calling both for Mahalanobis and ISI. Mahalanobis was appointed country's statistical adviser, and ISI was contracted to both help with the creation of India's second Five-Year Plan and design and direct the new National Sample Survey (NSS).

While working on the first draft of the Second Five-Year Plan, Mahalanobis realized that then-nascent computing technology could be invaluable for planning. 'We must proceed with electronic computers with all possible speed. Otherwise we will never be able to cope with the tremendous volume of primary information which is accumulating.... I know that real planning would require the use of such computers,' he said. However, computers were expensive and the knowhow to build one was scarce.

Mahalanobis directed ISI to build a computer.[17] In record time, they built an analogue computer using salvaged materials from Kolkata's Chandni Chowk Market.

---

[16] Ashok Rudra, *Prasanta Chandra Mahalanobis: A Biography* (New Delhi: Oxford University Press, December 1997).

[17] Nikhil Menon, '"Fancy Calculating Machine": Computers and Planning in Independent India', *Modern Asian Studies* 52, no. 2 (2018): 421–457.

This computer, however, was much less powerful than digital computers, so much so that it could not help with planning-related tasks.

Simultaneously, Mahalanobis had started asking different organizations and nations to help fund development of an Indian computer. Ultimately, then-USSR and the UN agreed in 1955 to fund the purchase of HEC-2M—a digital computer from the British Tabulating Machine Company. While the computer was not powerful enough for planning-related activities, Mahalanobis hoped that it would help the ISI and the government get experience with using and maintaining a digital computer. The computer arrived in 1956—this was the first digital computer in Asia. Two years later, another computer, URAL, arrived from the USSR. In no time, parts of economic planning and crunching of NSS data started happening on these computers.

Other computing-related activity soon followed in India. The Tata Institute of Fundamental Research (TIFR) commissioned India's first digital computer in 1960 under the stewardship of Homi Bhabha. The government partnered with UNESCO and several countries to set up five Indian IITs. IIT Kanpur—with help from the US government, the Ford Foundation and US academics—created educational programmes in computing, including programming classes which were mandated for engineering students. Several digital computers were imported and made operational in different parts of the country.[18]

At the same time, seeds of homegrown computer industry were being sown. Lalit Kanodia was a 1963 graduate of IIT Bombay and one of the beneficiaries of the

---

[18] R. K. Shyamasundar and M. A. Pai, *Homi Bhabha and the Computer Revolution* (New Delhi: Oxford University Press, February 2011).

widespread computer training at the IITs in the 1960s. After graduation, he went to MIT and received an MBA degree. He enjoyed his time at MIT enough that he decided to continue at MIT to pursue his PhD. The summer after receiving his MBA and before starting his PhD programme, he came back to India for a break. During the break, he met a woman, fell in love and decided to get married. Unfortunately, the priest declared the summer to be inauspicious for a wedding. Undeterred, Kanodia decided to defer his PhD for a semester. During this time, he met P. M. Agarwala, the managing director of Tata Electric Companies, and suggested to him in a series of three papers that Tata Group should use computers for billing and load dispatch system. He also suggested that computing would be so valuable in future that they should set up Tata Computer Center. Tata Group decided to implement all three of Kanodia's suggestions and invited Kanodia to start the Tata Computer Center. Kanodia agreed and TCS was born, perhaps India's first homegrown company in the computing space.[19]

Domestic Computer Industry's Growth Blocked by Policies

The uplifting, heart-warming stories made way for decades of frustration once policymakers got involved.

The first warning came in the mid-1960s. IBM was importing used computers into India, refurbishing them in Mumbai and renting them to Indian customers at prices as high as 190,000 dollars a year. These computers were of lower quality than those which were being sold in the

---

[19] Vaidyeswaran Rajaraman, 'History of Computing in India: 1955–2010',. *IEEE Annals of the History of Computing* 37 (January–Mar 2015): 24–35.

USA. Government officials noticed. IBM was accused of profiteering by the government.

In 1963, the government formed a committee chaired by Homi Bhabha to deliberate whether India should build electronic hardware locally or focus exclusively on software. Among many recommendations, the committee concluded that small computers must be manufactured locally and large computers could continue to be imported. The committee also recommended setting up of the Electronics Corporation of India Limited (ECIL) to manufacture electronics supervised by a new Department of Electronics.

These recommendations led to a set of governmental decisions which were debilitating for India's nascent electronics industry.[20] The government announced high tariffs on import of computers or computer parts. It also announced complex foreign exchange rules to discourage acquisition of foreign software and hardware. Severe restrictions were placed on domestic computer manufacturers. There were restrictions in terms of capital, foreign exchange, production volume and quality of the computer which could be manufactured. For example, private manufacturers were disallowed from manufacturing 32-bit machines, high end at the time. Private manufacturers also started getting disfavoured in government contracts.

Thriving under Protectionism Wasn't Possible

The straight-jacketing of the domestic computing industry might have been somewhat redeemable if the public computer sector had thrived because of this

---

[20] C. R. Subramanian, *India and the Computer: A Study of Planned Development* (New Delhi: Oxford University Press, 1992).

protectionism.[21] Unfortunately, ECIL struggled and could never scale up its production volume. From 1971 to 1978, ECIL sold only 98 computers, all but 4 of which were sold to government entities (including universities) which were 'required' to buy ECIL machines. There were several reasons for ECIL's struggles. First, instead of supporting a single flagship enterprise, ECIL, several other computer companies were also created by the Central government and different state governments in addition to ECIL. These companies ended up drawing resources and talent from ECIL while competing for customers and opportunities. Second, anti-computer sentiments had started forming within parts of the government. While Bhabha's committee was deliberating the mechanics of introducing and promoting computing in India, another committee chaired by V. M. Dandekar was studying the effects of computing and automation on employment and the government. The committee viewed computerization with suspicion. One reason was the ubiquity of IBM 1401s—small machines which were becoming popular for accounting, payroll processing and stores control. These machines reduced the number of people required for these tasks but did not accelerate the tasks much since the tasks still often required human intervention. So they started being viewed as labour-saving devices, not as devices which improved productivity. This negative attitude was reflected in the Dandekar committee's recommendations. The committee introduced in 1972 strict controls on computer introduction in both industry and government, including banking, railways and insurance. It also required a prior agreement

---

21 Dinsha Mistree, 'From Produce and Protect to Promoting Private Industry: The Indian State's Role in Creating a Domestic Software Industry' (Working Paper No. 07-2018, Stanford Law School, Rule of Law Program, 2018).

with labour before a computer could be introduced into an organization. This effectively killed the computer market in the country in the short term, and no amount of protectionism would have helped ECIL.

The anti-computer sentiment also made its way to the Parliament. The Public Accounts Committee submitted a report in 1975 where it remarked that the use of computers might be detrimental in a society like India with high population and high existing unemployment. It advocated a cautious approach to computerization, further dampening the domestic computer market.

Several other policies and internal and external events also affected the computer industry adversely. The foreign exchange restrictions became particularly prohibitive in 1973 due to the oil crisis which depleted India's foreign exchange reserves. Computer imports started taking one–three years. The computers were too slow for the target applications by the time they arrived. Similarly, the parts were too antiquated for building competitive computers by the time they arrived. Indo-Pak war of 1971, nuclear tests in 1974 and declaration of the Emergency in 1975 led to many countries placing embargoes on export of computer software and hardware to India.

A particular turn of events which had a long-term adverse impact on India's computing industry was government's treatment of IBM. In 1974, the Parliament passed the Foreign Exchange Regulation Act (FERA) which required all 'non-essential' international companies to dilute their ownership to 40 per cent and have a local (Indian) partner. IBM, which had a huge operation in India, was unwilling to dilute its equity. It decided instead to argue that it is 'essential' since it was deeply ingrained into both public and private sectors, including organizations of national importance. To strengthen its case, it also decided to let the government know that it would set up an export centre and an R&D centre in India. Unfortunately, the Emergency was declared right after the negotiations began. This stalled the negotiations. Then Indira Gandhi lost elections in 1977, right after the Emergency was lifted. The incoming government was much less friendly to foreign companies. IBM was asked to either dilute its stake or leave the country. IBM chose to leave India in 1978. This decision reverberated widely, discouraging an entire generation of multinational software companies from doing business in India.

Perhaps in a fitting finale before things started getting better for the computer industry, 1984 was declared an 'anti-computerization' year by various trade unions. So strong was the sentiment against computers that a committee formed to consider computerization of banking decided against using the words 'computer' in its name or its discussions. The committee was officially called the Committee on Mechanisation in the Banking Industry (1984), and computers were referred to as 'advanced ledger posting machines' (ALPMs)!

Condemned to Repeat

As is clear from the above examples, India's progress in technology has happened in spite of the numerous false starts, missteps and policy bungling. We truly have been reluctant technophiles—at once allured by the promise of technology as well as giving in to the instincts honed over centuries which keep pulling us towards traditionalism, if not Luddism. It is important for us to remember our technological history—past cavalier attitude around technology and its consequences—else we may be condemned to repeat it.

CHAPTER 9

THE DUBIOUS FUNDAMENTALS

As a country, why isn't there enough innovation? Why are we not quick at monetizing new technology at home? Fundamentally, it can be reasoned that we as a country are not risk-takers.

Perhaps the biggest roadblock to technological innovation is the simple fact that India is still a country of the poor.[1] According to a 2013 study on people's daily expenditure, last such headcount, over 22 crore people in India had a daily expenditure of less than ₹32. Almost two-thirds of the population—more than 80 crore—had a daily expenditure of less than ₹100. This also shows up in other metrics. Fourteen lakh children die in India before the age of five. Over 20 crore people do not have adequate access to food, including 6 crore children. Seventy-eight lakh infants have a birthweight of less than 2.5 kg. In spite of child labour being illegal, 1.25 crore children between the

---

[1] Chandra Sekhar Gupta Boggarapu, *What Explains Poverty in India* (Chennai: Notion Press, March 2018).

ages of 5 and 14 work. Over 6.5 crore children between the ages of 6 and 14 do not go to school. A quarter of children do not have access to education. Over 40 per cent girls get married before they reach the legal age. According to a 2017 Oxfam report, the richest 10 per cent control 80 per cent of the nation's wealth. The wealth of the top-16 richest people is equal to the wealth of 600 million people combined. Almost 75 per cent live in villages. At least one-third cannot read and write. Only 1 out of 10 owns a refrigerator.

Poverty Dampens Innovation?

So how does poverty impact the capability and motivation to create and innovate? There is an increasing evidence both based on behavioural psychology and neuroscience that poverty can dampen creativity and innovation. Eldar Shafir, a psychologist at Princeton University, and Sendhil Mullainathan, an economist at Harvard, gave 101 shoppers in a shopping mall in New Jersey, with an average income of $70,000 and income as little as $20,000, a series of problem-solving tests.[2] Tests included questions such as how they would handle a 5 per cent salary cut, a 15 per cent salary cut, a car emergency where the repair may cost $150 and a repair that may cost $1,500. In addition to these tests, the shoppers were given tests for basic IQ, focus and concentration. The study found that the shoppers with low incomes did as well as the high-income shoppers on the IQ, focus and concentration tests when they were considering a minor financial issue (e.g., a 5% salary cut or a $150 car repair). But when they were considering an expensive car repair or a large salary cut, they

---

[2] Anandi Mani, Sendhil Mullainathan, Eldar Shafir, and Jiaying Zhao, 'Poverty Impede Cognitive Function', *Science* 341 (2013): 976–980.

performed significantly worse than the high-income shoppers. In another experiment, Shafir and Mullainathan gave cognitive tests to sugarcane farmers in Villupuram and Tiruvannamalai in Tamil Nadu, India at different points of the year.[3] The farmers collect over 60 per cent of their yearly income right after the crop harvest. So they have a lot more cash right then compared to the rest of the year. The study found that the farmers performed significantly worse on the cognitive tests when they were comparatively poor! That is, test scores were much higher right after the harvest than at other times of the year. These experiments first suggested that poverty and financial hardship impacted the quality of decision-making and the creativity needed to solve a problem.

Several subsequent studies were able to refine exactly how the decision-making gets impacted as it relates to creativity.[4] These studies found that poverty changes the decision-making progress to be exploitative—focused on day-to-day survival—instead of being exploratory, open to creativity and innovations. Those who need to cope with significant financial stress simply run out of the mental bandwidth to create and invent. Similarly, they found that poverty changes the behaviour to be habit-directed, instead of goal-directed. A goal-directed behaviour is usually associated with creativity and innovation.

New studies are increasingly tying poverty-related metrics to creativity-inhibiting behaviour.

One study, for example, showed that subjecting a person to a stressor such as financial hardship which increases the level of stress hormone cortisol made them more likely to rely on exploitative decision-making, instead of exploratory

---

[3] A. Shah, S. Mullainathan, and E. Shafir, 'Some Consequences of Having Too Little', *Science* 338, no. 6107 (2012): 682–685.

[4] Stephanie Plamondon Bair, 'Impoverished IP', *Ohio State Law Journal* 81 (2020): 523.

decision-making.[5] This reduces the likelihood of innovation or creative pursuit.

Yet another research studied the relationship between sleep deprivation and an individual's behaviour—whether it is habit-directed or goal-directed. The study found that sleep deprivation reduced the likelihood of goal-directed behaviour. Poverty has often been associated with lack of sleep quality.

Neuroscience paints an even bleaker picture in terms of relationship between poverty and innovation and creativity. While the experiments discussed above may suggest that a person's quality of decision-making can be improved simply by changing their economic conditions (e.g., stressors can be removed), a large body of neuroscience research suggests that the impact of poverty on decision-making and ability to innovate may be permanent. In particular, if poverty is experienced during childhood, it can lead to cognitive impairments such as deficits in memory, language ability and goal-directed behaviours. These impairments last a lifetime.[6]

A 2008 study, for example, looked at the brain activity in the prefrontal cortex for children between 7 and 12 years of age belonging to different socio-economic backgrounds. Prefrontal cortex is often associated with creativity and problem-solving. The study found that the brain activity looked very different depending on the economic background. The differences were so large that a

---

[5] Eleanor D. Brown, Kate E. Anderson, Mallory L. Garnett, and Erin M. Hill, 'Economic Instability and Household Chaos Relate to Cortisol for Children in Poverty', *Journal of Family Psychology* 33, no. 6 (September 2019): 629–639.

[6] J. L. Hanson, A. Chandra, B. L. Wolfe, and S. D. Pollak, 'Association between Income and the Hippocampus', *PLoS ONE* 6, no. 5 (2011).

researcher observed that the poor children's brain activity looked similar to adults with brain damage![7]

The primary takeaway from both neuroscience and psychology research is that India's poverty is a significant impediment to the nation's ability to innovate. In particular, the impact of poverty on today's children's cognitive abilities and decision-making will take decades to overturn.[8]

The Economic Model Is Also at Fault

A nation's economic model may also determine its focus and success at innovation and entrepreneurship. For example, as was clear from the rapid advances of technology in the capitalist countries in the 19th and 20th centuries and as was acknowledged even by the prominent opponents of capitalism such as Karl Marx and Friedrich Engels, capitalism and competition-based economy promote technological progress. It works like this: Private entities pursue innovation to maximize profits and outperform competition. For example, a product innovation pries customers away from the competition and retains existing customers, while a process innovation reduces cost and allows undercutting the competition. The potential of increased profits from increased innovation encourages potential investors to financially support innovation. Well-financed, successful innovations, in turn, diffuse quickly, since competition attempts to replicate a success. India's decision to pursue socialist economic policies after Independence, instead of setting up a capitalist, competition-based economy, ended

---

[7] Kimberly G. Noble, M. Frank Norman, and Martha J. Farah, 'Neurocognitive Correlates of Socioeconomic Status in Kindergarten Children', *Developmental Science* 8, no. 1 (2005).

[8] Nicole L. Hair, Jamie L. Hanson, Barbara L. Wolfe, and Seth D. Pollack, 'Association of Child Poverty, Brain Development, and Academic Achievement', *JAMA Pediatrics* 169, no. 9 (2015): 822–829.

up creating salary and import substitution businesses instead of encouraging innovation and entrepreneurship.

An important concept in explaining the innovation and entrepreneurship benefits of a capitalist system is 'creative destruction'.[9]

Joseph Schumpeter was a political economist from Austria, who had once declared that he had three goals in life—becoming Europe's greatest lover, its greatest horseman 'and perhaps also its greatest economist'. He served as a professor at Harvard from 1932 till his death in 1950 and is now widely recognized as one of the most influential economists from the early 20th century. He is perhaps most known for popularizing the concept of 'creative destruction'. He argued that economies are primarily driven by entrepreneurs who generate growth through their successes and failures. In his book *Capitalism, Socialism & Democracy*, he observed that capitalism is marked by constant disequilibrium where new products and markets keep getting born which drive less innovative or less efficient products and markets out. He made his case using horse and buggy transportation as an example. In the late 19th and early 20th centuries, even incremental innovations in the buggy and buggy whip were valuable and could fetch a significant price in the open market. However, once Ford's Model T was introduced in 1908, the horse and the buggy technologies were driven out by an effectively superior innovation. In fact, even Model T was phased out to make way for (incrementally) better models.

Schumpeter considered creative destruction an 'essential fact about capitalism' and described it as the 'process of industrial mutation that incessantly revolutionizes the

[9] Joseph A. Schumpeter, *Capitalism, Socialism & Democracy*, 3rd ed. (New York, NY: Harper Perennial Modern Classics, November 2008).

economic structure from within, incessantly destroying the old one, incessantly creating a new one'. In other words, creative destruction refers to continuous process and product innovation which replaces less innovative products and processes which become obsolete over time. Creative destruction leads to waylaying of producers and workers committed to old technology, while the entrepreneurs and innovators create new profit opportunities. So social and economic churn accompany productivity benefits.

Recent economic history is replete with examples of creative destruction. One example is the electric power market where steam turbines were replaced by today's power generation technologies, including natural gas plants, nuclear power, solar panels and wind turbines. Another example is the Internet (and computers) which ended up replacing a large number of traditional jobs (e.g., typists and secretaries) and businesses (e.g., disc rental companies) by new categories of jobs (such a software programmers) and businesses (e.g., Netflix and Amazon).

A capitalist, competition-based system promotes creative destruction and the associated innovation and productivity benefits (some studies suggest almost 50 per cent productivity benefit from creative destruction). However, it also exacts its toll in the form of socio-economic disequilibrium. Hence, India decided instead to opt for a socialist system which minimized disturbance of social conditions and maximized job security (Marx and Engels famously castigated the bourgeoisie for its 'constant revolutionizing of production [and] uninterrupted disturbance of all social conditions'). India's rejection of creative destruction was ironic considering that some trace the source of the concept of creative destruction to the Hindu god Shiva, who is considered both a destroyer and a creator. In fact, perhaps the most popular representation of Shiva is as Nataraja, the lord of the dance, dancing Tandava in a ring of flames on top of the back of a dwarf demon named Apasmara Purusha. Tandava dance (along with its gentler version Lasya) symbolizes the rhythm of the universe where creation and destruction happen in cycles.

India's embrace of socialist, salary and import substitution-based economy ended up dampening innovation and entrepreneurship. As to Schumpeter, he admitted later in his life coyly that he had achieved two out of his three goals.

Why Soviet's Strategies Work and Don't Work

The advocates of the Indian economic choice point to the Soviet model which did achieve rapid industrialization and technological progress. The Soviets were the pioneers in space exploration and produced world-class scientists, military, industrial and civilian technologies, and also had high labour productivity.

There were several reasons why the Soviets did well. Lack of intellectual property protection and wasteful competition made innovating efficient. Large state investments were made into scientific education and research. State-mandated routine increase in productivity targets forced managers to innovate.

However, the lack of competition and the top-down structure of the Soviet economy ultimately led to stagnation. While incremental process and product innovations allowed productivity targets to be met, there was no incentive for disruptive innovation. In fact, such innovation was considered too risky since any failure or error could lead to targets being missed. Another challenge was the lack of feedback and demand signal from the Soviet population. Without such feedback, production started getting dictated by 'planner's preferences'. The Soviet central planners started investing into prestige projects (e.g., military) instead of focusing on what would have been demand-driven growth areas. This made investments, technologies and innovations ultimately out of step with society's needs. Finally, the Soviet system prioritized job preservation over productivity. That ultimately led to obsolescence of a vast number of fraction of technologies, products and processes.[10]

The dilemma about whether one should prioritize innovation or stability of jobs is a fundamental one. India made its choice. The consequence of that choice has been that the world largely does not look to India for new technologies. Most technologies being used in India were developed elsewhere.

Licence Raj's Necessary Dismantling

India's choice of economic model also impacted techno-logical innovation and progress due to significant impact of licensing and regulations typically associated with a socialist economy. When introducing the Second Five-Year Plan, Nehru outlined his vision of the role of government in economy and industry: 'The public sector must grow not only absolutely but also relatively to the private sector.' The Licence–Permit–Quota Raj[11] was thus born where the government decided which company would produce what, what would be their amount of production, and

---

[10] Robert Strayer, *Why Did the Soviet Union Collapse? Understanding Historical Change* (Oxfordshire: Routledge, April 1998).

[11] Gurcharan Das, *India Unbound: The Social and Economic Revolution from Independence to the Global Information Age* (New York, NY: Anchor Books, April 2002).

what would be the price of commodities. The Licence Raj, for example, required private companies, on occasions, to satisfy 80 governmental agencies before they could produce something. Once a company would receive a licence to start production, the government would step in again and regulate production. Understandably, this sapped any motivation for innovation or entrepreneurship. Also, several industries were either kept off limits for private enterprise or required majority control by the state. So these industries anyway discouraged entrepreneurial ventures. Imports were severely restricted in most sectors of the industry. So industries such as the electronics industry which relied on foreign-made components could not flourish either. To make matters worse, large businesses often acquired licences not to produce, but to prevent competition, especially from upstarts. The nationalization of banks in 1969 and the Monopolies and Restrictive Trade Practices (MRTP) Act of 1970 further snuffed out technological innovation and entrepreneurship.

In 1991–1992, India made a decision to dismantle its Licence– Permit–Quota Raj to improve competition, innovation and entrepreneurship (then Finance Minister Manmohan Singh had quoted Victor Hugo, 'No power on earth can stop an idea whose time has come'). Today, there are significantly fewer regulations than before. However, many regulations still remain.[12] In fact, licensing and regulations make India still one of the worst nations in the world in terms of the ease of starting a business. In World Bank rankings, India consistently ranks worse than 125 in the ease of setting up a business. Starting a restaurant business in New Delhi requires 45 documents just to obtain one of the 26 necessary licences. Starting a restaurant

---

[12] See Note 11.

business in Bengaluru takes 36 licences. Mumbai, India's financial capital, requires 22 licences to start a restaurant business. In contrast, it takes only four licences to start a restaurant business in Singapore and China. In general, it takes an average of 18 days to set up a business in India. This is much better than the 30 days it took in 2009. However, this is still completely uncompetitive compared to countries such as New Zealand which allow one to set up a business in half a day!

Diversity and Dissent Important for Innovation

Another challenge to technological innovation in India has been lack of diversity in the workplace. There are several social and moral reasons to increase the amount of diversity in India's institutions and reduce social biases. However, the lack of diversity in technological companies and institutions, especially at the upper echelons, as well as different biases which exist within these institutions, may also serve as a significant impediment to technological progress and innovation.[13] For example, caste system, gender discrimination and communalism may prevent collaboration and dissemination of ideas, discourage technological contributions from large sections of the society, and dampen innovation and productivity.[14]

Diversity's impact on innovation and productivity has not always been obvious.

Anthony Lising Antonio, a Stanford professor, designed an interesting experiment with his colleagues to study the

---

[13] Ruchika Tulshyan, *The Diversity Advantage: Fixing Gender Inequality in the Workplace* (Scotts Valley, CA: CreateSpace Publishing, April 2018).

[14] Carol Fulp, *Success through Diversity: Why the Most Inclusive Companies Will Win* (Boston, MA: Beacon Press, October 2018).

impact of diversity on the quality of discussions.[15] Over 350 students from 3 universities were divided into groups. Each group was asked to discuss a controversial social issue (the death penalty or child labour practices) for 15 minutes. Both black and white members were asked to deliver dissenting opinions (written by the researchers) to their respective groups. The researchers recorded how each group perceived the delivered dissenting opinion. They found that a group of whites perceived a dissenting perspective much more novel and worth further consideration when it was delivered by a black person than when the same perspective was delivered by a white person. The researchers concluded that hearing dissent from someone who is different provokes more thought than someone who is similar (in terms of their race, in this case).

In a similar 2006 study, researchers created three-person groups of undergraduate students enrolled in business classes at the University of Illinois such that some groups had all-white members while other groups had two whites and one non-white members. Each group was asked to work on a murder mystery exercise. Each member of the group had both some information shared with other members of the group and information that only he or she had. To solve the murder mystery, the group needed to share information with each other. The researchers found that the racially diverse groups significantly outperformed the racially homogeneous groups in unravelling the murder mystery. The researchers concluded that homogeneous group members assume that they already have the information and perspective that the others do. This prevents them from effectively

---

[15] Anthony Lising Antonio, Mitchell J. Chang, Kenji Hakuta, David A. Kenny, Shana Levin, and Jeffrey F. Milem, 'Effects of Racial Diversity on Complex Thinking in College Students', *Psychological Science* 15, no. 8 (2004).

processing information, adversely impacting their innovation and creativity.[16]

Social psychologist Samuel Sommers from Tufts University conducted mock jury trials to understand the impact of diversity on decision-making. A group of real selected jurors were decomposed into several six-person juries, each jury with either all white members or two black and four white members. He found that the racially diverse juries were better at considering evidence, made fewer oversights and were more open to consider the role of race in the case presented before them. Sommers concluded that people are more diligent and open-minded in the presence of diversity.

Another fascinating study asked 186 students to read a murder mystery, think about who committed the crime and write an essay to communicate their perspective with another person who disagreed on who the culprit was. The goal of the essay was to convince the partner to come around to their side. Half the students were asked to make a case to a partner they knew belonged to the same political party. The other half was asked to make a case to a partner they knew belonged to a different party. The researcher found that the students who were making an argument to someone from their own party tended to prepare less well than the students who were making an argument to a partner belonging to a different party. The researchers concluded that diversity encourages people to work harder and be more creative in order to come to an agreement and make progress.

An increasing body of research shows that socially diverse groups produce more innovation than homogeneous groups.[17]

---

[16] Katherine W. Philips, 'How Diversity Works', *Scientific American* (October 2014), https://www.scientificamerican.com/index.cfm/_api/render/file/?method=inline&fileID=9F4FCDB9-A5B3-40AB-A9A525FDC71156AB

[17] Scott Page, *The Diversity Bonus: How Great Teams Pay Off in the Knowledge Economy* (Princeton, NJ: Princeton University Press, September 2017).

Richard Freeman and Wei Huang from Harvard explored the Thomson Reuters's Web of Science database to examine 1.5 million scientific papers published between 1985 and 2008 for the ethnic identity of their authors. They found that papers with ethnically diverse author list received more citations than papers with ethnically homogeneous list of authors. They also found that papers with author list with higher geographical diversity had higher number of citations.

Cristian Dezsö and David Ross studied the gender composition of top management teams of the companies in the Standard & Poor's Composite 1500 list from 1992 to 2006 and correlated it to the financial performance of these companies. They found that 'female representation in top management leads to an increase of $42 million in firm value' on average. They also measured the 'innovation intensity' at these companies using R&D expenses to assets ratio as the metric. They found that greater female representation in the top echelons of management led to greater financial gains for companies which prioritized innovation.

A similar study by Orlando Richard surveyed executives at 177 US banks to prepare a database of the banks' financial performance, degree of emphasis on innovation and racial diversity, and observe correlation between these parameters. The study found that higher racial diversity was often associated with better financial performance for innovation-focused banks.

A much larger 2012 study by the Credit Suisse Research Institute examined 2,360 companies globally from 2005 to 2011, looking for correlation between gender diversity on corporate management boards and financial performance. They found that companies with at least one woman on the board had higher average growth, higher average returns on equity and lower net debt to equity ratio.

Boston Consulting Group (BCG) surveyed 1,700 companies globally to determine the portion of revenue each company earned from products and services it launched within the last 3 years, a metric of value from innovation and the diversity which existed within the company. They discovered that companies with below-average diversity produced 19 per cent smaller amount of revenue from innovation than companies with above-average diversity.

A typical professor in a selective technology-based educational institution in India or a typical member of management for a technology company in India is an upper-caste, Hindu male. As the above experiments suggest, this lack of diversity affects both innovation and growth.

The above experiments also point to the different reasons why diversity improves innovation and productivity.[18] Diversity promotes greater preparedness and open-mindedness, since people anticipate alternative and unexpected viewpoints and greater effort in reaching consensus. On the other hand, homogeneity induces complacency and sameness in thinking. A diverse team can also better appreciate unmet market needs and recognize new and different market opportunities. For example, a diverse team is more capable of addressing market segments with demographics similar to the team composition. A 2013 *Harvard Business Review* study found that a team is more than twice as likely to understand a client's needs if at least one member of the team shares the client's ethnicity than when no one does. This is especially important for India, since enormous social, cultural and economic diversity in the country often prevents technology-based

[18] Sylvia Ann Hewlett, Melinda Marshall, and Laura Sherbin, 'How Diversity Can Drive Innovation', *Harvard Business Review* (December 2013), https://hbr.org/2013/12/how-diversity-can-drive-innovation

businesses from understanding the potential customer needs and customer base (imagine mostly well-off urban youth trying to build products for a 70% rural population!). The lack of Dalits, Muslims, other minorities, those who grew up in poor families, etc., especially on the teams of founders or the management boards must be redressed to unlock innovation and creativity.

Weak Welfare Safety Net

Another key factor in the relative lack of technological innovation and entrepreneurship in India is the lack of a welfare safety net. Poor social security and fragile agricultural practices (that over 70% Indians depend on) discourage risk-taking.

Gareth Olds studied the relationship between entrepreneurship and food stamps.[19] He found that the expansion of the food stamp programmes in several states in the USA in the early 2000s was associated with a 16 per cent increase in the likelihood of someone starting an incorporated business. He also found that most of the new entrepreneurs did not actually participate in the food stamp programme. They simply found comfort in the fact that the existence of such a programme would enable them to take greater risks as they could fall back on food stamps if their venture(s) failed.

In another work, Olds examined Census data from before and after the creation of the Children's Health Insurance Program (CHIP) in 1997 to estimate its impact on entrepreneurship. The programme provides publicly funded health insurance for children whose families do not qualify for Medicaid, but whose incomes still fall below a

---

19 Gareth Olds, 'Entrepreneurship and the Social Safety Net' (PhD Thesis, Brown University, May 2014).

threshold. He compared self-employment rate of those whose incomes were just below the CHIP threshold to those whose incomes just exceeded the threshold. He found that the self-employment rate for CHIP recipients was 23 per cent higher. When considering the rate of ownership of incorporated businesses, entrepreneurship increased by 31 per cent. These increases could be attributed to the families knowing that their children's heath would be insured even if their business(es) failed. A different study also found that CHIP's eligibility increased the likelihood of an immigrant starting an incorporated business by 28 per cent.

RAND Corporation performed a study in 2010 to assess the impact of Medicare on entrepreneurship.[20] The study found a significant increase in the likelihood of an American man starting a business at 65 years of age than at 64 or at other ages in the 55–64 and 66–75 ranges. Sixty-five is the age at which a person qualifies for Medicaid. Again, this showed that a safety net greatly promotes entrepreneurship.

Another study found that single American women with health coverage were 10 per cent more likely to be self-employed than their counterparts who did not have access to health coverage.

A University of Cambridge study investigated the link between entrepreneurship and the harshness of the conse-quences of personal bankruptcy law using self-employment data over 16 years (1990–2005) from 15 countries in Europe and North America.[21] The study found that more

---

[20] Robert W. Fairlie, Kanika Kapur, and Susan M. Gates, 'Is Employer-based Health Insurance a Barrier to Entrepreneurship?' (Working Paper No. WR-637-1-EMKF, RAND Corporation, September 2010).

[21] John Armour and Douglas Cumming, 'Bankruptcy Law and Entrepreneurship', *American Law and Economics Review* 10, no. 2 (Fall, 2008): 303–350, https://www.jstor.org/stable/42705535

forgiving bankruptcy laws encouraged self-employment and business creation. If the fear of financial ruin was low, entrepreneurs took more risks.

France saw a 25 per cent increase in the rate of creation of new businesses when it decided in 2001 to lower the barriers to receiving unemployment insurance. Earlier, someone on unemployment insurance would lose benefits as soon as they started a business. The new system allowed anyone starting a new business to keep drawing benefits for a fixed period. Also, the entrepreneurs were guaranteed that they would again be eligible for unemployment insurance if their business failed.

There have also been surveys asking people directly what drew them away from entrepreneurship and towards employment. An EU survey found that 71 per cent of respondents who preferred employment over entrepreneurship did so due to job security. Forty-one per cent respondents cited stable income as a factor. Ten per cent cited insurance and social welfare benefits as a factor.

How Other Countries Encourage Risk-taking and Innovation

Different countries have strengthened their safety net for innovators and risk-takers.[22] Sweden passed the Right to Leave to Conduct a Business Operation Act in 1998, which allows employees to take unpaid leave of absence from their employment, for up to six months to start a new business. This addresses the 'job-lock' problem where the employed do not pursue entrepreneurial ventures due to

---

22 Directorate-General for Employment, Social Affairs and Inclusion (European Commission), *Access to Social Protection for Workers and the Self-employed: Best Practice Examples from EU Member States* (Luxembourg: Publications Office of the European Union, 2018).

the fear of losing existing benefits related to insurance, pension, etc. Sweden also provides unemployment benefits for up to six months if the entrepreneur can demonstrate business potential. Israel allows the unemployed who started a business that failed within 24 months to still collect unemployment benefits as long as the business was started within the benefits period. France's PARE scheme introduced in 2002 allowed business creators to retain access to their unemployment benefits for up to three years after the business was set up. A recent scheme called ARCE is more aggressive and allows one to use 45 per cent of the remaining employment benefits to be used to start or acquire a business. Portugal has a similar scheme called ACPE, which allows new business owners to either access unemployment benefits for some period or use a grant worth the remaining benefits to fund their business. Portugal also allows social security to entrepreneurs under qualifying events. Austria has a social security scheme, run through the Social Security Institution for Trade & Industry (SVA) and funded through beneficiary contributions and the government, specifically targeting entrepreneurs and self-employed. Finland also has a mandatory social security scheme called YEL, specifically targeting business owners and entrepreneurs. Both the Austrian and the Finnish schemes relax the contribution requirements for new business owners.

In contrast, India does not provide its innovators and risk-takers much protection.[23] The *World Social Protection Report 2017–19* found that India spent only 1.3 per cent of its GDP on social security schemes in 2017; Asian average was 7.4 per cent. Similarly, India covered only 19 per cent of its population using at least one social protection

---

[23] Ravi Prakash Yadav, *Social Security in India* (Jaipur: Aavishkar Publishers, January 2014).

scheme; again, Asian average was much higher at 39 per cent. Moreover, existing schemes do not focus on the entrepreneurs. This significantly dampens likelihood of someone taking risks to invent, develop and monetize technology. As Raghuram Rajan, an ex-governor of the Reserve Bank of India, had remarked,

> Entrepreneurs need to take risks.... We need to create a safety net, not one which we can't afford, but a minimum safety net that allows people to go out and take risks. And workers have the willingness to join small enterprises where there is a high risk of failure but knowing that if it fails, they have something to fall back on.[24]

Struggles with Social Harmony and Conflicts

India's well-publicized struggles with social harmony, rule of law and rights enforcement also adversely affect its capability to innovate and make technological progress.

There are several reasons.

First, a country marred by social hostilities and conflicts does not present a good business climate. Social instability discourages investments, especially into innovative ideas, since risks get multiplied. A study by Brian Grim, Greg Clark and Robert Edward Snyder found, for example, that countries with significant religious hostilities also did poorly on metrics such as technological readiness and innovation.[25] India has famously struggled with

[24] Karnik, Madhura. 2016. What India must do to create a billion entrepreneurs, according to Raghuram Rajan. 23 May, https://qz.com/india/689795/what-india-must-do-to-create-a-billion-entrepreneurs-according-to-raghuram-rajan/.

[25] Brian J. Grim, Greg Clark, and Robert Edward Snyder, 'Is Religious Freedom Good for Business? A Conceptual and Empirical Analysis', *Interdisciplinary Journal of Research on Religion* 10 (2014).

communalism and casteism, often leading to violent attacks and considerable social and political tensions. Similarly, social friction discourages participation into economy by a subset of the society. This reduces economic productivity. Damian Ruck and Daniel Lawson estimated that a single unit increase in secularism corresponds to an increase in per capita GDP by $1,000 after 10 years, $2,800 after 20 years and $5,000 after 30 years.[26]

Second, considerable human and monetary resources need to be spent on dealing with social conflicts; these resources could have been otherwise used for programmes which directly or indirectly impact innovation and progress. For example, the Institute for Economics & Peace (IEP), an Australian think tank, estimated that violence (of all kinds) cost the Indian economy $1,190.51 billion (over ₹80 lakh crore) in 2017 in constant purchasing power parity (PPP) terms.[27] This is $595.4 (over ₹40,000) per person and approximately 9 per cent of the country's GDP. This is over three times what India spends on education and over nine times what it spends on healthcare. Globally, violence cost $14.76 trillion or 12.4 per cent of the global GDP!

Third, the rule of law provides a framework for everyone involved in the business cycle to operate and interact and makes every participant accountable for their actions. The resulting certainty, consistency and stability provide reassurance, especially to the innovators, upstarts and new business owners. A lack of such stability discourages innovation and entrepreneurship. This also discourages entrepreneurs from investing their earnings into existing or new ventures.

---

26 Damian J. Ruck, R. Alexander Bentley, and Daniel J. Lawson, 'Religious Change Preceded Economic Change in the 20th Century', *Science Advances* 4, no. 7 (July 2018).

27 Institute for Economics & Peace, *Economic Value of Peace 2017: Measuring the Global Impact of Violence and Conflict* (Sydney: Institute for Economics & Peace, 2021).

Weak intellectual property protection is especially harmful. It discourages investing in innovation and development of new ideas, since competitions can simply copy and undercut on prices as they did not incur the research and innovation costs. Similarly, weak enforcement of competition laws discourages upstarts and late entrants from investing in follow-on innovation to due barriers to entry.

The Economic Freedom of the World (EFW) Index measures 'the ability of individuals to make their own economic decisions without government or crony interference'. Unsurprisingly, countries with high EFW Index (such as the USA, Canada and the UK), where the rule of law is followed, have higher rates of growth and entrepreneurship than countries where interference is rampant.

Lagging Education

Technological innovation and progress also require human resources with necessary skills, background and preparedness. A big factor in India's challenges with innovation and progress is the poor quality of technology education.[28] While India produces among world's largest number of technology graduates, it is difficult to hire skilled employees as most schools do not produce graduates with sufficient practical knowledge (over 80% graduates are considered unemployable!). In fact, youth unemployment rate has stubbornly stayed close to 10 per cent.

A close examination yields several causes.

First, there is a big supply–demand gap. India has one of the largest higher education systems in the world with over 50,000 institutions and over 35 million students enrolled in colleges and universities. However, even these

---

[28] Krishna Kumar, *Routledge Handbook of Education in India: Debates, Practices, and Policies* (New Delhi: Routledge India, March 2019).

numbers are not enough, considering that half of population is under 25 years of age. The gross enrolment ratio (GER) in India is below 30 per cent. Only half the children enrolled in a school in India become high school graduate. Only half of the high school graduates enrol in colleges. This is significantly lower than over 50 per cent enrolment in higher education in China or over 80 per cent enrolment in much of Europe and North America. A GER of at least 50 per cent is needed in order to start providing a seat for everyone who wants to get higher education.

The supply–demand problem is even worse when some breakdowns are considered. Twenty per cent of Indian colleges offer only a single programme of study. Only a third of institutions offer a postgraduate programme. Only 2.5 per cent offer PhD programmes. The ones that do offer these programmes are usually private and often operate without accreditation or regulation. Twenty per cent of the colleges, especially in the rural area, have under 100 students. On average, an Indian higher education institution has less than 700 students. In contrast, a Chinese higher education institution has over 16,000 students.

The second key problem is the poor quality of higher education.[29] There is a chronic shortage of faculty due to difficulty with both hiring and retention of well-qualified teachers. One estimate suggests that, on average, half the faculty seats in government institutions lie vacant. Shortage of faculty leads to poor student-to-teacher ratio. The student-to-teacher ratio in India is around 30:1. The corresponding numbers in the USA, China and Brazil are around 12.5:1, 19.5:1 and 19:1, respectively.

The pressure to hire faculty leads to significant degradation in the quality of teaching. Since the number of PhDs in India has stayed largely constant in spite of a large

---

[29] Pawan Agarwal, *Indian Higher Education: Envisioning the Future* (New Delhi: SAGE Publications, July 2009).

increase in the number of higher education institutions in the last decade, any teaching expansion is largely ad hoc and substandard even in the premiere institutions. Several surveys of the deans of India's top higher education institutions suggest that degrading faculty quality is their number one concern. China addressed a similar problem by attracting PhD diaspora with attractive salaries and research infrastructure and funding. There are over a *million* India-born PhDs in universities around the world, most of them focused on technology. However, it is unclear if any existing scheme is attractive enough for them to consider returning to teach at colleges and universities.

Third key problem is the disconnect of India's higher education system from the needs of the industry. Over half of the students in India's higher education system are pursuing one of the following three-year degrees with poor linkages to the industry: bachelor of arts (BA), bachelor of science (BSc) and bachelor of commerce (BCom). Without industry relevance and connections, many graduates do not find employment in the formal economy, falling instead into the trap of informal or temporary employment. Also, the separation of teaching and research within Indian universities prevents exposure to cutting-edge ideas, especially in the technology field. Ultimately, India's poor investment into R&D (0.6%–0.7% of the GDP) translates into poor quality and lack of research and industry relevance at its higher education institutions. For comparison, the USA, China, Israel and Korea invest much higher fraction of their GDP into R&D at 2.8 per cent, 2.1 per cent, 4.3 per cent and 4.2 per cent, respectively.

Fourth key problem is inequity in higher education.[30] Access to higher education is highly non-uniform across

---

[30] Manabi Majumdar and Jos Mooij, *Education and Inequality in India: A Classroom View* (New Delhi: Routledge, July 2015).

different socio-economic classes and regions. Millions cannot simply afford higher education since much of it is provided through expensive private institutions. Less than 10 per cent enrolled students have access to financial aid. Fewer women are enrolled than men. Fewer lower-caste students are enrolled than upper-caste students. While some states have a large concentration of colleges (e.g., Telangana has almost 60 colleges per lakh of eligible population), other states lag greatly in providing access to college (Bihar has only 7 colleges per lakh eligible population). All-India average is 28. The best universities and colleges are in metropolitan and urban areas, depriving the rural population access to high-quality higher education.

It should not be a surprise, therefore, that a large fraction of those who can afford, leave to get higher education in a different country. Over 750,000 Indians went to study abroad in 2018, a majority of them focused on engineering and technology. This was second only to China. The above problems also manifest in terms of the rankings of the higher education institutions. Not a single Indian institution was ranked in top 300 in the 2021 Times ranking of world's best higher education institutions.

India's Struggles with Education Start Much Earlier

India has 3 times number of schools (15 lakh) than China (nearly 5 lakh). However, educational outcomes are poor. The 2017 *Annual Status of Education Report* (ASER) brought out by Pratham, an educational non-profit agency, found that 57 per cent of surveyed 14- to 18-year-olds could not perform simple division, 59 per cent had used a computer and 40 per cent did not intend to go to a college. The survey also found that a large fraction of students had trouble calculating and telling time, fared poorly in foundational skills of reading and arithmetic, struggled with proper use of the unitary method, and were incapable of solving complex mathematical problems. Pratham's 2016 report had found that less than 20 per cent third-grade students in government schools could solve a two-digit subtraction problem. Over half of surveyed fifth graders could not read second-grade text.

These outcomes should not be surprising. One lakh elementary and secondary schools have only one teacher. Four lakh schools have just two teachers and fewer than fifty students. Even when teacher are on roll, teacher absenteeism is high. A World Bank report estimated that one out of four teachers is absent in a typical government-run primary school. Low-income states such as Bihar and Jharkhand report teacher absenteeism rates higher than 40 per cent. Simply teacher absenteeism is estimated to cost 2 billion dollars in India every year.

Facilities and infrastructure are also not conducive to learning. Data from District Information System for Education (DISE) shows that only half of the government schools (most schools in rural areas are run by the government) have access to electricity. Less than 30 per cent of the schools and less than one-fifth of the government schools have a computer. One out of ten schools and one out of twenty government schools have an Internet connection. Laboratory facilities are similarly inadequate.

A nation which provides poor foundation in math and science and educates only a fraction of its children would indeed struggle with technology-based innovation and progress.

CHAPTER 10

THE BUILD–BUY CONUNDRUM

Innovation and technology challenges at home does not mean that massification of technology can wait. A pragmatic combination of homegrown technologies and technologies acquired from elsewhere may be needed to allow us to reap the considerable benefits from technology (Chapter 7). It will also start improving country's technological DNA.

What is the right build vs buy combination, however. One argument is that the most efficient approach for a developing nation such as India is to acquire the technology it needs. The technology could then be absorbed by the local industry, which can then help the nation catch up quickly. But a contrasting argument is that the adoption of a foreign technology is not easy or cheap. It depends on the technological readiness of the receiving nation. Also, a foreign technology, especially one developed in a developed country, may not be a good fit in a unique socio-economic setting. In fact, studies repeatedly show that foreign direct investment (FDI) in technology sectors do not automatically lead to technology transfer to local firms. So what is the right approach for India: buy or build?

Indigenous Solutions to Unique Problems

Devendra Raj Mehta was a promising IAS officer and the collector of Jaisalmer in 1969 when he got into a road accident in Pokhran which shattered his femur into over 40 pieces. The doctors were not sure if he would survive. Mehta spent several months in bed. He was then advised to start physiotherapy at the Sawai Man Singh (SMS) Hospital in Jaipur where he first noticed the interest in 'Jaipur foot'.[1]

Jaipur foot is a rubber-based prosthetic leg for under-knee amputees. It was invented at the SMS Hospital a year earlier by an artist named Pandit Ram Chandra Sharma. Sharma had been invited to the hospital by an orthopaedic surgeon, Dr P. K. Sethi, to teach art as therapy to polio victims. When Sharma saw the polio victims fitted with imported, expensive artificial limbs, he decided to design one himself, in consultation with Dr Sethi, using wood with vulcanized rubber hinged to it. The resulting design was functional, and an order of magnitude less expensive than the imports. It also allowed a wider range of movements compared to other artificial limbs.

Jaipur foot started getting attention right after it was designed. The needy thronged SMS Hospital to get fitted. However, the prosthesis was still too expensive for most, and the scale was limited. When Mehta noticed the interest in Jaipur foot, he made a mental note. A few years later, in

---

[1] Sara Hendren, *What Can Body Do: How We Meet the Built World* (New York, NY: Riverhead Books, August 2020).

1975, when the 2,500th birth anniversary of Mahavira—the founder of Jainism—was being celebrated and Mehta had risen to be the principal secretary to the chief minister of Rajasthan, he founded Bhagwan Mahaveer Viklang Sahayata Samiti (BMVSS) with the goal of helping the disabled. BMVSS started designing Jaiput foot at scale and started offering it to the needy for free. Very quickly, Jaipur foot started being used widely both within India and in other countries and over time became the most used prosthetic foot in the world. *Time* hailed it among the greatest inventions of the 20th century. It also inspired an entire industry in India. India is now considered a world leader in low-cost prosthesis.[2]

The story of Jaipur foot is one of a need which could not be met simply by importing technology. The unique problem—supporting a large population of needy at a low cost—required developing a new technology at home. The indigenously developed technology helped launch a successful industry.

The 1980s saw an increase in popularity of super-computers. The USA and several European countries had started building these massive computing machines which could be used for applications as diverse as satellite construction, nuclear weapon development and weather monitoring. India also wanted one. In 1985, Rajiv Gandhi, the then prime minister of India, visited the USA and requested the then US president, Ronald Reagan, to sell India its Cray supercomputer. Reagan politely declined. The USA was worried that India would use the supercomputer for developing its nuclear programme. India then approached the USSR for purchase or lease of a

---

[2] C. K. Prahalad, *The Fortune at the Bottom of the Pyramid: Eradicating Poverty through Profits* (Upper Saddle River, NJ: Wharton School Publishing, August 2004).

supercomputer. USSR agreed. However, the USA pressured the then fast-disintegrating USSR to withdraw from the deal. Another opportunity to acquire a supercomputer was through IBM. IBM had left India in 1977 due to excessive regulations and was now preparing to enter the Indian market again. The Government of India was able to convince IBM to develop a supercomputer in India. However, the US government again intervened and scuttled the deal.

By 1987, it became clear that India would not be able to acquire supercomputing technology from elsewhere.[3] Gandhi gave CSIR the go-ahead to develop the technology at home. A Centre for Development of Advanced Computing (CDAC) was established in Pune which started working with a 30-million-dollar budget and a timeline of three years. India's top computer scientists and electronics engineers were summoned to work on the project under the leadership of Vijay Bhatkar.[4] Finally, in 1991, CDAC delivered PARAM 8000—an indigenously developed supercomputer which at the time was not only world's cheapest supercomputer (by a wide margin) but at 5 GFlops (billion operations per second) was also the second-fastest supercomputer in the world. It achieved this feat in spite of being restricted to use components which were not export-controlled by the USA. It was also the first supercomputer built by a developing country.

The PARAM story is an example of a technology which could not be bought—due to geopolitical restrictions in this case—and the technology had to be built at home in order meet the country's needs.

---

[3] Stuart Auerbach, 'Cray Deal a Casualty of Atomic Weapon Fears', *The Washington Post*, 19 March 1993, washingtonpost.com/archive/business/1993/03/19/cray-deal-a-casualty-of-atomic-weapon-fears/24f11e87-effe-4a2c-8976-d3d844cb4275/

[4] Ankita Katdare, 'Dr. Vijay Bhatkar – Father of Indian Supercomputers', CrazyEngineers, 3 May 2012, https://www.crazyengineers.com/threads/dr-vijay-bhatkar-father-of-indian-supercomputers.65610

Digital payments were non-existent before the early 1990s when India liberalized its economy and decided to establish an Electronic Clearing Service (ECS) to handle bulk or periodic payments. However, this served the payment needs for a small fraction of the society. India then set up several payment systems (or 'rails'), managed by the National Payments Corporation of India (NPCI), to increase the coverage. However, these rails barely made a dent since they required that people be part of the formal economy. Most Indians were not part of the formal economy—less than 2 per cent of eligible Indians pay taxes, while over 95 per cent transactions were cash-only.[5]

In the 2010s, three important trends emerged.[6] India started providing Aadhaar—a permanent, unique and secure digital identity to its citizens. It now covers almost 95 per cent of the population.[7] Second, mobile phones became ubiquitous. There are now over 1 billion mobile subscriptions—most of which are tied to Aadhaar for identity. Third, the government created in 2014 a financial inclusion programme—PMJDY—which brought a vast fraction of the population into the banking system. Over 40 crore Jan Dhan accounts have been opened. These trends created an opportunity to interlink mobile numbers, bank accounts and Aadhaar numbers for easier disbursement of subsidies and execute welfare programmes.

At the same time, mobile-first businesses took off, creating a demand for digital payments. To address this, government started allowing corporations with broad

---

[5] Jaspal Singh, *Digital Payments in India: Background, Trends and Opportunities* (New Delhi: New Century Publications, November 2019).

[6] Nandan Nilekani and Viral Shah, *Rebooting India: Realizing a Billion Aspirations* (Gurgaon: Penguin Random House India, November 2016).

[7] N. S. Ramnath and Charles Assisi, *The Aadhaar Effect: Why the World's Largest Identity Project Matters* (New Delhi: Oxford University Press India, October 2018).

customer reach, such as postal system and telecom providers, to create payment banks whose primary goal was to provide basic payment and deposit services. The demonetization exercise of 2016 only accelerated the demand for mobile payments and, therefore, these payment banks.

A new problem emerged. An alphabet soup of traditional banks, payment banks, rails and mobile wallets built on top of these payment systems, each targeting a different set of customers and with different sender authentication and receiver identification procedures, meant that interoperability became a challenge. That is, someone using one payment system could not seamlessly transact in real time with someone on a different payment system. This is a problem which exists in most of the world today. It can take multiple days to transact across different payment systems.

India decided that this is not acceptable for its population. Somehow the silos had to be broken. Unified Payments Interface (UPI) was developed.

UPI is a mobile payment interface which connects multiple bank accounts into a single application, facilitating real-time monetary transactions even across different banks. The bank accounts, in turn, can be linked to any payment app, including peer-to-peer payment apps such as PhonePe, Google Pay, Paytm and BHIM, thereby allowing users to pay each other, as well as UPI-enabled institutions and banks in real time through simply a phone number, an Aadhaar number, a QR code, a Virtual Payment Address (VPA), an UPI ID or an account number. It is also open— so technology companies and even non-financial institutions can build applications on top of UPI. This has changed the payment landscape in India, since most of the population can now participate in digital economy due to ubiquity of

Aadhaar, bank accounts and phones. This has also led to a boom in mobile-first businesses, which are using UPI in creative ways. Billions of UPI transactions are being conducted every month, running into at least a tenth of India's GDP.

UPI is widely celebrated as one of the most innovative, advanced, inexpensive and financially inclusive payment technologies in the world. Google, in fact, recommended UPI as the model for US Federal Reserve System to implement to enable faster digital payment in the USA.

The story of UPI is one of an opportunity which was created which could be leveraged only by creating a new technology at home. There was no existing technology in the world to meet the need. The newly developed technology is now a model for the rest of the world.

Things to Consider before Build or Buy

Several factors must be considered before deciding whether a technology should be built at home or simply imported from outside.[8]

Technical knowhow improves through movement of goods, capital, people and information between nations. Specifically, FDI, especially by MNCs, often brings with it technical and managerial knowledge, since these companies need to import machinery, train their employees and transfer knowledge to their local subsidiaries. Knowledge is also transferred to local firms through demonstration and movement of people from foreign firms to local firms as well as linkages between the MNC and the local suppliers and customers. Foreign firms also create competition, which forces local firms to be more innovative.

---

[8] Paul Krugman, *Rethinking International Trade* (Cambridge, MA: The MIT Press, March 1994).

On the other hand, allowing foreign firms to operate may crowd out domestic firms if they are not competitive. Local firms may reduce R&D investment if competition from foreign firms is strong. In many cases, foreign firms may simply take advantage of cheap labour and resources but not establish any linkages with the local economy.

Studies over time have established that technology transfer is best affected in a non-import-substitution regime and when the intellectual property protection is strong and the foreign company is not placed under heavy restrictions. Sufficient linkages should also be achieved between foreign and local firms through joint ventures, local content requirements, training requirements, etc.

Technology transfer also happens best when there are existing in-house R&D efforts. In fact, it has been observed that domestic firms can absorb indigenous technology much more easily due to such technology being more tuned to local needs. Indigenous development of technology also has the advantage of skill formation and capability building.

There is also an interesting dynamic where both allowing FDI cheaply and not allowing FDI dampen local innovation. For technology sectors where FDI is not allowed, the lack of foreign competition takes away any incentive for local firms to innovate. For technology sectors where FDI is allowed cheaply, the local firms would not innovate, since local innovation would not be cost effective. In fact, some have suggested taxing technology imports even in sectors where FDI is allowed so that incentive for local innovation remains.

Protectionism vs Free Trade

Of course, any limit on technology import would be quickly labelled as protectionism, especially by the developed nations. However, technology protectionism is as old as humankind.

According to Greek mythology, Minos and his brothers were vying for the kingship of Knossos on Crete. Minos prayed to Poseidon to send him a snow-white bull as a sign that God supported his quest. He promised to sacrifice the bull to Poseidon as a mark of gratitude. Poseidon granted his wish. However, once the bull arrived, Minos was enchanted by its beauty. Instead of sacrificing the snow-white bull, Minos decided to sacrifice one of his own white bulls to Poseidon. The broken promise infuriated Poseidon. Poseidon caused Minos's wife Pasiphae to fall in love with the bull. The bull and Pasiphae mated and produced a child Minotaur who was half-man, half-bull. Minotaur fed on human flesh and could not be controlled. Minos then asked Daedalus to design a labyrinth which would hold Minotaur. Men and women would be sent to the labyrinth periodically to feed Minotaur.

The labyrinth that Daedalus built was a thing of beauty. It was so complex that even Daedalus could barely navigate it. However, once Minos noticed that Daedalus could indeed get out of the labyrinth, he decided to imprison Daedalus and his son Icarus in a high tower so that they would never reveal the secret of the labyrinth. The technology was thus protected.[9]

Lokapannati, Pali translations of old Sanskrit texts, have stories about *yantakaras*—robot makers of Rome—who built robots which could assist in trade, farming and law enforcement. The secret robotic technology was closely guarded. The *yantakaras* were forbidden to leave Rome or divulge the secrets of robot making. If they did, they were

---

[9] Jacob E. Nyenhuis, *Myth and the Creative Process: Michael Ayrton and the Myth of Daedalus* (Detroit, MI: Wayne State University Press, January 2003).

hunted down and killed by robotic assassins so that the technology could be protected.

There is also a likely apocryphal story of Shah Jahan ordering to cut off the hands of the 20,000 artisans who worked for 22 years to build Taj Mahal after the building was completed. Shah Jahan did not want a comparable building to ever be built.

Protectionist West

In modern times, free trade (or antithesis of protectionism) has been promoted by the USA and Britain. However, both have had a protectionist past before they started championing free trade from a position of strength once they became developed countries.

The 14th-century England looked very much like a poor developing country today. It produced a lot of wool which would then be exported across the channel where Flemish weavers would create cloth which would then be exported back to England and other countries. King Edward realized how lucrative the weaving business was. So he imposed a complete ban on import of cloth and exhorted his countrymen to only wear English cloth. He led by example. He and his courtiers would only wear English cloth. He also imposed controls on wool exports to deny the Flemish weavers the raw materials they needed to compete. The protectionism continued even after Edward. Henry VII and Elizabeth I instituted several policies to protect and promote the textiles sector, including passing of the Navigation Acts to restrict colonies from trading with anyone other than Britain. In fact, the British colonies were forced to produce raw materials which would then be converted into finished goods by British factories. The colonies, on the other hand, were forbidden from manufacturing goods. Prime Minister William Pitt had famously said in 1770 that the colonies should 'not be permitted to manufacture so much as a horseshoe nail' and should they 'manufacture a lock of wool or a horse shoe, I would fill their ports with ships and their towns with troops'. Adam Smith, in *The Wealth of Nations*, similarly stated that America should simply grow agricultural products and leave manufacturing to Britain. Britain also imposed high tariffs on imported manufactured goods. The average tariff in Britain around 1860 was 45–55 per cent. For context, France imposed an average tariff of 20 per cent around that time.

Britain's transition to a champion of free trade happened primarily due to local factors.[10] After the Napoleonic Wars ended in 1815, European trade resumed in earnest, flooding Britain with imported corn. This led to a collapse of corn prices in Britain. In response, landowning, corn-producing aristocrats used their influence to erect a set of laws, called Corn Laws, imposing high tariffs on all grain imports. However, this made bread expensive, causing starvation and hunger for hundreds of thousands. This incensed local merchants and manufacturers—later known as 'Manchester Men'—since they had to then pay higher wages to the workers just so that they could feed themselves. These mostly self-made men also did not like that aristocracy with inherited wealth was dictating their lives and livelihood. A campaign to repeal the Corn Laws began, which then expanded into a demand for other countries to also remove their tariffs and allow free trade. The Corn Laws were repealed in 1846, and Britain started a crusade for other countries to stop protectionism.[11]

---

[10] From the Corn Laws to Free Trade: Interests, Ideas, and Institutions in Historical Perspective. Cheryl Schonhardt-Bailey. The MIT Press. June 2006.

[11] William D. Grampp, 'How Britain Turned to Free Trade', *Business History Review* 61, no. 1 (1987): 86–112.

As historian Paul Bairoch wrote, the USA, in its early years, was the 'bastion of modern protectionism'.[12] A tariff was the second bill signed by the first president, George Washington. The key proponent of protectionism right after American independence was Alexander Hamilton. Hamilton submitted to Congress in 1791 his *Report on the Subject of Manufactures*, where he made an 'infant' industries argument for economic protectionism. Hamilton was born in West Indies, then a British Colony, and had experienced first-hand how the British prevented colonies from competing while selling their manufactured good all over the world. As an aide-de-camp to General Washington, he had also seen the USA nearly lose the Revolutionary War due to lack of local weapons-manu-facturing capacity (France had sent 80,000 muskets and other war equipment to the Americans to rescue them during the war). He also worried that the USA would continue to be a producer of raw materials and agri-cultural products for British manufacturing even after independence. He believed that infant nations, such as the newly independent USA, needed to develop local industry and technology before they could compete against existing industrial powers. In his words:

> The superiority antecedently enjoyed by nations who have preoccupied and perfected a branch of industry, constitutes a more formidable obstacle than either of those which have been mentioned, to the introduction of the same branch into a country in which it did not before exist. To maintain, between the recent establishments of one country, and the long-matured establishments of another country, a competition upon equal terms, both

---

[12] Michael Lind, *Land of Promise: An Economic History of the United States* (Manhattan, NY: Harper, April 2012).

as to quality and price, is, in most cases, impracticable. The disparity, in the one, or in the other, or in both, must necessarily be so considerable, as to forbid a successful rivalship, without the extraordinary aid and protection of government.[13]

In fact, he even engaged industrial espionage when he sent men into British textile mills to spy on them and steal their technology.

Hamilton suggested 11 concrete measures[14]:

1. 'Protecting duties.'
2. 'Prohibition of rival articles or duties equivalent to prohibitions.'
3. 'Prohibition of the exportation of the materials of manufactures.'
4. 'Pecuniary bounties.'
5. 'Premiums.'
6. 'The exemption of the materials of manufactures from duty.'
7. 'Drawbacks of the duties which are imposed on the materials of manufactures.'
8. 'The encouragement of new inventions and discoveries at home, and of the introduction into the United States of such as may have been made in other countries; particularly those, which relate to machinery.'
9. 'Judicious regulations for the inspection of manufactured commodities.'
10. 'The facilitating of pecuniary remittances from place to place.'
11. 'The facilitating of the transportation of commodities.'

---

[13] Report on the Subject of Manufactures, Alexander Hamilton. 1791.

[14] Ian Fletcher, 'America Was Founded as a Protectionist Nation', HuffPost, 12 September 2010, https://www.huffpost.com/entry/america-was-founded-as-a_b_713521

Several recommendations in his report were accepted by the government, and the USA began its history as a protectionist state. The only hindrance to full embrace was the domination of Congress by southern planters who wanted free trade (since they supplied most of world's cotton). However, even they relented after the war of 1812 due to a surge of anti-British feeling. Tariff was increased to an average of 25 per cent. It was raised to 35 per cent in 1816. By 1820, the average tariff was 40 per cent. It was widely known that protectionism was Lincoln's second most important concern after slavery. He had famously declared in 1847: 'Give us a protective tariff, and we will have the greatest nation on earth.'

The average tariff in the USA at the end of the 19th century was as high as 45 per cent. These numbers were higher than anywhere else in the world.

Many believe that it was Hamilton-promoted economic protectionism that made America the world's fastest-growing economy in the 19th century and well into the 1920s.[15] Free trade started being considered only after the Second World War as a way to prevent further wars and restore European economies. Also, it was self-serving since the USA had already achieved global industrial and technological dominance by then, and free trade would allow the US producers to take advantage of foreign markets. Free trade became an American article of faith in Reagan era when it started being presented as a counterpoint to the socialist and communist economic systems.

America's protectionist tendencies keep showing every time its dominance is threatened. This happened in the 1980s due to the rise of Japan. It is happening now due to the rise of China.

---

15 Ha-Joon Chang, *Bad Samaritans: The Myth of Free Trade and the Secret History of Capitalism* (London: Bloomsbury Press, January 2009).

Learning from Asian Counterparts

To understand where India should choose to lie on the build vs buy scale, perhaps it is instructive to observe what India's Asian counterparts have done.

Korea's Rise

Korea was mostly a poor agrarian state occupied by Japan in the first half of the 20th century.[16] Before the end of the Second World War, a set of *chaebols* started emerging. A *chaebol* is a family-owned large business (*chae* means wealth and *bol* means a clan or clique in Korean) with interests across a diverse set of industries. These *chaebols* were modelled after *zaibatsu*, the powerful Japanese financial and industrial conglomerates which rebuilt Japanese economy after the Meiji Restoration of 1868. After the Korean War, the government started routing foreign loans to *chaebols* to rebuild the economy. Once General Park Chung-hee came to power after a military coup in 1961, the government also started guaranteeing these loans. That is, the government would act as a guarantor if a *chaebol* could not repay a foreign loan. In addition, the government started providing guaranteed domestic loans. Chung-hee had a technology-driven vision for South Korea's progress. His government started encouraging *chaebols* to focus on technology-based exports through preferential loans to technology-based export businesses. Simultaneously, he lowered taxes and blocked or handicapped technology-based foreign goods and services (through high tariffs, regulations and other protectionist policies) so that the *chaebols* could be guaranteed to make steep profits in the

---

[16] Seung-hun Chun, *The Economic Development of South Korea: From Poverty to a Modern Industrial State* (Oxfordshire: Routledge, February 2018).

local market. This led *chaebols* to transform themselves into technology-based businesses. For example, Samsung, founded in 1938 as a company exporting goods such as dried fish, fish and noodles, eventually grew into one of the largest technology-based companies in the world (it continues to have non-technology subsidiaries). Hyundai was founded in 1947 as a small construction business. It is now one of world's largest carmakers. SK Group was founded in the early 1950s as a textile company. It is now run as SK Telecom, South Korea's largest wireless carrier, as well as SK Hynix, the world's second-largest memory company. LG, founded in 1947, derives its name from the merger of Lucky and Goldstar, and was focused on chemical and plastics sectors. However, it transformed itself in the 1960s to become one of world's largest consumer electronics and technology companies. Essentially, the *chaebols* enthusiastically realized the government's blueprint for technology-based industrial progress in return for protectionism. This protectionism, among other things, thus allowed South Korea to become a technology giant and transformed it from an agrarian economy to one of world's largest and most advanced economies.[17]

Japan's Reconstruction

Japan had famously closed itself off for 200 years till 1853 when US Commodore Matthew Perry arrived in 'black ships' into Tokyo Bay and demanded trading rights. Japan decided to open up, but on its own terms, under the slogan of *fukoku kyohei*, 'rich country equals strong army'. The government decided to guide private enterprise thereon

---

[17] Daniel Tudor, *Korea: The Impossible Country—South Korea's Amazing Rise from the Ashes: The Inside Story of an Economic, Political and Cultural Phenomenon* (Clarendon, VT: Tuttle Publishing, November 2018).

through *zaibatsu*, largely family-based financial and industrial conglomerates.[18]

The Second World War devasted Japan economically. America wanted Japan to reconstruct itself through the principles of free trade. Japan had other ideas. In 1955, the USA and Japan were negotiating their first post-war trade agreement. The US side was led by C. Thayer White, who told Japan to reduce its tariffs on imported automobiles since, according to him, their tariff on imported cars was too high.

In a fascinating exchange which encapsulates the entire post-war free trade debate, White argued,

> 1. The United States industry is the largest and most efficient in the world.
> 2. The industry is strongly in favor of expanding the opportunities for world trade.
> 3. Its access to foreign markets in recent years has been limited by import controls.
> 4. Although the United States Government appreciates that it is necessary for some countries to impose import restrictions for balance of payments reasons ... it would be in Japan's interest to import automobiles from the United States and ex-port items in which Japan could excel.[19]

The Japanese trade negotiator, Kenichi Otabe, responded,

> 1. If the theory of international trade were pursued to its ultimate conclusion, the United States would specialize in the production of automobiles and Japan in the production of tuna.

---

18 Mark Ravina, *To Stand with the Nations of the World: Japan's Meiji Restoration in World History* (New York, NY: Oxford University Press, September 2017).

19 Testimony of Alfred E. Eckes' to U. S. Trade Deficit Review Commission. November 16, 1999. https://govinfo.library.unt.edu/tdrc/hearings/16nov99/aeeckes.pdf

2. Such a division of labor does not take place ... because each government encourages and protects those industries which it believes important for reasons of national policy.[20]

Of course, Japan did not decide to become a nation solely focused on fishing.[21] Instead, it decided to close its markets to foreign companies, enacted trade barriers and implemented exchange rates which discouraged imports and promoted exports. Only those foreign investments were allowed which transferred technology and helped its local companies grow. Japan also identified a few promising industries which were mostly technology-based and decided to develop those through tax breaks, high tariffs (on imports), 'administrative guidance' and cheap credit. For example, Japan decided to limit imports in the automobiles sector to $500,000 per year. Another interesting element was the development of *keiretsu*—a set of companies, including industrial houses, banks and trading companies, with interlocking ownerships and exclusive business relationships. *Keiretsu* allowed individual companies to undercut foreign competitors. It also allowed individual companies to aggressively enter high-capital, high-growth sectors with long-term potential such as electronics, robotics, automobiles, computing, heavy industries and semiconductor technologies. Protectionism helped Japan transform into one of the world's most advanced technology-based economies.[22]

---

[20] See Note 19.

[21] John W. Dower, *Embracing Defeat: Japan in the Wake of World War II* (New York, NY: W. W. Norton & Company, June 2000).

[22] Andrew Gordon, *A Modern History of Japan: From Tokugawa Times to the Present* (New York, NY: Oxford University Press, July 2019).

The Build–Buy Conundrum |

China Has Been Famously Protectionist When It Comes to Technology-based Industries

The year 1978 was a watershed year in China's economic history.[23] It was then that China started to move from state planning to a market-based economy. However, the new policy was selective. Only those sectors were opened to foreign investment which could ignite local growth. For example, sectors which needed new technology and infrastructure and sectors which required labour-intensive manufacturing were opened first. The international community protested the restricted liberalization, but not much moved. When the World Trade Organization (WTO) was formed, China wanted to join. In exchange for WTO membership, more areas of economy were opened. In practice, however, a combination of high tariffs, foreign equity restrictions, weak intellectual property protection, forced technology transfer, export subsidies and state trading ensured that foreign companies could not compete with local companies, except in select sectors.

The protectionism was perhaps the most blatant in the IT sector. Trade and information security restrictions, investment barriers and discriminatory taxes prevented foreign participation. The technical and legal infrastructure for online censorship blocked most foreign Internet-based platforms and intermediaries. It is widely believed that the primary reason to prevent foreign participation in the IT sector was to shield local companies so that national champions might emerge. The practice of preventing foreign players has continued, even though there are now several large IT companies in China. This is likely to

---

[23] Barry J. Naughton, *The Chinese Economy: Adaptation and Growth* (Cambridge, MA: The MIT Press, March 2018).

protect investments into these companies by the various investment vehicles controlled by different municipal and provincial governments. National security has also been often used as a reason to restrict supply of foreign equipment, software and services into China, especially into public sector and government.

This protectionism, however, has worked for China thus far. China has grown at over 9 per cent per year for last 30 years.[24]

India Has Also Had a Largely Protectionist Past

After India became independent, the successive governments sought economic self-sufficiency instead of globalization. International trade and investment were discouraged, and import substitution was the primary economic goal. India was home to the infamous Licence–Permit–Quota Raj. All production was tightly regulated with industrial licences. All competition to licensed entities was eliminated through outright import bans or excessive tariffs.

In fact, some protectionism decisions were infamously extreme. In 1977, the Janata Party had just come to power after defeating the Congress party and Indira Gandhi in the first election held after two years of the unpopular Emergency. The new prime minister, Morarji Desai, asked all foreign companies operating in India to reduce their ownership stake per FERA and find an Indian partner. He also wanted these companies to transfer their technology. Some agreed. However, many packed their bags and left India. One of the companies to leave India was the soft

---

[24] Loren Brandt and Thomas G. Rawski, *China's Great Economic Transformation* (Cambridge: Cambridge University Press, April 2008).

drink giant, Coca-Cola. Coca-Cola was enormously popular in India at the time and employed thousands of people. When it decided to leave India instead of partnering with an Indian business and sharing its secret recipe with it, it left a large number of people unemployed. Undeterred, the government decided that India would develop its own soft drink.

The government tasked the Central Food Technological Research Institute (CFTRI) at Mysore to develop the formula. CFTRI had previously famously developed the formula for making baby food from milk powder on government calling in 1956. The formula was a great success in India and was marketed by Amul.

CFTRI developed a formula. Modern Food Industries, a government-owned company, started manufacturing a soft drink, and Double Seven was born. The drink was named Double Seven (or satattar in Hindi), as the winning name in a national competition to name the drink, to mark the year the emergency had ended, the mighty Congress party had been defeated for the first time, the new government had come to power and the soft drink was launched (with great fanfare at the annual trade fair in Pragati Maidan in Delhi). The government provided employment to those who had lost jobs when Coca-Cola left and projected Double Seven as a gift to the masses who had to live through the draconian Emergency.

All the fanfare, however, did not translate into success. Competitors such as Thums Up emerged, which grew more popular while Double Seven's market share kept declining after a popular launch. Also, the Janata Party government fell in 1980, and Indira Gandhi returned to power. Gandhi's government decided to not support a product which was named to celebrate her defeat. By the end of 1980, the Modern Food Industries, which manufactured and marketed Double Seven, had slipped into red and, due to lack of government support, decided to stop producing the drink.[25]

The story of Double Seven is a reminder that it is not always a good idea to forsake a foreign technology in favour of a domestic one. Sometimes it may be better to simply let a foreign technology thrive, since it may lead to large-scale employment and economic value and help create local industry in the long term.

Why They Succeeded Despite of Protectionism

So why is it that countries such as Korea, Japan and China thrived while closing their markets (other countries such as Hong Kong and Singapore have similar stories), but India did not. India's share of global trade dropped from 2.2 per cent in 1950 to 0.45 per cent by 1985. Average GDP growth was 3.5 per cent for three decades after Independence. This was half of what was achieved by the other discussed Asian economies.

There are several reasons. First, these countries had spent heavily into high-quality education and training to prepare a low-cost workforce which could take advantage of advanced manufacturing and other technologies. Second, these countries identified a small number of technologies where they endeavoured to become world leaders and, in most cases, succeeded. In fact, they continue to do so. Again, China presents an instructive example. China launched in 2017 a National Champions programme to support and fund private companies to become world

---

[25] Sam Dolnick, 'Waning Days of an Indian Soda Pop', *The New York Times*, 23 February 2009, https://www.nytimes.com/2009/02/23/technology/23iht-cola.1.20365713.html

leaders in AI. The current 15 champions appear to be well on way to close the technology gap with the USA by 2030. Third, they recognized that successful competition against developed nations required scale. So they actively promoted creation of conglomerates (e.g., *keiretsu*, *chaebols* and state-owned large enterprises).

In contrast, India's investment into education has been minimal, and the quality of higher education and training continues to be poor (Chapter 9). Except for space technology, India did not achieve technological leadership or parity in any area. The number of large Indian corporations and institutions (e.g., banks) remained too small to compete effectively. In fact, far from being world champions, most of these institutions harmed investors and consumers alike.

Right Approach

What is the right approach for India going forward? First, for uniquely Indian problems which need technological solutions, India must build the required technologies. Examples include low-cost pharmaceuticals and prosthesis. Then there are technologies which are strategic to own—AI, semiconductors, nuclear energy, advanced manufacturing, quantum computing, etc. India must try in earnest to build and develop those technologies in-house. For all other technologies, India must be careful about the balance between build and buy. For example, the Chinese model of cutting off access to foreign technology companies may adversely impact India's booming digital economy. Similarly, any world champions borne out of protectionism may not do well externally as they may be viewed as nationalistic entities, instead of being viewed as corporations which maximize shareholders' value. This is especially true in the enterprise software market where the buyers will be wary of buying software from protectionist regimes due to geopolitical risks. Another challenge would be that protectionism at home may trigger similar tendencies in richer markets impacting exports. India should not operate under the false assumption that domestic market is large enough to sustain homegrown businesses. India's per capita GDP is only US$2,000. China's is five times more. Also, investors may be wary of investing into a controlled market.

At the same time, India should recognize that free trade disproportionately benefits resource-rich countries (e.g., oil suppliers), countries which serve as trading hubs (e.g., Hong Kong and Luxembourg) and countries with entrenched export advantages. Therefore, free trade should not be followed as a dogma either. India's large market, low-cost plentiful labour, large environmental footprint, and existing strengths and global supply chain integration in areas such as pharmaceuticals and IT provide ample leverage to create a conducive trade environment.

THE PATH FORWARD

India's complicated relationship with technology notwithstanding, which reflects both in our technological past and the present, it can still become a center of technological innovation and technology-based prosperity. In fact, it must. One must not forget how much power technology has to transform a nation. There does not exist a better, more instructive example in history than the transformative impact of the Industrial Revolution on Great Britain.

Technology Can Indeed Change the World[1]

The first set of advances began in Britain in the early 18th century on the agricultural field. Jethro Tull invented a seed drill in 1701, which greatly improved the efficiency of planting. Other advances such as crop rotation and

---

[1] William Rosen, *The Most Powerful Idea in the World: A Story of Steam, Industry, and Invention* (Chicago, IL: University of Chicago Press, March 2012).

selection of crops to improve soil nutrient content for the next rotation significantly improved yield and income. Farmers then had more time to pursue other employment opportunities.

Textile production was mostly based on hand weaving then. Spinning was mostly done at home (and occasionally in workshops) mostly by women and some men. John Kay invented in 1733 the flying shuttle which allowed a weaver to create more cloth in the same amount of time by allowing the use of much wider fabrics. It also needed only one person to operate it as opposed to the two needed to operate a traditional loom. It, therefore, quadrupled the efficiency of weaving. In addition, it could also be connected to mechanized looms.

In 1764, James Hargreaves invented the spinning jenny (named after his daughter Jenny) which allowed one person to work on eight spools at a time (instead of working off only one ball of yarn). This increased the productivity dramatically. By the time Hargreaves died in 1778, over 20,000 spinning jennies were in use in Britain.

Richard Arkwright, a successful wigmaker, was approached by John Kay, a clockmaker, and Thomas High, an engineer, with an idea of a new spinning machine which used a set of rollers to twist fibres together to create a strong thread. Arkwright decided to finance the idea, and the spinning frame was born. The spinning frame was a huge piece of machinery and could not be hand powered. Arkwright first used horsepower and then waterpower (using a water wheel) from River Derwent to operate the spinning frame. The water-powered spinning frame (later renamed to water frame) inspired many innovators and entrepreneurs at the time.

In 1779, Samuel Crompton created the spinning mule—a combination of the spinning jenny and the water frame—which could produce soft but strong yarn, support as many as 400 spools at a time and that could be water powered and later be powered using a steam engine.

When Edmund Cartwright visited an Arkwright factory, he was impressed by the level of automation. In 1784, he invented the power loom which fully automated the entire weaving process. Humans were needed only to repair broken threads. By the middle of the 19th century, a quarter million power looms were already in use in Britain. From being an importer of textiles in the early 18th century, Britain had become a textile powerhouse with textile factories dotting the entire landscape. In fact, so common were the factories and the smog and the haze they caused due to their emissions that world's first air pollution laws, the Alkali Act of 1863, had to be instituted!

Perhaps the invention which is the most emblematic of the Industrial Revolution is the steam engine.[2] Coal had become the primary fuel of the 17th-century Britain. Large usage of coal meant that one had to dig deeper to look for coal. Deep coal mines and shafts would invariably get flooded by groundwater or rainwater, and some solution better than using buckets had to be found to get water out. An English engineer Thomas Savery had been familiar with a steam-powered pressure cooker which a French scientist Denis Panin had built. The cooker used a cylinder and a piston. Savery decided to use a similar principle to build a steam-powered engine to get water out of a mine. The engine with two steam boilers could run almost constantly—Savery referred to it in his patent as an 'engine to raise water by fire'. However, it did not have enough power to draw water from really deep. Blacksmith Thomas Newcomen improved upon Savery's design in 1711, where

---

[2] Eric Hobsbawm, *Industry and Empire: The Birth of the Industrial Revolution* (New York, NY: The New Press, September 1999).

the engine pumped steam into a cylinder, cold water then condensed the steam, which, in turn, created a vacuum strong enough to operate a piston with enough power to go much deeper than Savery's machine. This machine became very successful and started being used widely. One problem with the Newcomen machine was that it was very energy inefficient, since the cylinder had to be reheated over and over. Enter James Watt, an instrument maker at the University of Glasgow, who realized that the reheating problem could be easily solved by having a separate condenser for the steam, since the cylinder would then remain hot. Watt's modification took one-fourth the fuel of Newcome's design for the same work. He made further modifications which allowed speed control and constant load, and the piston could operate in both directions. Watt's engines soon started powering textile mills, blast furnaces and over time steam boats, train engines and airships. They really did change the world.

Iron production before the Industrial Revolution relied on the blast furnace which was slow and produced iron not strong enough for many needs. Abraham Darby demonstrated in 1709 that coal could be heated to produce coke which could then be used to smelt iron. Abraham Darby II used a steam engine to power a water wheel which then powered the making of iron. Abram Darby II built the first cast iron bridge. To improve strength, Henry Cort invented a technique to create wrought iron by frequent high heat stirring of iron.

As iron became strong and started being produced at high volume, it led to a rapid development of railways, tunnels, bridges and weapons, affecting British and world economy and geopolitics greatly. Parallel innovations in mass production of steel (e.g., Bessemerization), leading to cheap, high-quality, high-volume steel, had a similar impact on the world. Rapid machine tool inventions, for example, machines for milling, planning, shaping and boring, followed, greatly increasing worker productivity.

The Industrial Revolution also dramatically changed transportation.[3] John Madam, then the Surveyor-General of roads for the Turnpike Trusts, came up with the idea to improve roadways by using multiple layers of stones during road construction such that the top layer used much smaller stones than the bottom two layers. This method, which became popular as the McAdam method, then effectively knitted the stones together by compacting them using a heavy roller. The resulting roads, sloping slightly downwards at the sides for drainage, were much stronger and longer-lasting than previous roads and supported an explosion in the use of the roadways by horses, carriages, wagons and coaches. Of course, the most consequential transportation innovation during the Industrial Revolution was the railroad. Production of cheap and high-volume iron facilitated laying of railroads all over Great Britain. Steam-powered locomotive was invented by Richard Trevithick in 1802 who advertised it by driving it down a street. Subsequent innovations by John Blenkinsop and Matthew Murray and then by George Stephenson made the locomotive ready to be driven down railroads as a mode of mass transportation. By the middle of the 19th century, railways were a dominant mode of transportation.

The explosion of the textile, iron and other industries and the advent of the railways gave rise to the division-of-labour-based factory system, wherein men, women and children worked 6 days a week for 12–14 hours a day at

---

[3] Emma Griffin, *Liberty's Dawn: A People's History of the Industrial Revolution* (New Haven, CT: Yale University Press, August 2014).

low wages without many guards for health or safety. People started moving from farms to cities to work in a factory, often living in squalid conditions in shared living spaces, giving rise to diseases and epidemics. Reforms gradually started. Factory Acts were passed in 1833 and 1834 to improve working conditions. Poor Law created workhouses for the poor. Trade unions, Chartists and Luddites demanded better working conditions and work security. These reforms and movements ultimately formed the bedrock for modern expectations regarding labour.

Finally, the technological changes during the Industrial Revolution also led to mass production of food and manufactured goods, redistribution of political and economic power, increased international trade, wider distribution of wealth, and decline of land as source of wealth.[4]

Every time someone is sceptical of the impact technology can have in changing the face of India for the better, the above refresher should turn them into an optimist.

India as a Centre of Technological Innovation

One could overthink the question of how to make India a centre of technological innovation. The answer ultimately starts with the basics—eliminate poverty, reduce inequality and improve education.

Since poverty is a key reason behind limited innovation (Chapter 9), poverty must be targeted directly in order to increase the nation's innovation capabilities. Similarly, reducing inequality (Chapter 5) will enable broader technological opportunities.

---

[4] Gavin Weightman, *The Industrial Revolutionaries: The Making of the Modern World 1776–1914* (Greenwich Village, NY: Grove Press, May 2010).

Reducing poverty and inequality, of course, will require a multipronged sustained approach.[5]

For example, it is important to invest into labour-intensive economic sectors. Labour-saving, capital-intensive approaches may create growth but may not generate employment at the needed rate. We have seen that the rate of growth of employment has continually lagged India's GDP growth rate.

We need to improve agricultural productivity, since the poverty ratio in India has been inversely related to the growth rate in agriculture. Perhaps more importantly, improved agricultural productivity can enhance the income of small farmers and agricultural labourers. Measures may include public investment in agricultural infrastructure, low-cost credit to farmers and weather insurance. Training related to infrastructure, nutrients and production practices would also be helpful.

Targeted agricultural policies are needed to reduce inequality. Even rich farmers are excluded today from taxation. They also arrogate most of the farm subsidies. A targeted approach should ensure that farm subsidies, farm loan waivers, minimum support price (MSP), etc., are available only for the most vulnerable farmers.

Greater investment in infrastructure (e.g., transportation, housing, power and irrigation) can create both growth and employment. Availability of infrastructure can also improve labour productivity, accelerating poverty reduction.

One very effective measure for tackling poverty and inequality is investing into education and health. Educational institutions promote literacy and import skills—both increase employment opportunities and

---

5 Abhijit V. Banerjee and Esther Duflo, *Poor Economics: Rethinking Poverty and the Ways to End It* (Gurugram: Penguin Random House India, March 2013).

productivity. Investment into hospitals, dispensaries and primary health centres improves healthcare, increases productivity and generates employment.

Non-farm employment opportunities should be created in rural areas to compensate for stagnation of farm income. Examples include dairy, food processing, forestry, marketing, repairs and processing of other agricultural and animal products.

Land reforms are also essential. Excessive fragmentation of agricultural land due to rising population has made the condition of small farmers and agricultural labour untenable. Measures such as land redistribution by establishing a ceiling on landholdings, protection of tenants against eviction by establishing a minimum tenancy period and placing an upper bound on rent could help alleviate rural poverty.

Since a large fraction of a poor household's income is spent on food, one way to target poverty is by strengthening the public distribution system (PDS) which provides targeted households (e.g., those below the poverty line) food and other essential commodities at subsidized prices.

In some cases, specialized schemes such as MGNREGA, whose sole goal is employment generation, may help. The poor are provided employment to build durable assets (such as roads and school buildings) for the community. These assets can, in turn, generate sustained employment. Creative schemes may make such programmes more sustainable. For example, registered farmers may be allowed to avail of MGNREGA labour in exchange for MGNREGA minimum amount payable to the worker. Labour reforms such as minimum wages and universal basic income should be seriously considered.

India should invest in women to both improve growth and reduce inequality. A startling International Monetary

Fund (IMF) data suggests that Japan's GDP could grow at 9 per cent per annum and India's GDP could grow at 27 per cent per annum if women's participation in the economy matched men. A 2016 McKinsey report estimated what while women contributed only one-sixth to India's GDP, 700 billion dollars could be added to India's GDP in 2025 by closing the gender participation gap. To close the participation gap, both public and private sectors should support family-friendly work policies such as paid parental leave and childcare. In addition, the problem of low asset ownership by women should be addressed. For example, one survey estimated that women own less than 2 per cent of India's farmland. This is not a surprise considering the historical and prevalent patriarchy. To reverse this trend, tax rebates can be given in certain labour-intensive sectors such as textiles and food processing based on female asset ownership. Similarly, women participation in the management structure should be incentivized.

Finally, India should strive for growth to eliminate poverty and inequality. Growth often creates employment opportunities, increases wages due to improved productivity, and reduces prices leading to increased savings. The rich who benefit first from growth spend their money, which increases employment and income for the poor. Growth also increases revenue of the government, which can then invest this money into infrastructure and human resource development and direct poverty reduction schemes.

How Can India Improve Education?

Education is also a key factor in enabling technological innovation (Chapter 9). How can India improve education?[6]

---

[6] Cathy N. Davidson, *The New Education: How to Revolutionize the University to Prepare Students for a World in Flux* (New York, NY: Basic Books, September 2017).

The public education system should be made more accountable There are public schools in different parts of the country where not a single student passes their Class X board examination! There are many public schools where a single student achieves distinction in the board examination and many more where less than half of the students clear the examination. These schools must be called upon to account for their poor performance, in absence of which teachers' effort at educating children will remain a choice rather than a responsibility. Teachers and principals should be required to undergo periodic, ideally specialized and individualized, training programmes and clear tests to retain eligibility. Autonomy should be given to teachers, principals, block officers, etc., to adapt education to the local context.

Privatization of schools may allow market forces to improve educational quality, enhance scale and increase cost effectiveness. A public–private collaboration model may also be considered, similar to Charter schools in many Western nations, where a school is funded by the government but run by private bodies. This creates accountability. Another option is to require quality-assurance mechanisms on government-backed loans to private schools. This could help ensure quality. Yet another option would be to rationalize fee structure such that well-to-do pay more than the disadvantaged.

One of the reasons for the large dropout rate at the secondary level is the inability of the high school graduates to find jobs. Greater introduction and emphasis on vocational subjects at the high school level can improve job prospects and encourage retention. In general, technical and vocational education and training should be expanded—this improves employability. Some laws may be needed to guarantee equal access to technical education to all disadvantaged groups, including women who often fall behind due to societal attitudes and lack of family and childcare support.

Affirmative action should continue and be applied aggressively. Data shows that it does increase enrolment from the targeted disadvantaged groups. However, it also displaces students from non-targeted disadvantaged groups. The target set should be made more comprehensive or tweaked to include all disadvantaged groups.

Like many similar countries, India supports public-funded universities where no tuition is charged. However, access to these universities is restricted due to limited budgets. Cost-sharing strategies should be explored where the students are required to bear a portion of their education expenses while coupling it with a strengthened educational loan infrastructure (e.g., by supporting a strong debt refinance market). This will allow the government to widen access to higher education.

It would be useful to conduct regular assessments to measure progress and bring visibility to the state of education. Regular participation in international assessments (e.g., Trends in International Mathematics and Science Study and Program for International Student Assessment) will allow benchmarking and facilitate goal setting. Improvement in domestic assessment infrastructure will allow better tracking of progress of individual students and teachers. Tests should be made multidimensional to promote overall development and well-being and encourage learning rather than reproduction.

Use of technology in education should be encouraged. Specific focus areas could include intelligent software tools and applications to teach, hone and remediate reading and math skills, creation of multilingual content and Internet access to enable online education.

Awareness of the 'concrete' value of education should be made widespread through public education campaigns targeting potential teachers (to enable high-quality recruitment), existing teachers (to help them better appreciate their value), parents (to motivate them to support their child's education and help them choose school) and students (to improve retention).

Higher education system, especially in technology areas, needs particular rethinking to improve quality and sustainability.[7]

For example, the value of a technical college education should be maximized to encourage enrolment and retention. India's higher education system has largely remained the same since Independence. Innovations should be encouraged to increase the college premium—the short-term and long-term economic value of attending college.

One area of improvement is increased emphasis on team-based experiences. The unique opportunity that universities provide is that they allow in-person interaction and engagement with peers. This opportunity can be leveraged to promote team-based learning and evaluation.

Another area of improvement is increased focus on hands-on, project-based learning. There is still no true replacement for an in-school, hands-on, project-based experience in spite of considerable advances in digital twin technologies and remote learning. The new and emerging educational resources, such as online and software tools and apprenticeships, can be used to supplement these in-school, hands-on, project-based experiences. These emerging alternate higher education channels, therefore, become allies rather than threats.

---

[7] Ibid.

Universities should also consider loosening the structure of modern degree programmes. India's colleges largely operate in terms of fixed-credit courses, fixed-course-list majors and fixed-length semesters. However, fixed-length and fixed-credit courses and rigid majors do not recognize the wide diversity in student needs, especially in a country like India where differences in socio-economic status and background are large. Eliminating these barriers and focusing instead on tracking progress through outcome-based assessment will accommodate the diverse needs of students better. It will also arguably leave students better prepared for innovation and the job market, since the students would graduate only when certain learning outcomes have been met.

Another suggestion is to cleanly compartmentalize teaching and research. It is fashionable today to advocate for a tight coupling between research and teaching. In fact, it did make sense historically, since access to robust academic knowledge was scarce. However, it is unclear if the same model works well today. Using the same resources (e.g., teachers and professors) today to target both teaching and research may adversely impact both; for example, a great teacher may be a lousy researcher, while a fantastic researcher may have no interest in teaching. Creating research-focused academic institutions[8] may allow them to become world-class if they are not distracted by the requirement to teach and manage students at scale. At the same time, large public universities with strong linkages to industry can impart cutting-edge, high-quality education.

Technology universities must also be encouraged to experiment with new, innovative business models to

---

[8] Clayton M. Christensen and Henry J. Eyring, *The Innovative University: Changing the DNA of Higher Education from the Inside Out* (San Francisco, CA: Jossey-Bass, July 2011).

enhance their sustainability and scale. An example to consider is supporting lifelong learning. Since skills needed in the job market continually shift, universities can sign long-term agreements with students to retrain their graduates on demand in return for a retainer or a recurring fee. Another out-of-box model charges students upon exiting their educational programme, not on entry as it is done today. This encourages accountability. Yet another interesting model, for some technology universities, could be to target only adult and professional learners. Such universities may not need to subsidize education for such learners, allowing them to truly specialize themselves into world-class institutions.

Data-driven and timely interventions can also help with enrolment and retention as well as fundraising. Some potential retention issues can be addressed proactively. For example, selective microgrants can be used to ease the financial struggles for at-risk students. Similarly, the most effective teachers should be cultivated. It may pay dividends in the long term, since studies suggest that the most common reason for donation from alumni is some inspirational teacher who deeply impacted their life.

India's higher education system should become the fountainhead of Indian innovation going forward. While university administrators routinely look for government for solutions, the responsibility should be increasingly placed on the college systems themselves to innovate to sustain themselves and thrive.

On the Policy Front

While reducing poverty and inequality and improving education are key to unlocking technology-based prosperity, the government's role in directly promoting technological innovation should also be clearly defined. For example, considering that resources are scarce, a hard look is needed at how India allocates public funding for science and technology.

A common complaint is that a key cause of India's laggard performance in science and technology is the limited funding for science and technology research. India allocates no more than 0.6 per cent of its GDP to R&D funding, while comparable numbers for China and the USA are 2.1 per cent and 2.8 per cent, respectively. An assumption made in this lament is that increased research funding will lead to increased economic activity, increased innovation, and enhanced prestige and problem-solving capacity.

However, is this assumption correct?

How Much Benefit Does Government Funding for R&D Directly Deliver?

From launching Aryabhata, India's first satellite, to the SITE satellite TV-based mass education, from Bhaskara, India's first remote-sensing satellite, to world-class GSLV rockets, from Chandrayaan-1, India's first mission to moon, to Mangalyaan, India's first mission to Mars, India's achievements in space and rocketry have been exemplary. However, the concrete impressive outcomes from government research funding have been much more sparing in other fields. For example, while India can claim a sharp increase in the number of papers and patents over the last few years, it is unclear if any modern technological break-through has come out of India, let alone government R&D funding being responsible for it. Similarly, it is unclear if government R&D funding has had any industrial impact. One is hard-pressed to name a commercial Indian product which came out directly as a result of government R&D funding. While entrepreneurship is exploding in India (there are close to 70 unicorns in India at the time of writing—start-up companies with over 1-billion-dollar valuation), again, it is difficult to trace any start-up's origin directly to government-funded research. There also does not appear to be any correlation between India's economic growth rate and increases in governmental research funding. So it is also unclear if government research funding has given a fillip to economic activity. India's science and technology capability has obviously increased over time— one only has to look at the nature and sophistication of science and technology projects being executed routinely— however, this capability may be attributable to better education and training, not to an increased governmental investment into science and technology research. Moreover, a large fraction of these projects rely on imported core technologies in spite of massive government R&D funding. Even projects often touted as indigenous rely heavily on technologies developed elsewhere. For example, India's Light Combat Aircraft, Tejas, marketed often as an indigenous aircraft, has less than 60 per cent of its components (by value) developed in India.

It is not clear if government R&D funding has ever been directly effective at spurring economic activity anywhere in the world.[9] There was a fascinating study done by the Organisation for Economic Co-operation and Development (OECD), where they attempted to understand the different factors which spur economic activity in a nation. They studied the impact of such factors as 'new technology and

---

[9] Terence Kealey, 'The Case against Public Science', *Cato Unbound* (August 2013), https://www.cato-unbound.org/2013/08/05/terence-kealey/case-against-public-science#:~:text=For%20libertarians%2C%20economic%20growth%20is,is%20the%20gift%20of%20government

R&D, macroeconomic policy, education and training, labour market flexibility, product market competition, and barriers to business start-up and closure' between 1977 and 1998. Going in, the expectation was that public-funded research would show as being a strong contributor to economic activity. However, the result of the study surprised everybody. They found that publicly funded research had no impact on economic activity for *any* OECD country—all economy-stimulating innovation arose from private investment! Interestingly, the history of science in the 19th and 20th centuries hinted at this data all along. Britain and the USA contributed greatly to science during that time with negligible public funding, while France and Germany had no better contributions in spite of heavily funding research using public money. Britain and the USA did fund science and technology heavily after the Second World War. But there is no evidence of increased economic growth, directly attributable to increased public funding.

There have been several studies which do argue the opposite – that public R&D funding can indeed spur economic activity.[10] Irrespective of where the truth lies, it is clear that we cannot attribute any significant number of economy-stimulating technology breakthroughs in India to government-funded research.

There are two key reasons why government R&D funding has been ineffective in the Indian context (Chapter 9).

First, as an underdeveloped country, indirect factors prevent both technology development and economic growth. For example, poor infrastructure, education and health limit broader engagement in R&D. Similarly, weak

---

[10] Mariana Mazzucato, *The Entrepreneurial State: Debunking Public vs. Private Sector Myths* (New York, NY: Anthem Press, June 2013).

protection of intellectual property rights discourages risk-taking. Another reason is that researchers and innovators cannot be trained, mentored and supported at scale due to the nascent innovation ecosystems.

Second, research funds are mostly allocated ineffectively. Countries, including India, increasingly allocate their research funds to applied science and technology rather than funding basic research. The underlying assumption is that applied research could lead to technologies which could be commercialized, spurring economic activity which could, in turn, both justify the funding and benefit the nation. However, there is scarce evidence that a government can predict what technology would be commercially successful. In fact, emerging wisdom is that technology evolves at a pace which cannot be sped up or slowed down through external intervention, let alone by a government.[11] For example, at least 23 people had some version of the incandescent bulb invented before Edison. The test tube baby created by the Indian physician Subhash Mukhopadhyay was born only 67 days after the world's first test tube baby was created by British physicians Robert Edwards, Patrick Steptoe and Jean Purdy. The patent for telephone was filed by two different people—Elisha Gray and Alexander Graham Bell—*on the same day*. There are multiple independent inventors credited for the invention of thermometer, vaccination, telegraph, photography, hypodermic needle, electric railroad and the steamboat.[12] Historian Alfred Kroeber had observed that the history of inventions is 'one endless chain of parallel instances'. Once technology is viewed as an autonomous, evolving entity

---

[11] Steven Johnson, *Where Good Ideas Come From: The Natural History of Innovation* (New York, NY: Riverhead Books, October 2011).

[12] Rebecca Stott, *Darwin's Ghosts: The Secret History of Evolution* (New York, NY: Random House, March 2013).

which cannot be made to commercially succeed through external stimuli, one realizes that applied science and technology should be the last thing a government should fund. Public funding of presupposed likely-winning technologies also means that it crowds out research in other technologies (since researchers get drawn to the technology areas with funding). It also crowds out any private commercial or philanthropic funding which other technologies could have received.

Since there is little evidence that allocation of government R&D funds impacts whether an emerging technology would be commercially successful, any monetary investment to drive a new technology to market adoption would be ineffective.

Better and Concrete Outcomes Necessary to Justify Increasing Government Funding

The following factors should be considered.

First, the government should primarily focus on funding basic research, but not perhaps for the reason one would imagine. Many argue that it should be because it is basic research that leads to innovative technologies. However, it is not clear if this is often true. Radios were invented before communication theory developed. Computers were invented before computer science developed. Telescopes were invented before the science of optics developed. Astronomy evolved in the age of the explorers. Steam engines contributed more to development of thermodynamics than thermodynamics helping the engines become more efficient. Even today, machine learning as a research field is taking off after some models were demonstrated to be successful.

However, there is still an argument for public funding of basic research, since the gestation period for any technology which is typically borne out of basic research is long.[13] Industry may not have patience for a long-term payoff and, therefore, only government funding can sustain such research.[14] Even in the case of payoffs, it is not clear if the original funder gets rewarded. Transistor was invented at Bell Labs, but other companies such as Intel and AMD profited the most. Modern graphical user interface was invented at Xerox PARC, but billions were made by other companies such as Apple and Microsoft. IBM incubated research on magnetoresistance, but most resulting hard drives were subsequently sold by Western Digital and Seagate. This makes the industry hesitant to fund basic research even if the payoffs are clear. Finally, much of basic research may not have much of a payoff at all besides enhancing human understanding. Again, the industry may balk, and only public funding can sustain such research.

Second, the government should consider funding a select number of moon shots or prestige projects. Such projects enhance pride and national identity.

The Laser Interferometer Gravitational-Wave Observatory (LIGO) is a large-scale physics experiment to directly detect cosmic gravitational waves. First predicted by Einstein's general theory of relativity in 1916, gravitational waves can be used to detect cosmic events such as supernova explosions, collisions or coalescence of neutron stars and black holes, or possibly even birth of the universe. Two large observatories have already been built in the USA. The third LIGO observatory is being planned to

---

[13] William H. Janeway, *Doing Capitalism in the Innovation Economy: Reconfiguring the Three-player Game between Markets, Speculators and the State* (Cambridge: Cambridge University Press, May 2018).

[14] Naomi R. Lamoreaux and Kenneth L. Sokoloff, *Financing Innovation in the United States, 1870 to Present* (Cambridge, MA: The MIT Press, August 2009).

be built in India as a collaboration between the LIGO Laboratory (operated by Caltech and MIT) and three institutes in India: the Raja Ramanna Centre for Advanced Technology (RRCAT, in Indore), the Institute for Plasma Research (IPR in Ahmedabad) and the Inter-University Centre for Astronomy and Astrophysics (IUCAA, in Pune). Adding more detectors improves the 'ability to locate sources, test theories of gravity, space, and time, and provide important clues to puzzles in astrophysics and cosmology'. The project, often referred to as LIGO-India, is one of humankind's most sophisticated and collaborative scientific projects.[15] India's participation adds to its prestige and knowhow. Any success at detecting new cosmic events will be a source of immense national pride. As such, projects such as LIGO-India are worthy of public support.

India declared in 2017 its intention to send humans to space by 2022. The ISRO announced that it will send three astronauts into space for seven days using Gaganyaan, an indigenously developed crewed orbital spacecraft, as a part of India's first human space flight. The capsule will orbit the earth at a 400 km altitude. In that process, India may become one of the four–five countries to have an independent manned spaceflight programme. India's Gaganyaan will join Chandrayaan-1, India's first lunar probe launched in 2008, and Mangalyaan, the Mars Orbiter Mission project, launched in 2014 as flagbearers of India's leadership in space. India's space programme unites India in its pride and is an envy of the world. Just for that reason alone, human spaceflight programme is worthy of continued public support.

---

[15] Harry Collins, *Gravity's Kiss: The Detection of Gravitational Waves* (Cambridge, MA: The MIT Press, January 2017).

In general, any cost-effective and peaceful instrument which enhances identity and pride is valuable for a diverse country like India with a large number of disuniting contradictions and should be publicly supported.

Moon shots also often lead to development of intermediate technologies which can have applications in other settings. Consider ISRO, for example. It developed an artificial polyurethane foot using the same material used in its rockets. After extensive tests at the Government Medical College, Thiruvananthapuram, the technology was transferred for free to the BMVSS of the Jaipur foot fame. The new Jaipur foot weighed only 500 g. Similarly, ISRO developed ISROSIL, a cloth containing 98 per cent silicon dioxide as a nozzle liner reinforcement material for its vehicles. Subsequently, ISROSIL was trademarked by ISRO and is now used as a thermal blanket for furnaces, seals, gaskets and pipes in various industries. As another example, ISRO developed several fire-extinguishing powders for safety during rocket launches and other high-risk environments. At least two ISRO-patented powders—ternary eutectic chloride (TEC) for metal fires and OLFEX for flammable gas and liquid fires—are now in the market and are used in industry and government departments.

If applied research must be funded, the government should consider specifying only desired research outcomes, not approaches. For example, if the goal is to digitize land records in a way that these records can be tamper proof and publicly accessible, this goal should be specified as the desired outcome of research funding. A specific approach (e.g., blockchain) to achieve the goal should not be mandated or desired. This flexibility will allow market forces to determine the best approach. This will also prevent crowding out of all, but one, technologies to address the same problem. This market-driven approach to technology development may increase the rate of commercialization of funded research, making it more palatable to publicly fund R&D in future.

A Market-driven Approach to Funding Also Prevents Expensive Mistakes

The list of expensive government science and technology projects that did not go anywhere is long.

Enamoured by nuclear power, US President Richard Nixon authorized in 1971 construction of an experimental nuclear power plant, the Clinch River Breeder Reactor, which would produce both nuclear power and plutonium to power other nuclear reactors. The Atomic Energy Commission estimated that it would cost 400 million dollars. Private utilities agreed to pitch in 175 million dollars. So the government was to provide over 225 million dollars of funding. However, initial estimates were wrong. Costs ballooned, but the government continued to pay for the overruns. When Ronald Reagan came to power in 1981, he considered killing the project. However, then Senate Majority Leader Howard Baker successfully lobbied to save the project—the project was in his home state of Tennessee. However, the death knell was sounded in 1983 when the Congressional Budget Office estimated the overall cost to be 4 billion dollars, 10 times larger than the original estimate. The project was killed before the actual construction began (even though components had been ordered). The government had already spent 1.7 billion dollars by then (4 billion dollars in today's money).[16]

---

[16] James Mahaffey, *Atomic Awakening: A New Look at the History and Future of Nuclear Power* (New York, NY: Pegasus Books, June 2009).

When Jimmy Carter came to power in 1977, energy security weighed on his mind. He worked with Congress to allocate 17 billion dollars to set up Synthetic Fuels Corporation, an investment bank-like vehicle which would fund projects which turned coal and shale which the USA had a lot of into oil and gas. The vision was that this would secure energy independence; the goal was to produce two million barrels a day of synthetic fuels by 1990.

The project had a decent start. Several auto and coal manufacturers banded together to use the funds to build a large synthetic oil production facility. However, oil prices started tapering and then falling around the same time. This made the project uneconomical in spite of government funding, and the private entities abandoned the project. Congress forced the corporation's president out in 1983 on corruption charges, and the corporation shut down in 1986 after spending two billion dollars of government money (more than four billion dollars in today's value).[17]

George W. Bush similarly poured 1.2 billion dollars into hydrogen-powered vehicles. The project went nowhere.[18] Almost a billion dollars have been spent on 'clean coal' projects without much success. Obama provided more than half a billion-dollar guaranteed load to Solyndra, a solar-panel maker, which then promptly went bankrupt.

India's own nuclear programme has been a colossal public money sink by many measures (Chapter 8)

Focus More on Facilitation Than Funding

In general, the government's focus should be more on facilitation than funding. For example, markers for health,

---

[17] Ralph L. Bayrer, *The Saga of the U.S. Synthetic Fuels Corporation: A Cautionary Tale* (Washington, DC: Vellum, October 2011).

[18] Joseph J. Romm, *The Hype about Hydrogen: Fact and Fiction in the Race to Save the Climate* (Island Press, April 2013).

education and infrastructure need to be improved; entrepreneurship needs to be encouraged as well as taught as a skill; intellectual property rights which are fairly weak in India need to be strengthened. The private sector needs to be incentivized to take risks and invest more into R&D. Only a third of the overall research investment in India is private. Over two-thirds of R&D investment in the USA is private. In China, the private sector accounts for almost nine-tenths of the overall R&D investment.

In today's connected and hypercompetitive technological world, not much economic or strategic value is accrued by those who are also-rans; it is mostly winners who take all. Therefore, one goal for R&D funding should be to create world leaders in a small number of areas, instead of dispersing resources widely. Other than some strategic areas which must be funded, focus should be on achieving technological superiority or parity in the chosen areas. This would also be a necessity, since the costs of developing new science and technology are high—large and sustained investment would be needed. Since it may be difficult, expensive and time-consuming to build strengths from the ground up, preference should be given to areas where India already has existing strengths or built-in advantages. For example, considering India's strengths in space, it could aspire to be a leader in commercial space aviation. Similarly, considering India's strengths in data-driven technologies and IT systems and its large population producing digital data, it could aspire to be a leader in AI and Internet-of-things-based software technologies.

In terms of mechanisms for funding, US Defense Advanced Research Projects Agency (DARPA) program or China's 863 programme should be held as inspiration.

By many measures, the US DARPA has the longest track record of sustained radical innovation in the history,[19] which has produced world-changing technologies and multi-billion-dollar industries such as the Internet, global positioning system (GPS), RISC computing, stealth technology, unmanned aerial vehicles or 'drones', and micro-electro-mechanical systems, while being a tiny and nimble organization with a modest budget. To run its programmes which last only three–five years, it recruits about 100 programme managers and contract performers to work on carefully chosen, fixed-duration, use-driven ambitious basic research projects. Both the fixed-term programme managers and the contractors are world-class experts from academia and industry. Most importantly, DARPA has autonomy in selection and execution of projects, which allows it to move swiftly, take bold risks and recruit the best.

Funding should not be a one-way street. Outcomes should be measured periodically through careful and periodic evaluation. Unless outcomes are measured, there may be lack of accountability and adaptation on part of both the funders and the performers. India cannot afford the luxury of funding without evaluation of outcomes.

To summarize, government-funded research has had a mixed record, particularly when compared against private investment, especially in terms of stimulating innovation and economy per rupee/dollar invested. This has been true in India as well as internationally. However, there is a continued case of public investment in science and technology as long as it is done with clarity. Potential payoffs may be an enhancement of national problem-solving capacity,

---

[19] Sharon Weinberger, *The Imagineers of War: The Untold Story of DARPA, the Pentagon Agency That Changed the World* (New York, NY: Alfred A. Knopf, March 2017).

occasional commercialization or simply national pride. At the same time, funding decisions as well as mechanisms should be data-driven and return-oriented to ensure effective use of public's hard-earned money.

Change in Cultural Mindset

Beyond policies, a cultural mindset change is also needed. Old customs and rituals emphasize *santosha* (equanimity), instead of ambition and restlessness. India needs to become a greedier, more restless nation.

Steve Jobs's 'Stay Hungry, Stay Foolish' mantra applies even at the national scale. This applies to both the government and the people, since restlessness is key to innovation. Brad Bird, a director at Pixar who is behind some of the most iconic animation movies, often talks about *relentless restlessness*: 'that often uncomfortable urge for constant innovation, driven by the nagging feeling that things are never quite good enough'.[20] Joseph Schumpeter of the creative destruction fame routinely attributed creative innovations and entrepreneurship not only to the potential of reaping economic rewards but also to the ability and desire of potential entrepreneurs and innovators to move away from the status quo. Facebook's motto of 'Move Fast and Break Things' is indeed a good recipe for innovation.

Restlessness Is Also Key to Technological Survival

Nine out of ten companies which were on the Fortune 500 list in 1955 are no longer on the list. These companies

---

[20] George Couros, *The Innovator's Mindset: Empower Learning, Unleash Talent, and Lead a Culture of Creativity* (San Diego, CA: Dave Burgess Consulting, October 2015).

went bankrupt, got acquired or simply fell off the perch, as other newer, more innovative, more restless companies took over.[21]

There are several examples of spectacular failures caused due to a company resting on its laurels.

Founded in 1985, Blockbuster was a home movie and video game rental company which was an unquestioned leader in its space. At one point, it had over 84,000 employees and over 9,000 stores worldwide. It did not recognize, however, the impending digital entertainment boom. In 2000, it declined a 50-million-dollar offer to buy the upstart Netflix, since it thought that online entertainment was a niche business. Sitting pat, it missed the rapid growth of online entertainment, which ended up eating into its business. Blockbuster filed for bankruptcy in 2010.[22]

Founded in 1937, Polaroid was synonymous with instant film and cameras. It could not anticipate the impact digital cameras would have on its business and neglected where the market was going. It had to file for bankruptcy in 2001.[23]

Kodak was world's biggest film company. However, it decided against developing digital camera, since it feared that digital cameras would cannibalize its business. Of course, digital cameras boomed, making Kodak's core film business obsolete. Kodak filed for bankruptcy in 2012.[24]

Borders sold books and music through its worldwide chain of stores. It could not anticipate either online

---

[21] Tim Phillips, *Fit to Bust: How Great Companies Fail* (London: Kogan Page, April 2011).

[22] Alan Payne, *Built to Fail: The Inside Story of Blockbuster's Inevitable Bust* (Muskego, WI: Lioncrest Publishing, March 2021).

[23] Christopher Bonanos, *Instant: The Story of Polaroid* (New York, NY: Princeton Architectural Press, September 2012).

[24] Douglas Collins, *The Story of Kodak* (New York, NY: Harry N. Abrams, October 1990).

bookselling or e-reading. It had to ultimately close all its retail stores and sell off its customer loyalty list to Barnes & Noble for less than 14 million dollars.[25]

As India keeps opening up and as protectionist barriers are brought down, several of India's companies are likely going to meet the same fate unless they display greater restlessness and penchant for innovation. Even as a country, India will keep being mired in mediocrity unless it sheds complacency and acts restlessly. It needs to make bold bets and take pragmatic risks. It needs to recognize its imperfections and weakness and work on them.

As Benjamin Mays said, 'The tragedy of life is often not in our failure, but rather in our complacency; not in our doing too much, but rather in our doing too little; not in our living above our ability, but rather in our living below our capacities.'

---

[25] Shira Ovide, 'Bookstore Chain Borders Is Dead', *The Wall Street Journal* (18 July 2011), https://www.wsj.com/articles/BL-DLB-34047

BIBLIOGRAPHY

Chapter 1: The Perfect Scapegoat

Howard, Philip. *Lie Machines: How to Save Democracy from Troll Armies, Deceitful Robots, Junk News Operations, and Political Operatives.* New Haven, CT: Yale University Press, May 2020.

Pomerantsev, Peter. *This Is Not Propaganda.* London: Faber and Faber, July 2019.

Rid, Thomas. *Active Measures: The Secret History of Disinformation and Political Warfare.* New York, NY: Farrar, Straus and Giroux, April 2020.

Sinha, Pratik, Sumaiya Shaikh, and Arjun Sidharth. *India Misinformed: The True Story.* Noida: HarperCollins India, April 2019.

Woolley, Samuel. *The Reality Game: How the Next Wave of Technology Will Break the Truth.* New York, NY: PublicAffairs, January 2020.

Chapter 2: The Delusion of Grandeur

Abbott, Elizabeth. *Sugar: A Bittersweet History.* London: Duckworth Books, October 2009.

Figiel, Leo. *On Damascus Steel.* Woonsocket, RI: Andrew Mowbray Publishers, December 1991.

Harari, Yuval Noah. *Homo Deus: A Brief History of Tomorrow.* Manhattan, NY: Harper, February 2017.

Kelly, Kevin. *The Inevitable: Understanding the 12 Technological Forces That Will Shape Our Future.* London: Penguin Books, June 2017.

Lipson, Hod, and Melba Kurman. *Driverless: Intelligent Cars and the Road Ahead.* Cambridge, MA: The MIT Press, September 2016.

Radjou, Navi, and Jaideep Prabhu. *Frugal Innovation: How To Do More with Less.* Paris: Hachette, 2015.

Reiffel, Eleanor, and Wolfgang Polak. *Quantum Computing: A Gentle Introduction.* Cambridge, MA: The MIT Press, August 2014.

Taplin, Ruth. *Innovation, Investment and Intellectual Property in South Korea: Park to Park.* New York, NY: Routledge, March 2020.

Taulli, Tom. *Artificial Intelligence Basics: A Non-technical Introduction.* New York, NY: Apress, August 2019.

West, Darrell M. *The Future of Work: Robots, AI, and Automation.* Washington, DC: Brookings Institution Press, May 2018.

Chapter 3: The Faith Paradox

Bell, Charlotte. *Mindful Yoga, Mindful Life: A Guide for Everyday Practice.* Berkeley, CA: Rodmell Press, February 2005.

D'Souza, Dilip. *Narmada Dammed: An Inquiry into the Politics of Development.* New Delhi: Penguin Books, January 2002.

Hawk, Kyczy. *Santosha/Contentment How Gratitude and Acceptance Can Bring Contentment.* Los Gatos, CA: Smashwords, June 2014.

Iyer, Lakshmi, Laura Alfaro, and Namrata Arora. 'Tata Motors in Singur: Public Purpose and Private Property'. *Harvard Business Review* (11 February 2009). https://www.hbs.edu/faculty/Pages/item.aspx?num=36940

Major, Andrea. *Sati: A Historical Anthology.* Oxford: Oxford University Press, February 2007.

Roy, Tirthankar. *The Economic History of India, 1857–1947.* New Delhi: Oxford University Press, September 2011.

Roy, Tirthankar. *An Economic History of India 1707–1857.* New York, NY: Routledge, September 2021.

Satchidananda, Sri Swami. *The Yoga Sutras of Patanjali.* Buckingham, VA: Integral Yoga Publications, September 2012.

Swenson, Richard. *Contentment: The Secret to a Lasting Calm.* Colorado Springs, CO: NavPress, June 2013.

Thurston, Edgar. *Omens and Superstitions of Southern India.* Scotts Valley, CA: CreateSpace, February 2015.

Weber, Thomas. *Hugging the Trees: The Story of the Chipko Movement.* London: Penguin Books, June 1990.

Chapter 4: The Misguided Utopianism

Astill, James. *The Great Tamasha: Cricket, Corruption, and the Turbulent Rise of Modern India.* New York, NY: Bloomsbury USA, July 2013.

Marsten, R. B. 'ATS-6 Significance'. *IEEE Transactions on Aerospace and Electronics Systems* AES-11, no. 6 (November 1975): 984–993.

Chapter 5: The Unequal Opportunity

Azad, Rajiv. *Gender Discrimination: An Indian Perspective.* London: Atlantic, January 2014.

Dutt, Yasicha. *Coming Out as a Dalit.* New Delhi: Aleph, February 2019.

Kaur, Harmeet. 'Even in the US, South Asians Say Caste Has Proved Hard to Escape'. CNN (8 September 2020). https://edition.cnn.com/2020/09/04/us/caste-discrimination-us-trnd/index.html

Wadhwa, Vivek. *The Immigrant Exodus: Why America Is Losing the Global Race to Capture Entrepreneurial Talent.* Philadelphia, PA: Wharton School Press, October 2012.

Chapter 6: The Legitimate Fear

Aly, Anne, Stuart Macdonald, Lee Jarvis, and Thomas Chen. *Violent Extremism Online: New Perspectives on Terrorism and the Internet.* New York, NY: Routledge, February 2018.

Beckert, Sven. *Empire of Cotton: A Global History.* New York, NY: Vintage Books, November 2015.

Bracegirdle, R. *William Lee and the Stocking Frame.* Leicester: Leics Museums, December 1979.

Diamond, Jared. *Collapse: How Societies Choose to Fail or Succeed.* London: Penguin Books, January 2011.

Erickson, Jon. *Hacking: The Art of Exploitation.* San Francisco, CA: No Starch Press, February 2008.

Frey, Carl Benedikt. *The Technology Trap: Capital, Labor, and Power in the Age of Automation* Princeton, NJ: Princeton University Press, June 2019.

Fry, Hannah. *Hello World: How To Be Human in the Age of the Machine.* London: Transworld Digital, September 2018.

Gans, Joshua, and Andrew Leigh. *Innovation + Equality: How to Create a Future That Is More Star Trek Than Terminator.* Cambridge, MA: The MIT Press, October 2019.

Greene, Daniel. *The Promise of Access: Technology, Inequality, and the Political Economy of Hope.* Cambridge, MA: The MIT Press, April 2021.

Hansson, Sven Ove. *The Ethics of Technology: Methods and Approaches.* Lanham, MD: Rowman & Littlefield Publishers, March 2017.

Holland, Michael. *Swing Unmasked: The Agricultural Riots of 1830 to 1832 and Their Wider Implications.* Newcastle upon Tyne, UK: FACHRS Publications, December 2004.

Jones, Steven E. *Against Technology: From the Luddites to Neo-Luddism.* New York, NY: Routledge, April 2006.

Kaplan, Jerry. *Humans Need Not Apply: A Guide to Wealth & Work in the Age of Artificial Intelligence* New Haven, CT: Yale University Press, August 2015.

Klein, Naomi. *This Changes Everything: Capitalism vs. the Climate.* New York, NY: Simon & Schuster, August 2015.

Kolbert, Elizabeth. *Under a White Sky: The Nature of the Future.* New York, NY: Crown, February 2021.

Marantz, Andrew. *Antisocial: Online Extremists, Techno-Utopians, and the Hijacking of the American Conversation.* New Delhi: Viking, October 2019.

Millington, John T., and Stanley Chapman. *Four Centuries of Machine Knitting: Commemorating William Lee's Invention of the Stocking Frame in 1589.* Leicester: Knitting International, January 1989.

Mitnick, Kevin. *The Art of Invisibility: The World's Most Famous Hacker Teaches You How To Be Safe in the Age of Big Brother and Big Data.* Boston, MA: Little, Brown and Company, February 2017.

Noble, Safiya Umoja. *Algorithms of Oppression: How Search Engines Reinforce Racism.* New York, NY: New York University Press, February 2018.

O'Harney, Andy. *Automation and Job Creation.* Richmond, VI: International Policy Digest, 2 August 2018.

Oppenheimer, Andres. *The Robots Are Coming! The Future of Jobs in the Age of Automation.* New York, NY: Vintage Books, April 2019.

Reese, Byron. *The Fourth Age: Smart Robots, Conscious Computers, and the Future of Humanity.* New York, NY: Atria Books, April 2018.

Ross, Alec. *The Industries of the Future.* New York, NY: Simon & Schuster, February 2016.

Schneier, Bruce. *Data and Goliath: The Hidden Battles to Collect Your Data and Control Your World.* New York, NY: W. W. Norton & Company, March 2015.

Van Norman, Brian. *Against the Machine: Luddites.* Montreal: Guernica Editions, April 2020.

Wallach, Wendell, and Colin Allen. *Moral Machines: Teaching Robots Right from Wrong.* Oxford: Oxford University Press, June 2010.

Chapter 7: The Motive to Succeed

Barker, Juliet. *Agincourt.* Paris: Back Bay Books, August 2007.

Bradford, Travis. *Solar Revolution: The Economic Transformation of the Global Energy Industry.* Cambridge, MA: The MIT Press, July 2006.

Budiansky, Stephen. *Battle of Wits: The Complete Story of Codebreaking in World War II.* New York, NY: Free Press, January 2002.

Deighton, Len. *Blitzkrieg: From the Rise of Hitler to the Fall of Dunkirk.* Glasgow: William Collins, December 2014.

Kumar, Alok. *Electricity Sector in India: Policy and Regulation.* New Delhi: Oxford University Press, November 2012.

Pillalamarri, Akhilesh. '3 Problems with War and Strategy in Medieval India'. *The Diplomat* (27 August 2016). https://thediplomat.com/ 2016/08/3-problems-with-war-and-strategy-in-medieval-india/

Rust, Nancy, and Carol Stubbs. *Andrew Higgins and the Boats That Landed Victory in World War II.* New Orleans, LA: Pelican Publishing, May 2020.

Sebag-Montefiore, Hugh. *Enigma: The Battle for the Code.* Hoboken, NJ: Wiley, February 2004.

Smil, Vaclav. *Energy and Civilization: A History.* Cambridge, MA: The MIT Press, November 2018.

Strahan, Jerry E. *Andrew Jackson Higgins and the Boats That Won World War II*. Baton Rouge, LA: Louisiana State University Press, October 1998.

Zetter, Kim. *Countdown to Zero Day: Stuxnet and the Launch of the World's First Digital Weapon*. New York, NY: Crown, September 2015.

Chapter 8: The Cavalier Attitude

Bassett, Ross. *The Technological Indian*. Cambridge, MA: Harvard University Press, February 2016.Gupta, Uma Das. *Science and Modern India*. Noida: Pearson India, June 2010.

Heeks, Richard. *India's Software Industry: State Policy, Liberalisation, and Industrial Development*. London: SAGE Publications, 1996.

Khanna, Tarun, and Krishna Palepu. 'The Evolution of Concentrated Ownership in India: Broad Patterns and a History of the Indian Software Industry'. In *A History of Corporate Governance around the World: Family Business Groups to Professional Managers*, edited by Randall Morck. Chicago, IL: University of Chicago Press, 2005.

Kohli, Atul. 'Politics of Economic Liberalization in India'. *World Development* 17, no. 3 (1999): 305–328.

Prakash, Gyan. *Another Reason: Science and the Imagination of Modern India*. Princeton, NJ: Princeton University Press, August 1999.

Ramadorai, A. *TCS Story . . . and Beyond*. New Delhi: India Portfolio, February 2013.

Sharma, Dinesh C. *The Outsourcer: The Story of India's IT Revolution*. Cambridge, MA: The MIT Press, March 2015.

Chapter 9: The Dubious Fundamentals

Bhagwati, Jagdish, and Arvind Panagariya. *Why Growth Matters: How Economic Growth in India Reduced Poverty and the Lessons for Other Developing Countries*. New York, NY: PublicAffairs, April 2014.

Bhushan, Sudhanshu, ed. *The Future of Higher Education in India*. Singapore: Springer, November 2019.

Kishiyama, M. M., W. T. Boyce, A. M. Jimenez, L. M. Perry, and R. T. Knight. 'Socioeconomic Disparities Affect Prefrontal Function in Children'. *Journal of Cognitive Neuroscience* 21, no. 6 (2009): 1106–1115.

Kohli, Atul. *Poverty amid Plenty in the New India*. Cambridge, MA: Cambridge University Press, February 2012.

Kumar, Shail. *Building Golden India: How to Unleash India's Vast Potential and Transform Its Higher Education System. Now*. Jaipur: ONS Group Press, October 2015.

Nyenhuis, Jacob E. *Myth and the Creative Process: Michael Ayrton and the Myth of Daedalus.* Detroit, MI: Wayne State University Press, January 2003.

Rooth, Tim. *British Protectionism and the International Economy: Overseas Commercial Policy in the 1930s.* Cambridge: Cambridge University Press, April 2002.

Schoonveld, Ed. *The Price of Global Health: Drug Pricing Strategies to Balance Patient Access and the Funding of Innovation.* Abingdon: Routledge, June 2020.

Taussig, Frank William. *The Tariff History of the United States.* Boston, MA: Adamant Media Corporation, December 2000.

Todd, David. *Free Trade and Its Enemies in France, 1814–1851.* Cambridge: Cambridge University Press, June 2015.

Trentmann, Frank. *Free Trade Nation: Commerce, Consumption, and Civil Society in Modern Britain.* Oxford: Oxford University Press, May 2009.

Von Glahn, Richard. *The Economic History of China: From Antiquity to the Nineteenth Century.* Cambridge: Cambridge University Press, March 2016.

Chapter 11: The Path Forward

Alexander, Bryan. *Academia Next: The Futures of Higher Education.* Baltimore, MD: Johns Hopkins University Press, January 2020.

Asmus, Barry. *The Poverty of Nations: A Sustainable Solution.* Wheaton, IL: Crossway, August 2013.

Bartusiak, Marcia. *Einstein's Unfinished Symphony: The Story of a Gamble, Two Black Holes, and a New Age of Astronomy.* New Haven, CT: Yale University Press, June 2017.

Collins, Daryl, Jonathan Morduch, Stuart Rutherford, and Orlanda Ruthven. *Portfolios of the Poor: How the World's Poor Live on $2 a Day.* Princeton, NJ: Princeton University Press, December 2010.

Guillen, Mauro F. *2030: How Today's Biggest Trends Will Collide and Reshape the Future of Everything.* New York, NY: St. Martin's Press, August 2020.

Ingebretsen, Mark. *Why Companies Fail: The 10 Big Reasons Businesses Crumble, and How to Keep Yours Strong and Solid.* New York, NY: Crown, May 2003.

Jacobsen, Annie. *The Pentagon's Brain: An Uncensored History of DARPA, America's Top-secret Military Research Agency.* New York, NY: Back Bay Books, June 2016.

Lamb, David. *Multiple Discovery: The Pattern of Scientific Progress.* Aldershot: Avebury, January 1984.

Larish, John J. *Out of Focus: The Story of How Kodak Lost Its Direction.* Scotts Valley, CA: CreateSpace, June 2012.

Sachs, Jeffrey. *The End of Poverty: Economic Possibilities for Our Time.* London: Penguin Books, February 2006.

Sanburn, Josh. '5 Reasons Borders Went Out of Business (and What Will Take Its Place)'. *Time* (19 July 2011). https://business.time.com/2011/07/19/5-reasons-borders-went-out-of-business-and-what-will-take-its-place/

Selingo, Jeffrey J. *College (Un)bound: The Future of Higher Education and What It Means for Students.* Seattle, WA: Amazon Publishing, April 2015.

Snyder, Paul. *Is This Something George Eastman Would have Done? The Decline and Fall of Eastman Kodak Company.* Scotts Valley, CA: CreateSpace, February 2013.

Weir, Bob. *Why Businesses Fail: … And the Journey through Our Irrational Minds.* Hamilton: Pinpoint Business, September 2018.

Wijeakumar, Sobanawartiny, Aarti Kumar, Lourdes M. Delgado Reyes, Madhuri Tiwari, and John P. Spencer. 'Early Adversity in Rural India Impacts the Brain Networks Underlying Visual Working Memory'. *Developmental Science* 22, no. 5 (September 2019): e12822.

Chapter 10: The Build–Buy Conundrum

Bhaskarabhatla, Ajay. *Regulating Pharmaceutical Prices in India: Policy Design, Implementation and Compliance*. Singapore: Springer, August 2018.

Capie, Forrest. *Depression & Protectionism: Britain between the Wars*. Abingdon: Routledge, November 2010.

Eban, Katherine. *Bottle of Lies: The Inside Story of the Generic Drug Boom*. Manhattan, NY: ECCO Press, May 2019.

Farris, William Wayne. *Japan to 1600: A Social and Economic History*. Honolulu, HI: University of Hawaii Press, August 2015.

Feldman, Robin. *Drugs, Money, and Secret Handshakes: The Unstoppable Growth of Prescription Drug Prices*. Cambridge: Cambridge University Press, April 2019.

Francks, Penelope. *The Japanese Consumer: An Alternative Economic History of Modern Japan*. Cambridge: Cambridge University Press, November 2009.

Greenspan, Alan, and Adrian Wooldridge. *Capitalism in America: A History*. New York, NY: Penguin Press, October 2018.

Helpman, Elhanan. *Understanding Global Trade*. Cambridge, MA: Belknap Press, April 2011.

Heo, U. K., and Terence Roehrig. *South Korea's Rise: Economic Development, Power, and Foreign Relations*. Cambridge: Cambridge University Press, October 2014.

Huang, Yasheng. *Capitalism with Chinese Characteristics: Entrepreneurship and the State*. Cambridge: Cambridge University Press, September 2008.

Irwin, Douglas A. *Peddling Protectionism: Smoot-Hawley and the Great Depression*. Princeton, NJ: Princeton University Press, February 2011.

Jansen, Marius B. *The Making of Modern Japan*. Cambridge, MA: Belknap Press, October 2002.

Kinch, Michael, and Lori Weiman. *The Price of Health: The Modern Pharmaceutical Enterprise and the Betrayal of a History of Care*. New York, NY: Pegasus Books, April 2021.

Kroeber, Arthur R. *China's Economy: What Everyone Needs to Know*. Oxford: Oxford University Press, March 2016.

Memon, Ayaz, and Ranjona Banerji. *India 50: The Making of a Nation*. Mumbai: Book Quest Publishers, January 1997.

ABOUT THE AUTHOR

Rakesh Kumar is a Professor of computer engineering at the University of Illinois. His research in computer system design has pioneered technologies which are used widely today. Several of his papers have been recognized as the most influential papers in computer systems; many of them have won best paper awards. His research has received coverage and mentions in outlets such as *BBC*, *Fortune* and *The New York Times*. In addition to being an award-winning researcher and teacher, Rakesh thinks deeply about issues at the intersection of technology, policy and society, especially in the Indian context. His opinion articles have appeared in *The Telegraph*, *The Statesman*, *The Tribune*, *Nature India*, *Business Today* and the *Washington Examiner*. Rakesh received a BS from IIT Kharagpur in 2001 and a PhD from the University of California at San Diego in 2006. He is often seen eating adventurously at a restaurant or spending time with his very active eight-year-old.